LIFE, TIMES AND POETRY OF MIR

T0078198

LIFE, TIMES AND POETRY OF MIR

S R SHARMA

PARTRIDGE
A Penguin Random House Company

To order additional copies of this book, contact
Partridge India
000 800 10062 62
www.partridgepublishing.com/india
orders.india@partridgepublishing.com

<u>DEDICATION</u>

To my family-my wife Santosh, sons Tarun and Sachin, daughters-in-law
Manisha and Purabi, Grand Kids Shrutika,Rohan and Ashim
To them, who are always there for me . . . .

Mir ke shair ka ahwal kahon kya Ghalib
Jis ka deewan kam az gulshan-e-Kashmir nahin
Mirza Ghalib

Ghalib, what to say of Mir's Verse
His poetry is no less than the garden called Kashmir.

CONTENTS

PART I

PART II
Zikr-e-Mir (The Story of Mir)

PART I

PREFACE

This Book is a study of the poet Mir-Taqi-Mir (1722—1810), spanning his life and times, his poetry and personality and his Select Verse, broadly representative of his poetry, which has been trans-created and elucidated. Besides, Mir's mental state and his hallucinatory experiences, as narrated by the poet in his Masnavi (a longish narrative poem) Khawab-o-Khayal (Dream or Fantasy) have been inquired into from psychological angle. The Masnavi is given in original in Appendix II and its English translation in Appendix III of this book.

Life and Times of Mir are given very briefly in the text of the book since the detailed narration of these appears in the translation of Mir's autobiography given at Appendix I. It may be clarified here that the poet's autobiography 'Zikr-e-Mir' written by him in Persian was translated by Dr. Nissar Ahmed Farooqi in Urdu as 'Mir Ki Aap Beeti' which I have translated into English. As will be seen from there that a large part of historical events of his times. Incidentally I may mention here that I have not confined myself to translating footnotes given by Dr. Farooqi in his book, but have given, by and large, my own footnotes particularly about historical events based on recorded history.

The purpose of this study is not academic, I have, therefore, not gone at length into the prosodical and literary niceties of Mir's poetry even though salient features of his poetry have briefly been commented upon. Main thrust of this book is to bring out thought-emotive content of his verse and compare it with that of other poets, thinkers and philosophers including experiences of Sufi Saints such as Rumi, Rabla, Kabir, Khusro, Bulley Shah and a few others.

A substantial part of the book relates to translation of Mir's poetry and comments thereon. While on the subject of translating poetry, it must be conceded that task involved is rather difficult. A few interesting observations on the subject made by different writers may be mentioned here. To begin with, Tagore has out rightly castigated translators of poetry as traitors. The Polish poet Zhigniew Herbard compares them with an awkward bumble bee handling on the flower which it cannot reach through its head to its roots but hums proudly that he has been inside showing its nose yellow with pollen. However, a more spicy comment has been made by a French translator who holds that translation of poetry is like a mistress who is either faithful or beautiful but cannot be both.

Notwithstanding the limitations involved in translating poetry, it may be observed that if a translator has fairly good grasp of the poetic idiom of the two languages and has himself a poetic temperament, there is no reason why the translation cannot combine the twin attributes of beauty and faithfulness at least to the essence of the original. This is demonstrated by a couple of Mir's verses given in the last chapter of this book which are translations of Persian verses of Sheikh Saadi. As explained there, Mir's translation is an improvement or the original Persian verse (see verse 27 and write up there under). Another instance is that of Fitzgerald's translation of Omar Khayyam from Persian to English which reads equally good if not better than the original. Nearer home Dil Mohammed rendering of Hindu's and Sikh's scriptural poetry into Urdu makes an excellent reading.

I do not, however, presume in any way to imply that my translation of Mir's poetry into English is anywhere near that excellence. Far from it, I am aware of my own limitations as also of the limitations inherent in translating poetry of one language into another; particularly when the idiom of the two languages is at vide variance with each other. Nevertheless, an effort has been made, to the best of my ability, to convey the intent and essence of Mir's verses while translating them and to bring out their nuances without, at the same time, deviating from the original idiom as far as possible.

CHAPTER 1

MIR—TAQI—MIR (1722-1810)
HIS LIFE AND TIMES

As already mentioned about the life story of Mir, his autobiography 'Zikr-e-Mir' written by him in Persian and translated into Urdu by Dr. Nissar Ahmad Farooqi as 'Mir ki Aap Beeti' has been retranslated into English and is given at Appendix I of this book. A large part of the autobiography deals with historical events of his times to some of which he was a witness or even a victim and in a few of which he participated. The period of half a century covered in Mir's autobiography corresponds to the fifty years of historical events narrated in the two out of three volumes of Sir Jadu Nath Sarkar's 'Fall of the Moghul Empire'. While translating his life story wherever the narrative of historical events has been found to be inaccurate, abstruse, laconic or one of poetic exaggeration, footnotes have been added giving a description of events as recorded in history. For that I have depended largely on Sarkar's aforesaid book, even though a few other sources have also been relied upon.

As will be seen from his autobiography, Mir has written in detail about his childhood. He has, however, remained somewhat sketchy about his later life. To recount briefly the salient facts of his life, Mir was born in 1722 in Akbarabad (Agra). His father Ali Muttaqi was a Dervaish, a Sufi fakir well respected by all, high and low. Mir mentions in the very beginning of his autobiography that his ancestors had migrated to India from Hejaz (a part of Arabia where Mecca and Medina are situated). They first came to Deccan and from there they moved on to Gujarat. Mir's great grandfather, however, came to Agra where he soon died due to sudden exposure to a different climate. It was Mir's grandfather who settled there and became the Faujdar (Administrator) of areas adjoining Agra. Doubts have, however, been expressed about Mir's statement that his ancestors came from Hejaz. As will be seen from Appendix I that Dr. Farooqi in his Urdu translation of Mir's autobiography points out in a footnote that, sprinkling of water on a mirror as a good omen for journey, mentioned by Mir in the context his father's proceeding to Lahore, is an Iranian custom and not an Arabic one. Another authority Dr. Kamal Ahmed Saddique in his essay on Zikr-e-Mir has asserted[1] that the language used by Mir and his father and their quotations of Persian verses combined with their Sufi leanings would suggest an Iranian ancestry. Dr. Siddique further adds that there is a possibility of Mir having assumed Hejaz to be a city of Iran.

From his autobiography, it will be seen that Mir's childhood was deeply influenced by his father and his uncle Aman Allah who were both Dervaishes. The latter was in fact a disciple of his father whom he (his father) had adopted as brother. It was his uncle who was mainly responsible for nurturing and guiding Mir in his childhood. Again it was Aman Allah who took Mir along with him to visit various Dervaishes and Fakirs. Details of these visits to and meetings with these holy men along with their teachings are given by Mir in his autobiography. How far are these teachings an authentic recollection of Mir, and how far they are embellished and interpolated by the wisdom of the poet's hindsight is difficult to say. It has remained a controversial issue into which we need not go. Nevertheless, this exposure of Mir, at an impressionable age, to these fakirs and Dervaishes preaching and practicing abstinence and self-mortification had a marked impact on him, both on his personality as well as on his poetry. This has been brought out at some length in more than one place in the subsequent chapters of this book.

His uncle Aman Allah died when Mir was merely ten years' old and about a year later he lost his father. There followed for him a period of despair and destitution. His troubles were compounded by the callous indifference of his elder stepbrother who later turned hostile towards Mir.

---

[1]   Mir-Taqi-Mir-A critical and Investigative Evaluation—Ghalib Institute, New Delhi

Orphaned in early childhood with no visible means of livelihood, with no kind hand to help and guide him, Mir looks back on his childhood with a cry of

Apna hi haath sir peraha apne yan sada
Mushafuq koi nahin koi merharban nahin

My own hand has ever patted my head
No affectionate one, nor kind one, was there

Mir struggled in vain for survival in Agra. When things became unbearable there, he came to Delhi. He was then only a young lad of 13 or 14 years. Luckily for him he met in Delhi a youngman named Khwaja Basit who introduced Mir to his (Basits') uncle Nawab Samsam-ul-Daula, the Royal Paymaster who had great reverence for Mir's late father.

The said Nawab granted a stipend of one rupee per day to Mir from his own administration. More about his meeting with Nawab Samsam-ul-Daula is written in the later chapter on Mir's personality and poetry.

Following the grant of the stipend Mir returned to Agra. But as ill luck would have it, the stipend did not last long because the said Nawab was among the many nobles killed about a year later in Nadir Shah's invasion of Delhi. Consequently, Mir was constrained to return to Delhi for he had no means of substance in Agra. This time around he stayed with Khan Siraj-ud-Din Ali Khan Arzoo, the maternal uncle of his step-brother. Khan Arzoo was a well known poet and a polyglot scholar of repute. Mir learnt a great deal from him initially. However, at the instigation of Mir's step-brother, the said Khan started maltreating him. When Khan Arzoo's hostility became unbearable, he was constrained to seek shelter elsewhere. Mir writes in his autobiography that his step-brother wrote to his uncle, Khan Arzoo thus:

"Mir-Taqi-Mir is a veritable nuisance Take no interest in his upbringing. Better finish him off in the garb of Friendship"

Mir further writes:

"Khan Arzoo was a crass worldly man who turned suddenly hostile to me. He would treat me with contempt whenever I approached him . . . If I am to describe his animosity towards me in detail, it would require another book."

Soon after leaving Khan Arzoo, Mir had a mental breakdown which lasted for months. Mir was then 17 years in age. Later in life he wrote a long poem 'Khawab-o-Khayal' (Dream or Fantasy) in which he has narrated in detail his madness and his hallucinatory experiences of a fairy from moon visiting him in moonlit nights and leaving at dawn. A study of Mir's mental breakdown and the images of the feminine in her multiple moods experienced by the poet have been made separately in the next chapter.

Sometime after his recovery, Mir came under the influence of one Mir Jaffer who taught him. But this did not last long as Jaffer had suddenly to go away. However, soon thereafter, he came in contact with one Saadat Ali of Amroha who inspired him to choose Rekhta (Urdu) as medium of his poetic efforts. Mir writes about it in his autobiography thus:

"After sometime I happened to meet a gentleman named Saadat Ali of Amroha who advised me to write verse in Rekhta (Urdu) which resembled Persian Verse. Urdu was the language of Hindustan by the authority of the king and was now gaining currency. I worked at it very hard and practiced this art to such an extent as to be acknowledged by the literati of the city. My poetry became well known and reached the ears of the young and old in the poetic circles of Delhi."

As has already been mentioned, a greater part of Mir's autobiography is devoted to historical events of his times. As these events have been described in detail in Appendix I, there is the need to repeat them here. However, it may be mentioned that these events had a profound impact on Mir, both as a person as well as a poet. An intermingling of personal anguish with that of the horrendous times is often found in his poetry.

While describing historical events, Mir has narrated the large scale lootings, massacre and destruction of Delhi by successive invading borders of Afghans, Maharathas, Rohillas, etc., and the internecine wars between various feudal principalities and provinces consequent upon the decline and progressive erosion of the Moghul authority. The royal capital was rapidly changing hands bringing about a state of anarchy in its wake. In his poetry Mir has dwelt upon these woefully chaotic times. He bemoans the killing and blinding of kings. He mourns the dead friends and acquaintances killed in the mayhem. He feels sorry for nobles put to the sword and for those rendered homeless paupers. He became intensely conscious of the emptiness of glory for he had seen high and mighty done to dust.

As already mentioned, Mir was exposed to the influence of Sufis and Dervaishes in his early childhood. From this exposure, he learnt patience and fortitude which must have helped him in withstanding the hardships of those terrible times.

A few of his verses describing the horrendous times with its naked dance of death and destruction and the dire state into which nobility was pushed in the then prevailing anarchy are given below for readers' perusal:

> Woh dasht-e-khaufnak-raha hai mera watan
> Sun kar jise Khisr ne safar se hazr kiya

> Such a frightening jungle has been my land
> That hearing of which even Khidr[2] was afraid to travel

> Tu hal bechara gada Mir tera kya mazkoor
> Mil gaye khak mein yan sahib Afsar Kitne.

> Mir, you a hapless beggar what to talk of you
> How many high and mighty were done to dust here

> Dilli mein aaj bheek bhi milti nahin Unhein
> Tha kal talak dimag jinhein takht-a-taj Ka

> They do not alms in Delhi today
> Who till yesterday were proud of their thorn and crowns

Mir has described in his autobiography the blindings of the kings, first of Ahmed Shah by his minister Imad-ul-Malik and later of King Shah Alam by Ghulam Qadir Rohilla.

In his brutal acts against the king, princess, princesses and even the menials of the royal palace, Ghulam Qadir had surpassed the worst tyrants of history. Details of his gory misdeeds have been given in the footnotes towards the end of the translation of Mir's autobiography. Referring these blinding of Kings

---

2   Protector and guiding angel of travellers

Mir wrote:

Shahan ke kahal-e-jawahar thi khak-e-pa Jhinki
Unhein ki aankhon mein phirti slaein dekhein

Kings, the dust of whose feet was precious collyrium
I saw their eyes being pierced with

Having seen so much that had happened to kings, nobles, the mighty and the rich, Mir like Webster was left with no illusions about glory. Webster says through a character in his play 'Duchess of Malfi' that glory is like a glow worm from far off shining bright but seen from near it has neither heat nor light. In a similar vein Mir tells seekers of glory

Aai hub-jah walo jo aaj tajwar hai
Kal usko deekho tum ne taj hai na sir hai

O, you, the seeker of glory of high position
See the one who wears the crown today
For tomorrow he will have neither the
crown nor the head that wears

He further tells them:

Tha mulk jin ke zair-e-nageen saaf mit gaye
Tum is khayal mein ho ke naam-o-nishan rahe

Those who ruled over this country were totally wiped away
You are still toying with the idea of leaving your name behind

In the circumstance then prevailing, the poet finds contentment of fakiri (poverty) the only wealth left:

Sikh, Maharathe, chor-uchakkay, shah-o-gada zar khawahan hain
Chain se hain jo kutch nahin rakhte, fakr hi ek daulat hai ab Sikh,
Maharattas, thieves, ruffians, kings and beggars all greedy for wealth

At peace are those who have nothing, fakiri
poverty is the only wealth now

Apart from the foregoing verses which depict the tragedy of his times, Mir has, as already mentioned earlier, mirrored in many of his verses an intermingling of personal pain and the agony of his times. Dr. Nissar Ahmed Farooqi in his book 'Mir-Taqi-Mir' has made a very appropriate observation in this regard when he says "Mir writes not verse but elegies of Dil (heart and Dilli (Delhi). As wine distilled becomes sword so has the historical atmosphere been distilled into ghazal."

The traces of death, destruction and devastation he witnessed in Delhi on his return from the Jat Country, after the third battle of Panipat, having been described poignantly by Mir in his autobiography. He writes:

"Strolling about one day I went through Delhi which had recently been reduced to a ruin. I wept at every step. Each step left a lesson to be learnt. I was increasingly appalled as I went on. I could not recognize houses; there were no habitats, no inhabitants. Rows of houses were lying demolished, walls broken, mosques deserted, taverns desolate—a stretch of vast ruin met the eyes. I looked in vain for the old bazaar. Where were those good looking faces?

Where could one look for beauty? Where were the romantic lovers and charming beloveds? The pious old men had been driven out, Palaces had been razed to the ground; streets had been robbed of their citizens . . .

Wilderness reigned unhindered." "Suddenly I came to the street where I had lived . . . I came across none of the known people with whom I could talk of the happier times. I met no one worth the name whom I could have as a company. I left the ruin stood aside and looked at remnants of destruction with an anguished heart.

I was devastated and took a solemn vow never to come there and never ever to venture in the direction of the city as long as I lived."

In this verse too he has given a moving expression to the pain of losing friends and neighbours:

Dilli mein abke aa kar yaaron ko na dekha
Kuch woh gaye shatabi, kutch ham ba dair aaye

Coming back to Delhi, I saw no friends around
Either they departed (from the world) in ahurry or I was late in comin

Manzil na kar jahan ko ke ham ne safar se aa
Jis ka kiya surag suna woh guzr gaya

Make not this world your destination for returning from the journey.
Whomsoever I tried to trace, I heard he had passed away.

Mir found his own house destroyed. He, a man of unusual blend of contemplating and action now found himself homeless with no means of livelihood. The relief came in the form invitation on behalf of Nawab Asaf-ul-Daula, the ruler of Avadh asking Mir to come to Lucknow. Consequently, he migrated to Lucknow where he was materially well off and creatively active (four out of six collections of his poetry were published from Lucknow). Nevertheless, he never felt at home there for he remained discontented with the glossy superficiality of the place and its people and the decorative affectations of its culture. Consequently, he experienced an agonizing nostalgia for Delhi. His life in Lucknow has been described at some length in a subsequent chapter on Mir's personality and poetry. A mention here, however, he made to the fact that what hurt him most was the lack of understanding and appreciation of his poetry in Lucknow where in his own words:

Rahi nagufta mere dil mein dastan Meri
Na is diar mein samjha koi zuban Meri

My tale remained untold in my heart
For none in this city understood my language

To the frustration of not being understood and appreciated were added the personal tragedies in Lucknow with his son, wife and daughter dying in quick succession. His health broke down. He withdrew completely from society. And after protracted ailments, both physical and mental, Mir died in Lucknow in the year 1810 at the age of 88 and was buried by the side of the graves of his wife, son and daughter.

In so far as discontent with Lucknow is concerned, it may be recalled here that the seeds for it were sown soon after Mir's arrival there. In his very first appearance in a Mushaira (a poetry recitation symposium) he was greeted derisively by the gathering there, being simply attired in a dress which appeared alien to the people of Lucknow. Mir, an extremely sensitive and self-respecting man was cut to the quick. When his turn for recitation came, he was asked who he was and where he came from, he responded with verses extemporized on the spot in which his personal hurt gets submerged in the anguished cry for Delhi:

Kya bood-o-bash poocho ho poorab ke sakno
Ham ko gareeb jaan ke hass hass pukar ke
Dilli jo ek shahr tha aalam mein inthekhab
Rehte thay muntkhib hi yahan rozgar ke
Jis ko falak ne loot ke weerane kar diya
Ham rahne wale hein usi ujde diar ke

What ask ye, O, the people of the east
about where I belong to
And that too derisively considering me
to be a poor alien
Delhi, a city select of this world
Where the chosen ones of the times lived
A city reduced to rubble by Heaven's ire
To that ruined city I belong

Incidentally, it may be mentioned here that even before living in Lucknow under the patronage of Nawab Asaf-ul-Daula, Mir had enjoyed the favours and the support of Rajas, Nawabs and even of the king. Even though the main reason for this was his poetic excellence, Mir was well-versed in the art of State craft, diplomacy and warfare. In the employment of Nawab Rayyat Ali Khan, Mir had accompanied his employer as a part of the delegation of Delhi Durbar (royal court) sent to Sirhind to negotiate with Ahmed Shah Abdali. He also served as adviser to Raja Nagar Mal who held various assignments in the Moghul court ranging from Deewan for government land to that of Deputy Ministership. Mir's sagacity in these matters can be seen from his observations in state craft and art of warfare in his autobiography. For instance, with reference to the third battle of Panipat, he has observed that had the Marathas stuck to their traditional method of guerrilla warfare instead of arrogantly marching their army with heavy armour into the plains of north India for pitched battle in an unknown terrain, they would have, in all probability won, a perception that commonly shared by later historians.

CHAPTER 2

THE LUNAR VISITOR
(HALLUCINATORY EXPERIENCES OF THE POET)

A brief mention was made in the preceding chapter to Mir's mental breakdown and the Masnavi Khawab-o-Khayal (Dream or Fantasy) in which he has narrated what was happening to him during this mental illness. The Masnavi in original is given at Appendix II and its English translation at Appendix III.

As already mentioned, Mir was 17 years of age when this affliction struck him. His breakdown lasted four months. It is not known when the abovementioned poem narrating his hallucinatory experiences was written. So it is not possible to pinpoint the time gap between what he experienced and his recollections of it. However, it is seen from his autobiography (Appendix I) that Mir has been able to recollect and relate at length with a good deal of clarity the events of his early childhood and the persons who influenced him during the process of his growing up. We can, therefore, take Mir's recollections of his madness to be broadly accurate, giving allowance for some degree of poetic embellishments as also an element of conscious censoring of these experiences.

For understanding Mir's mind and the phantasmagoria of his delusionary state in which he experienced the benign and more often the malignant aspect of the feminine (a fairy descending from the moon very often torturing him) we may go back to his early childhood as described by

10

Mir in his autobiography. Two persons who influenced him in early years were his father Ali Muttaqi and his uncle Amaan Allah. Both of them were Dervaishes, Muslim Sufi fakirs vowed to poverty, austerity, abstinence and self-mortification. Mir has described in detail in his autobiography how his uncle used to take him along when he visited fakirs and Dervaishes whose lives and teachings emphasized the absolute need for self-denial and abstinence.

Earlier, when young Amaan Allah was getting married, Mir's father told him that marriage was prohibited to the worshippers of God adding that in his youth "he too was intoxicated with sensual pleasures" and he got nothing out of it but painful hangover. When one of God's men gave him deliverance, he created firmness of resolve and started burning like a lamp with a single wick. The result of this advice was that on the night following his marriage, Amaan Allah went forth in search of the Dervaish abandoning his wife. This Amaan Allah became a beacon light for Mir in his childhood and as already mentioned it was he who exposed his ward to Fakirs and Dervaishes given to severest austerities. While sensual love was projected on to the child's mind as an anathema, message on love, as such, was impressed upon him by his father with all the Sufi emphasis thus:

My child adopt the creed of love, for love is the presiding deity of this world. If love is withdrawn from the universe, cosmos will turn into chaos. Life without love is a barren weight. To lose yourself in love is real gain and joy. Love is fire, love is light. The fire burnth the dross in man. Love is the source and spring of all we perceive. The world, my boy is in a state of flux; we have no time to waste; utilize every minute of your time for self-awakening. Ups and downs characterize the path of life. Chasing the pleasures of this world is like chasing a mirage or an attempt to bind water with a string. Be the nightingale of the never fading rose. Dedicate yourself to God; catch the time by forelook and try to know thyself."

As has been mentioned in the preceding chapter, both his father and uncle had died when Mir was barely a boy of 10-11 years. In material terms, both of them left nothing behind. He had to struggle for survival in his early childhood. Besides now that the teaching and guidance of the father and uncle were no longer available, Mir's passage into adolescence must have been difficult. Teachings of love received from his father must have confused the boy more than enlightened him, with the libidinous urges pulling him in one direction and the teachings of absolute self denial and abstinence into another. Such a muddle is inevitable if we do not realize the reality of what

DH Lawrence says in the Fantasia of the 'Unconscious' about the upper centres of our being having corresponding responses in the lower centres.

Mir in his autobiography has, to say the least, oversimplified the cause of his madness which he attributes, though only implicitly, to the gross ill-treatment at the hands of his step-uncle Khan Arzoo at the instance of his (Mir's) step-brother. He describes this ill-treatment and follows it immediately saying "And I became mad". This is what he wrote in his autobiography about this ill-treatment and it alleged consequence, his madness.

"In Delhi Again"

"After that turbulence (Nadir's Invasion), cruel times again tortured me. The people in the lifetime of Dervaish (his father) used to treat the dust of my feet as collyrium, now looked down on me. Again I came to Delhi and bore the heavy load of obligation of my step-uncle Siraj-ud-Din Ali Khan Arzoo who was the maternal uncle of my elder brother. In short I stayed with him for sometime and read some books borrowed from friends in the city. When I became capable of conversing correctly with someone, a letter came from my brother to his uncle saying, "Mohd Taqi (Mir) was a trouble-maker. On no account should be brought up and in the guise of friendship should be finished off." That dear one (Arzoo) was a crass worldly man. Taking note of his nephew's enemity towards me, he started ill-treating me. If I went to him he would scold me and if I avoided him, he would abuse me. His eyes relentlessly followed me. He often treated me with hostility. What to say what I got from him? How to say what I went through? I used to remain, somehow, tongue tied. Even in the dire need, I would not ask even for a rupee but he did not refrain from ticking me off. If I have to narrate the details of the entire episode of his enemity, it would require another volume. My anguished heart was even more wounded."

"Madness"

And I became mad. My already depressed heart was thrown into more depression. I went wild. I would close the door of the cell in which I lived and would go into seclusion, misery stored around me. When the moon rose, a doom would land on me. If at a time a maid helping me wash my face said "moon, moon", I would look towards the sky, I would go very crazy.

The wildness increased so much that the people will close the door of my cell and would run away from my company."

"On a moonlit night a figure of beauty, both of face and body, would descend with elegance towards me from moon's circumference and drove me beyond myself. Whatever direction I looked I saw that envy of a fairy. Whichever way I saw that pride of hour less was in view as if the door, roof and courtyard of my house were sheets of paintings. In short all six directions that wonderful face was seen. Sometimes, she would appear before me like a full moon. Sometimes she would treat my heart as a playground to strut about. If I looked at the moon my restless self got singed. Every night I had her company and every morning in her absence I would remain in a wild state. When the dawn's dim light came, she would depart to return to the moon with a sigh from an afflicted heart.

I would go crazy throughout the day and would torture my heart in her memory. Like a madman in a trance, I would go around with a stone in my hand. I would stagger around and people would avoid me. For four months that glowing apparition of the night played havoc with me in a variety of ways and tortured me with her strident mischief. Suddenly, the spring came; the wounds of madness festered further. In other words, I went completely mad and became totally worthless, lost as I was in the delusionary face, and her fragrant tresses. I became ripe for being segregated, in other words, to be confined in chains.

Fukhur-ul-Din's wife who was a disciple of the Dervaish (my father) and was a near relation spent a lot of money on my treatment. The exorcist's used charms and spells to cure me. The physicians bled me and their efforts proved helpful. Autumn came and spring departed; my madness waned. The delusionary imprint was erased from the heart's page. The lesson learned in madness was forgotten. Tongue got acquainted with silence. The ravings of the disturbed mind ceased. With the massage of the head, sleep also came. Strength lost was regained. Thus, I became normal. Sleep was no longer disturbed and the moon face disappeared from the sight. After the lapse of sometime, I was completely cured and started reading Tarsul (a primer containing rhymes/prose to acquaint children with different letters of the alphabet)."

Mir's version of his ill-treatment at the hands of Khan Arzoo is discounted in many quarters. The said Khan was a well-known Persian scholar and Mir himself has elsewhere acknowledged him as one of his mentors. One version which appears plausible is that the visionary figure of his hallucinatory experiences had an earthly counterpart who belonged to

Khan Arzoo's family. The said Khan tried to dissuade Mir from his ardent overtures to the person in question for according to the then prevailing social norms, as open expression of love was considered an unforgivable offence. Since it did not have the desired effect on Mir, Khan Arzoo wrote about it to his nephew, Mohd. Hafiz Hassan, Mir's step-brother who wrote back that he (Mir) was a trouble maker and that he would ruin family's reputation. He should, therefore, be finished off. After that, Khan Arzoo had turned him out instead of Mir walking out of the said Khan's house as claimed by him in his autobiography.

Before we take up the hallucinatory experiences of Mir, as described by him in his autobiography and more so in his poem; a case parallel to that of Mir may be mentioned. In a case study of one Theodore, in 'The Road Less Travelled' by M. Scott Peck (reproduced in Appendix IV) in whom neurosis started setting in at the age of 18 (more or less at the same age at which Mir mentally broke down), ingredients found leading to neurosis were, unsuccessful love affair, absence of parental concern, childhood being a continued bloody battle ground and above all unparalleled viciousness of his brothers. Interestingly, all these ingredients were present in Mir's case too and the only difference in the two cases is merely a matter of minor details. Mir lost in the death of his uncle Amaan Allah a nurturing guardian-cum-mentor and his father's death a year thereafter left him rudderless. His elder step-brother showed gallous indifference and followed it with active hostility. Besides, he had to struggle from early childhood for sheer survival in the absence of any economic support. Suffering in both the cases was the primary cause of the neurosis. In the succinctly elegant words of Carl Jung, "Neurosis is always a substitute for legitimate suffering."

Reverting to Mir's lunar visitor, it may be mentioned that fairy from the moon visiting Mir on moonlit nights and departing at dawn is in consonance with folklore of children's fairy tales wold over. But in Mir's case, feminine is experienced in her multiple moods full of contraries mainly of malignant nature. Moon itself symbolizes three aspects covered by Mir in his poem, beauty, love and insanity.

The very nature of this work precludes any kind of in-depth psychological study of the poet's mental ailment. Nor do I presume to be competent to do so. Nevertheless in light of the childhood influences on Mir explained at some length earlier, it may be said with a fair amount of certainty that libidinous repression must have played a part in his mental breakdown in addition to other factors already explained. Incidentally, speaking from archetypal angle, the fairy from the moon is a seductive and torturing paradigm of a femme fetale experienced by the poet on the threshold of his consciousness. This reminds us of Keats' deluded knight of 'La Belle Dam Sans Merci' or Majnu languishing in the scalding sands of the desert.

In short, it may be said that living in precarious conditions with no kind hand to help and guide him, adolescence arrived for Mir with a bang on his head which together with other factors already detailed drove him mad. However, his madness brought about a mysterious transformation in Mir for soon after his recovery, he made serious efforts to educate himself and to start his poetic efforts in Urdu which did not take long to burgeon. In this he was lucky enough to come in contact with a couple of learned and talented individuals who helped him launch on the path of poetic creativity.

The transformation from the private hell of mental illness to a state of grace in which Mir blossoms as a poet finds a parallel in Greek myth of Orestes which embodies, beautifully, relationship between grace and mental illness. Orestes was a grandson of Atreus on whom Gods placed a curse on account of his arrogance vis-à-vis Gods. As a part of enactment of the curse, Orestes' mother, Clytemnestra, murdered his father (her husband). This crime in turn brought down the curse on Orestes' head because by the Greek code of honour, a son was obliged to slay his father's murderer. Yet the greatest sin a Greek could commit was the sin of matricide. Orestes was agonized over his dilemma. Finally, he did what he seemingly had to do and killed his mother. For this sin Gods punished Orestes by visiting on him the Furies, three ghastly harples who could be seen and heard only by him and / who tormented him night and day with cackling criticism and frightening appearance.

After many years of lonely reflection and self abrogation, Orestes' requested Gods to relieve him of the curse. A trial was held by Gods. Speaking in Orestes' defence God Apollo argued that he had engineered the whole situation that had placed Orestes in the position in which he had no choice but to kill his mother. Therefore, Orestes could not be held responsible. At this point, Orestes jumped up and contradicted his own defender stating, "It was I and not Apollo that murdered my mother." Gods were amazed. Never before had a member of the house of Atreus assumed such a total responsibility for himself and not blame the Gods. Eventually, Gods decided the trial in Orestes favour and not only relieved him of the curse on the house of Atreus, but also transformed the Furies into Eumenides, loving spirits who brought their wise counsel enabled Orestes to obtain continuing good fortune. (The details of the myth and relationship between grace and mental illness are given in Appendix IV).

Likewise in Mir's case the hallucinatory female, more often of malignant nature, appearing to him during his mental illness and tormenting him turned later to be a benign influence on the poet, acting as it would appear, an invisible guide in Mir's pursuit of the Muse (of poetry) as soon after his ailment be started burgeoning as a poet.

CHAPTER 3

A—His Poetry and Personality

Mir is often described as a poet of Ah (pathos) and Sauda, his worthy contemporary, a poet of wah (ebullience). It is only a part truth and not the whole truth. Even though sad wistfulness permeates his poetry at places, to dub Mir as a poet of pathos would be an over simplification. As will be seen from a careful perusal of his poetry transcreated into English and discussed in this book that he was a man of multi-dimensional sensitivities. The melancholy of his poetry is relieved by the poet's creed of love and his aesthetic sensitivity which combined with his liberal mind saved Mir from acerbity. In him we find more of a lingering shadow of sorrow as occasional plaintive note, but no wailing of any kind. In spite of all trials and tribulations in Delhi as also the precarious existence when he along with other families of Delhi had to take refuge in the Jat Kingdom of Suraj Mal where they struggled to keep the wolf from the door, there is no bitterness in Mir. Ironically the only trace of bitterness is found in him in later years in Lucknow where he was comfortably placed economically, thanks to the benevolent Nawab Asaf-ul-Daula, the then ruler of Avadh. I will revert to this subject at some length later in Section-D of this chapter.

Love in its myriad manifestations is the main concern of Mir in his poetry, the tragic element safeguarding it from banality. Here he was influenced by his father's teachings imparted to him in his early childhood.

These remained imprinted on his mind and got inevitably mirrored in his poetry. The thumb nail sketch of his father's advice to him about love has already been given in the preceding chapter.

The teachings of all embracing love together with teachings of Sufi mystics with whom he came in contact in his early childhood through his guardian uncle, Amaan Allah, are abundantly reflected in Mir's poetry. For him love is the very essence of existence, encompassing all dimensions;

> Zahir batin awall aakhir paien bala ishq hai sab
> Noor zulmat, maani soorat sab kutch aap hoa hai ishq

> External internal, first last upper lower all are love
> Bright darkness meaning appearance all have become love

Even though love is the primary concern of Mir's poetry, it is not the only concern. A good deal of his verse covers existential, ethical and philosophical subjects rendered in simple and direct language, yet in a scintillating style. Transcreation of some of Mir's verses have been given in this chapter wherever the context demanded. However, the transcreation and elucidation of verses broadly representative of his poetry has been given in the last chapter of the book.

In keeping with the Sufi influence on and inclination of Mir, organized religion, more so the priests were impediments in the way to God which lied through human heart; visiting places of worship and pilgrimage sight was of little consequence unless these led to spiritual regeneration. But unfortunately, in most cases we remain unregenerate. A few of verses on the subject are given here for reader's perusal:

> Mat ranja kar kisi ko apne to eitqad
> Dil dhaye kar jo Kaaba banaya to kya hoa

> Hurt no one, that is my faith
> What is Kaaba worth if built on the
> ruins of human hear?

> Maccay gaya Mediney gaya, Karbla gaya
> Jaisay gaya tha vaise hi chal phir aa gaya

I pilgrimaged to Mecca, Medina, Karbla
I came as I was after these perambulations

Kaabey jane ka nahin kuch sheikh mujko itna shauk
Chal woh batla ki mein dil mein kisi ke ja karon

O Sheikh, I have no such fondness for going to Kaaba
All right tell me how I can create a place
for myse in someone's heart

These verses remind us of Punjabi Sufi poet Bulley Shah who has expressed a similar idea with his usual directness and force thus, "Demolish if you must the temple, the mosque but not the human heart in which dwells the beloved (the Lord)."

Holding on, steadfastly, to the belief that religion was an individual's experience of the divine in which no intermediary was needed, he had great aversion to the priesthood of any genre for, as he says, God departs whenever and wherever priest enters. He is opposed to the collective will imposed on man by organized religions with their narrow walls of conflicting beliefs and rituals which sowed seeds of strife between man and man. Since it is only of the recurring themes, in his poetry, a few of his verses on the subject are quoted here. In a strident castigating tenor he writes:

Shirkat-e-Sheikh O Brahmin se Mir
Kaaba-o-dair se bhi jaaye ge
Apni daid eint ki judi masjid
Kisi weerane mein banaya ga

Once Sheikh and Brahmin join, Mir
Kaaba (mosque) and temple are both lost
So build tiny little mosque in secluded ruin
Dair-o-haram mein kyonke kadam rakh sake ga, Mir
Idhar is se but phire udhar khuda phire

How can Mir step into temple or mosque
Icons deserted the one and God the other

Ham na kehte the mat diar-o-haram ki rah chal
Ab yeh daawa hashr tak Sheikh-o-Brahmin mein raha

Did I not tell you not to go the way of temple or mosque
Now Sheikh and Brahmin will be at logger heads till doomsday

Rejecting all dogmatic notions or organized religions Mir writes:

Kis ko kehte hain nahin mein fanta Islam-o-kufr
Dair ho ya Kaaba matlab mujkho tere dar se hai

I know not what is Islam or Kufr*
Be it temple or Kaaba, I am concerned only with Your (God's) door.

In short, he is concerned with light and not where it emanates from like the Persian poet who said that moth differentiates not between the lamp of the Mosque and that of the temple. In a similar vein Mir says:

Uske firog-e-husn se jhamke hai sab main noor
Shammai haram no yak ke diya Somnat ka

His beauty's effulgence shimmers through all
Be it a lamp of the mosque or taper in Somnath temple

Mir's attitude here is in tune with that of Sufi mystics who held that the path to God did not lie through following religious ritual but experiencing Him through love. Believing that a sect or the people of particular religion will get special dispensation, being the chosen one of God is born out of ignorance. This attitude not only leads to division among human beings but also sows seeds of hatred among communities. For Sufi saints all such diversions are home made and God eclipsing and were to be transcended through love. Punjabi Sufi poet, Bulley Shah, conveys it through a simple utterance thus:

Na ham Hindu na turk zaroori
Naam isha di he manzoori
Aashiq ne har jeeta

With the blessing of love
I have no need to be Hindu or Turk
Love wins over God

Like Ghalib, Mir had earlier ridiculed the concept of heaven and hell
which priests used as carrot and stick for the people in furtherance of their
material goals. Ghalib says that we have to rid heaven of material props to
ensure untainted worship:

Tait mein tana rahe mei-o-angbein ki laaa
Doozakh mein dal do koi lai kar bahisht ko

Take away heaven and merge it with hell
So that obedience to God is freed from taints of heaven and hell

Mir had said a similar thing with direct spontaneity and more impact
fully with an air of impatience:

Jaye jo Nijat ke gham mein
Aisi jannat gai jahanam mein
Heaven that is craved for deliverance
Let be consigned to hell

This attitude is in conformity with Sufi love for God for God's sake and
not motivated by the desire for reward or the fear of punishment. Maula
Abdul Kalam Azad quotes in his book, 'Gubar-e-Khatir', the following
anecdote about Rabia Basria, the woman Sufi Saint who, as Huxley observed
in his 'Perennial Philosophy' "speaks, thinks and feels in terms of devotional
theism." One day Rabia left her house in a state that in one hand she held
cauldron of fire and in another a vessel full of water. When the people
questioned her she replied, "By this fire I want to burn down heaven and
by this water I want to extinguish the blaze of hell so that both may be
destroyed and people worship God for God's sake and not for the reward for
heaven or from the fear of hell."

Rabia also used to say "O, God, if I worship thee in the hope of
paradise, exclude me from paradise and if I worship thee in fear of hell, burn
me in hell; but if I worship thee for thine own sake, withhold not thine
everlasting beauty." This is the only boon a true religious person will ask for.

Another Sufi, Ansari of Herat begs of the Lord thus:

A beggar, Lord, I ask of thee
More than a thousand kings could ask
Each one wants something which asks of thee
I come to ask thee to give me thyself

As has already been stated, Mir is primarily a poet of love. It may be added here that he is felicitous both of Ishq-e-Majazi (Sensual love). Ishq-e-Haqiqi (Mystical love—Sufi seeking to merge with the Divine, a part becoming whole, a drop merging into the ocean). The verses covering both kinds of love have been dealt with at a number of places in this book. Suffice here to say that to his poetry of sensual love, Mir shows an admirably exquisite sensitivity and aesthetics:

Naaziki us lab ki kya Kahaye
Pankhadi ek gulab ki si hai
Mir in neem baaz aankhon mein
Sari masti sharab ki se hai

What to say of the delicacy of her lips
As if they were rose petals
And in those half open doe-eyes
Entire ecstasy is as if of wine

Two more aspects of Mir's poetry of sensual love that need mention are pathos and basokht (where lover complains of cruelty, infidelity, indifference of the beloved).

Hamare aage tera jba kisi ne naam liya
Dil-e-Sitamazada ko ham na tham tham liya

When someone mentioned your name to me
I had, somehow, managed to keep a hold on my afflicted heart

The pathos in Mir's poetry reminds us of Thomas Mann's words. "He who loves most is vanquished and must suffer". However, in so far basokht is concerned, it came to be adopted by later Urdu poets to an extent as to make it somewhat of a trite tradition. About Pathos, Majnu Gorakhpuri holds that one is constrained to say that "Mir is a poet of sorrow but there is some sort of a revolutionary and ethical message in his poetry".

He further adds: "Mir's time was one of sorrow and had he not been a poet of sorrow, he would have betrayed his times and would not have been such a great poet for us[3]."

In his poetry of Ishq-e-Haqiqi, love in mystical mould, Mir followed in the footsteps of Persian poet, Jalal-uddin-Rumi who proclaims:

"The beloved is all in all. The lover merely veils him. The beloved is all that lives the lover is a dead thing."

At another place Rumi says, "O let me not exist! For non-existence proclaims, To Him we shall return. In similar vein, Mir says:

Hasti apni hai beech mein purdah
Ham na hovein to phir hijab kahan

My self is a veil in between
(Self and Divine)
If I cease to be where is the veil

Mahay kar aap ko yun hasti main uski
Boond pani ki nahi aati nasar pani mein

Merge yourself into Him
Like a drop of water separately is not seen in water

Juz martaba-e-kul ko hasil kare hai aakhir
Yak qatra na dekha jo darya na hua hoga

Finally a part attains the whole
Not a drop is seen that did not become river.

This Fana (merger) culminates in Baga (immortality, having become one with the Divine and Sufies achieve it through love.

In so far as human consciousness is concerned, Mir has emphasized the imperative need to pay attention to it well in time and not leave it to twilight

---

[3]   As quoted by Professor Shama-ul-Rehman in his essay on 'Mir's personality and Poetry' In the book 'Mir-Taqi-Mir' published by Ghalib Institute, New Delhi (page 39)

years when the level of consciousness, with the progressive loss of the lucidity of mind, would have deteriorated. Mir puts it forcefully thus:

Kya chetne ka phaide jo sahib mein cheta
Sone ka saman aaya to bedar hua mein

Of what value it is to rise to awareness in old age
I woke up when it was the time to sleep

In the beginning of this Section a mention has been made to Mir being a poet of 'Ah' (sorrow) and his contemporary Sauda as a poet of 'Wah' (celebration) (Mir weeps while Sauda laughs). More, however, needs to be said on the subject. Sauda was senior to Mir by nine years and was already an established poet when Mir was just a fledgling in the field. The poetry of the two is distinctly different. As already mentioned pathos in Mir is a direct result of his grief and anguish both personal as well as of the times. He was not, however, weighed down by these trials and travails because of his hold on love in its various manifestations apart from his aesthetic and cultural sensitivity.

While Sauda's poetry was embellished with similes and metaphors, Mir used these sparingly but whenever he did it to a great effect:

Sham hi se bujha sa rahta hai
Dil hua hai chirag muflis ka

As the day dims, so does my heart
Like the lamp with waning wick in a poor man's hut

However, by and large Mir's language is simple and direct. Besides, he makes use of common proverbs to effectively convey an idea. The relationships of these two contemporaries, however, were marked with mutual respect. When someone asked Mir in Lucknow who were the poets of the times, he said that there were only two poets. Sauda and his humble self (Mir)—and all others were two-third, one-half, one-third poets or no poets at all. Ghalib was a great admirer of Mir. The literati of his (Ghalib's) time were divided into two groups, one that admired Mir and the other admiring Sauda. In his book 'Yaadgar-e-Ghalib', Maulana Hali recalls that in a gathering, Ghalib was praising Mir. His contemporary poet Zauq, who was also present and whom Ghalib considered to be one of the admirers of Mir;

expressed preference instead for Sauda's Poetry. Ghalib with his characteristic humour said, "I thought you were a Miri (Mir's fan) but, alas, you turned out to be a Saudai." There is a pun on the word Saudai for it means Sauda's fan as also a mad man.

Earlier, it has been mentioned at more than one place that Mir's poetry was affected by his personal trials and travails as also of the terrible times. In this context, one thing needs to be taken note of is that Muse cannot be free from the influences of the life around. The great classic 'Don Quixote' was conceived by Cervantes in prison, let us hear what he has to say of Muses in the Prologue to his classical novel:

"But I could not violate nature's ordinance whereby like engenders like. And so, what could my sterile and uncouth genius beget but the tale of a dry, shriveled, whimsical offspring, full of odd fancies such as never entered another's brain—just was might be begotten to a prison where every discomfort is lodged and every dismal noise has its dwelling."

A few verses in which Mir gives expression to his personal anguish are given here for reader's perusal:

Mujhko shair na kaho Mir ke Sahib main ne
Dard-o-Gham Kitne Kiye jamma to deewan kiya

Do not, Sir, call me a poet
I gathered so many pains and sorrows to create a book of verse

Marsaiy dil ke kai keh diye logon ka
Sehr Dilli mein hai Sab paas nishani uski

Many obituaries of heart has he recited to people
He left this souvenir for all in Delhi

Hai ghao itne tegh-e-zuban se sab ki
Tab dard hain hamare ai Mir har Sukhan mein

All inflicted wounds on me by their tongues' sword
This is why, Mir, every verse of mine cried in rain

Har Subah mere sir par ek hadsa naya hai
Paiwand ho zameen ka shewa us aasman ka

Every morning a new calamity hangs over my head
Doing me to dust is heaven's vocation

Notwithstanding what is stated above, it may be reiterated that Mir had marvelous quality of resilience which enabled him to withstand trials and tribulations and not let tragedies wear him down. As already stated, one finds hardly any trace of bitterness in his writings even though sad wistfulness or even sorrow at times permeates his poetry. Intense creativity and personal integrity enabled him to transcend the terrible times to let his spirit soar thus:

Ab bhi dimag rafta hamare hai arsh par
go aasman ne khak mein nam ko mila diya

Even now my spirit soars skywards
Although heavens have done me to dust

We have earlier discussed the contents of Mir's poetry that as a poet of love he placed human heart above everything else, three more concerns of Mir's poetry may be mentioned here. First he talks of masti (ecstasy) where self as separate ego is transcended.

Rahe ham salam-e-masti mein aksar
Reha kutch aur ni salam namara

Often I remained in a state of ecstasy
Remained thereby in mind's state unique

Bekhudi le gai kahan ham ko
Dair se intezar hai apna

Where has the state of abandon carried me
I have been waiting for myself for long

As already brought out earlier, Mir has dwelt, in his poetry, on the Sufi theme of merger of the element with the whole, the particle itself becoming the cosmic (divine). Incidentally, this matter of merger with the divine is to be found in the Sufi poetry of other languages such as Persian, Hindi and

Punjabi as well. To give a few examples, here: firstly a couple of Persian Verses on the subject read as follows:

Haich kas rat a-na gardad O, fana
Naisht rah durbar gahe Kibria
—*Jalal-ud-deen Rumi*

One cannot enter the abode of God
If he loses not himself through Fana (merger)

Man tu shudam tu man shudi man tan shudam to jan shudi
Ia kas na goid baad azeen man deegram to degree
—*Amir Khusro*

I became you, you became me
I became body, you the life therein
None can say after this that you and I are separate

Kabir, Hindi poet, saint, had a similar thing to say:

Kabir tu tu karta hu hoa mujh main rahi na hu
Jab aapa parka mit gaya jit dekhon tit tu

Kabir repeating you as Mantra I became you losing myself
When I was obliterated as separate ego, wherever I see I see you

And In a similar vein, Bulley Shah, a Punjabi Sufi poet says:

Main fani aap non door karan
Tain baaqi aap hazoor karan

I, the mortal one, remove myself
And what to left is God

The message contained in these verses may be viewed in the context of Aldous Huxley's observations in the chapter on "Suffering" in his book "Perennial Philosophy." According to him, one of the causes of suffering is "separation from an embracing totality." Speaking in Buddhist terms, "The cause pain is craving for individual life." How are we to end the suffering?

For answers let us go again to Huxley. "For the individual who achieves unity within this own organism and union with the divine ground, there is end of suffering. The goal of creation is the return of all sentient beings out of separateness and that infatuating urge to separateness which results in suffering through unitive knowledge into the wholeness of eternal reality."

The second aspect of Mir's poetry is that, he has in it raised man to a state of dignity and to a pre-eminent position in the scheme of things. He wants no man to bow to another, no man to place himself above others and no man to play God seeking others to genuflect before him:

Elahi kaise hotey hain jinhein hai bandgi khwahish
Hamein to sharam damangir hoto hai khuda hotey

O, God, of what type are they who crave obedience from others
Playing God would make me hang my head in shame

Sir kaso se fro nahin aata
Haif, bande hoay Khuda na hoay

The Head bows to none
Shame on you, you are a mere man and not God

Mir's attitude towards people in the position of authority resembles that of mystics whether it be Greek Diogenes or Muslim Sufies. "A mystic does not recognize slavery." Sheikh Nizam-uddin-Aulia, it is said expelled from his Khangah (hermitage) a senior disciple Maulana Burhan-ul-Din when the Sheikh came to know that the said Maula used to sit in an arrogant way leaning on a pillow while supervising the preparation of food in his langarkhana (common kitchen). When Alexander went to meet Diognese who was basking in the sun on the beach and told him to ask for any favour, the only favour Diognese asked of Alexander was to move aside as he was obstructing the sun. In a similar vein Mir says:

Ho koi baadshah ya koi vazir
Apni bla se baith rahey jab fakir ho

I care not whether one be a king or his minister
Since I am settled here as a fakir

Sabaat kasr-o-dar-o-baam khisht-o-gill kitna
Amarat-e-dil-e-dervaish ki rakho bunyad

How long will last the palaces with doors
and roofs of mud and mortar
Lay instead the foundation of a heart of the Dervaish

Professor S.U.R. Farooqi in his essay on Mir quoted earlier in this
chapter has raised the point that we may not make these verses as basis for
assessing Mir's personality. This observation of his is based on a general
ground of the dichotomy in what the poet says and what he really is. He
adds that all one can say is that the poet was interested in the subject of
'self-respect'. Nevertheless, preceding verses of Mir transcend egoistic
self-esteem by upholding dignity of man, going a step beyond Koranic edict
of man being 'Ashraf-ul-Mukhloogat', the best of all sentient beings. In the
first place, Mir holds that man is the one who lends beauty to this world.
Besides he elevates man to dizzy heights in recognizing his inherent Divinity
as compared to Sophocles speaking of man as the most wonderful among
many wonders in his play 'Antigone'. A couple of Mir's verses may be quoted
here to illustrate the point:

Aadam-e-khaki se salam ko jila hai verna
Aeina tha to magr qabil-e-deedar na

It is the mortal man who bestows
splendour on the world
Otherwise the mirror of this world was
there but not worth looking at

Sirapa Arzoo hone ne banda kar diya hamko
Wagarna ham Khuda the gar dil-e-bemuddaa hote

Being a creature of countless yearnings,
I remained a mere man
Had I been without desires I would have been God

Thirdly, one finds in Mir an intense awareness of transience of human
existence, yet he would not like us to be weighed down by it but to rejoice in
our being as long as it lasts. At one place, he would say that life is short-lived

like the morning dew and at another place his message for us is to rejoice in the transitoriness like blossoming of the bud, the flower fading away with a smile:

Bood-e-Aadam namood-e-Shabnam hai
Aik do dam mein phir hawa hai yeh

Man's existence is like dew drops
In a moment or two it vanishes into thin air

Kaha mein ne kitna hai gul ka Sabat
Kali ne yeh sun kar tabassam kiya

I asked how long flower's life be
Bud, hearing this blossomed

We now move on to Mir's language and style. In him we find a great gift of combining everyday spoken language with Persian and Hindi words. He considered the use of Persian expressions "legitimate which are in consonance with Rekhta (Urdu) and also provided their usage could be harmonized with the native speech. He wove, thereby, unique designs achieving rate eloquence of expression. He also uses conversational style with intimate tones which cannot but touch the heart. Mir's structuring of verse is natural without any perceptible labouring. Maulana Hali in his Mugaddam Shair—o—Shairi, a critique of Urdu poetry, has observed that Mir remains unique in simplicity and purity of expression and that even a trite idea is presented by him in a refreshingly original manner. He cites the following verse of Mir to illustrate the point:

Ab ke janoon mein fasla shaid na kuch rahe
Daman ke chalk aur gareban ke chalk mein

In madness now no distance may perhaps be left
Between the two seams one of the collar and the other of hem

Hali has further observed that Mir could convey in simple words a poignant idea:

Hamare aage jab tera kaso ne naam liya
Dil-e-sitamzada ko ham ne thaam tham llya

When someone mentioned your name before me
I had somehow managed to keep hold on my afflicted heart

And this quality extended to many of his verses. For instance he conveys in simple words sad wistfulness in whispering undertones thus:

Sirhane Mir ke ahista bolo
Abhi abhi rote rote so gaya hai

Talk only in whispers over Mir's bedstead
After incessant weeping he has just gone to sleep

Sorrow lingers in the air and someone is whispering in your ear to be quiet to let the sleep take care of the suffering. The grand old man of Urdu literature, Maulvi Abdul Haq, while commenting on this verse, observes: "This verse is so simple. What can be more ordinary everyday language? But the style of expression is replete with anguish and from each word drips longing and despair."

In another verse Mir conveys a profound existential truth in the simplest possible language, yet with a forceful impact:

Bawale se kab talak bakte the sab karte the pyar
Aqal ki baaten kiyan kya hum se nadani hoi

So long we chattered senseless gibberish everyone loved us
We talked sense what a folly we committed

Most of Mir's ghazals are in 'Choti Behr' (small lines). The brevity, simple construction, conversations-style give his poetry an exquisite flavour. While commenting on these qualities of his verse, Abdul Haq further writes in his book "Intekhab Kalam-e-Mir":

"Usage of correct expression and unique arrangement and construction of words land music to his poetry. This, if combined with simplicity and inimitable style raises poetry to a great height. All these qualities are to be found in Mir and along with this his poetry has poignancy of pain which cannot but touch the heart."

However, it is not that he does not use Persian words and phrases difficult to comprehend, Mir has, by and large preferred everyday spoken language to convey deep thought—emotive content. In his own simple words:

> Shair mere hain sab khas pasand
> Par mujhe guftgoo awam se hai

> All my verses are liked by the select
> But my language is of the masses

While comparing Mir and Sauda's poetry earlier in this chapter, it was stated that the former made use of common proverbs to effectively convey an idea or emotion. It will be in place to give here a few such verses to illustrate the point:

> Dil ke yek qatra-e-khoon nahin hai baish
> Aik alam ke sir bla laya
> Dil mujhe uske gali mein lay ja kar
> Aur bhi khak mein mila laya
> Ab to jate hain butkade se, Mir
> Phir milainge gar khuda laya

> Heart no more than drop of blood
> But it brought calamity to many
> Heart took me to her street
> Dragging me down even more into dust
> Now I depart from the abode of the beautiful ones
> God willing we will meet again

> Mir Sahib, Zamana nazuk hai
> Donon bathen se thamiye dastar

> Mir Sahib, times are precarious
> Keep a hold on your turban with both hands

Dil who nagar nahin jo aabad ho sake
Pachtaoge suno ho yeh basti ujad kar

Heart is no habitation which can be rebuilt
Listen, you will repent destroying at

Mir, amdan bhi koi marta hai
Jaan hai to jahan hai piare

Does anyone die deliberately Mir
World exists so long as you live

Shikwa-e-abla abhi se Mir
Hai Piare, hanooz Dilli door

Complaining of blister so soon Mir
O, dear, Delhi is yet far off

B—POET'S POET—TRIBUTES

No Urdu poet, past or present has been paid tributes in such abundance
as that to Mir. Rich encomiums have been paid to him by various poets.
They include both his contemporaries and successors whether of yester years
or of the recent past. Sauda, a great contemporary of Mir says of his poetry:

Sauda tu is ghazal ko ghazal dar hazal hi likh
Hona hai tujh ko Mir se ustad ki tarf

Sauda, keep on perfecting ghazal to achieve excellence
For you have to attain Mir's level

Mohd Hassan Azad writes in his book 'Aabe-e—Hyal Itat' for once in a
while these two contemporaries also indulged in light hearted banter against
each other. For example Sauda says of Mir:

Na Padheo yeh ghazal Sauda hargaz Mir ke aage
Who in tarzon se kya waqif woh lye andaz kya jane

Do not, Sauda, in any case recite this ghazal before Mir
What does he know of its idiom,
What does he understand its style?

And Mir retorts:

Taraf hone mera mushkal hai Mir is shair ke fun mein
Yunhi Sauda kabhi hota so jahil hai kya jana

It is difficult for one to come up
to Mir in the art of poetry
Even though Sauda is there sometime
but what does that ignoramus know

Two more of his contemporaries, viz., Nasikh and Mussafi have
expressed their appreciation of Mir thus:

Shuba Nasikh nahin kuchh Mir ki ustadi ka
Khud woh be behra hai jo muttagad-o-Mir nahin

There is no doubt, Nasikh, of Mir being a master
Ignoramus is he who believes not in it

Ai Mussafi tu aur kahan shair ke dava
Phabta hai yeh andaz-e-sukhan Mir ke munh par

O, Mussafi, you and your claim to poetic perfection
It behoves Mir alone to make such a caim

What sets Mir apart from his contemporaries is that while the latter
remained preoccupied with embellishment of the language of their verses,
Mir was equally meticulous about words and content as also about his
style.

Two more immediate successors of Mir; who were great poets of not only of their own era but also of all times, Ghalib and Zauq who barely agreed on anything except on the subject of Mir as a poet. Let us see what Ghalib had to say of Mir:

Rekhte ke tum hi ustad nahin ho Ghalib
Kehte hain ugle zamane main koi Mir bhi tha

Ghalib you are not the only master of Urdu (verse)
I hear said there had been Mir in days gone by

Mir ke shair ka ahwal kahon kya Ghalib
Jis ka deevan kam az gulshan-e-Kashmir nahin

Ghalib, what to say of Mir's verse
Whose poetry is not less than garden of Kashmir

Ghalib, apna yeh aqseda hai bagol-e-Nasikh
Aap be-behra jo mutaqad-e-Mir nahin

Ghalib I believe in the words of Nashik
Ignoramus is he who believes not in Mir's masterliness

Zauq, a contemporary of Ghalib, as also a rival in the Moghul court goes a step further in his compliments to Mir:

Na hoa par na hoa Mir ka andaz naseeb
Zauq yaaron ne bahut zor ghazal mein mara

Zauq, we all strove the utmost to
achieve in ghazal Mir's style but it was never to be

Maulana Hali (1837-1934), poet, critic and writer known for his two outstanding books of Urdu prose 'Yadga-e-Ghalib' (his reminiscences of Mirza Ghalib) and 'Muggadame Shair-o-Shairi' (a critique of Urdu

Poetry) (observations from both these books have been quoted easier) has acknowledged his debt to three poets, Shaifte, Ghalib and Mir thus:

Hali sukhan mein Shaifta se mustfeed hoon
Ghalib ka muttaqad hoon muglad hoon Mir ka

Hali I have benefited from Sheifta in my verse
I am admirer of Ghalib but I follow in the footsteps of Mir

It is a great tribute to the perennial nature of Mir's poetry that the twentieth century poets have not lagged behind in praising him as a poet. Two early twentieth century poets Akbar Ailahabad and Hasrat Mohani speak thus of Mir:

Main hoon kya cheese jo is tarz pe Jaon, Akbar
Nasikh o Zauq bhi chal na sakey Mir ke saath

What am I to follow this style, Akbar
When Nasikh and Zauq could not keep with Mir

Shair mere bhi hain pur dard lekhin Hasrat
Mir ka shewa-e-guftar kahan se laon

My verse too has poignancy of pain, Hasrat
But Mir's style' excellence is nowhere within my reach

And modern Urdu poets have shown similar appreciation of Mir's verse. Firaq Gorakhpuri says of Mir:

Sadgay Firaq ejaz-e-sukhan ke kaisi udai yen awarz
In ghazalon ke purde mein to Mir ki ghazalein bole lhain

Blessed, Firaq be the spell the style has cast on your verse
From behind the veil of your ghazals resound ghazals of Mir

Not only is there the spell of Mir's style on Firaq's poetry, he even seeks solace from Mir's poetry in his loneliness of nights:

Yaad ayyam ki parwaiyo dheeme dheeme
Mir ki koi ghazal gao ke kutch raat kate

Blow gently, o, breeze of days gone by
Sing some ghazal of Mir to make the night's loneliness endurable

Another modern poet Asar Luckhnavi says of Mir:

Main Mir ka dam bharta hoon Asar uske kalam ka shaida hoon
Haan shair to tum keh laite ho par bol banana mushkal hai

I admire Mir, I adore his verse
Well I too can write verse but it is
difficult to bring about that tone and tenor

From accolades paid to Mir as a poet, it does not, however, follow that excellence extended to all or bulk of his verse. It is generally true of all great poets that all their verses are not and cannot invariably be of high quality. Mir too shares with them the verses of low quality and in his case there is also an element of bathos at places.

Hali in his Muggadma (Critique), quotes Maulana Azurda having said of Mir-poetry:

Pastish bagair past, blundish busain blund
When low extremely low when high of great height

The grand old man of Urdu literature Abdul Haq endorses this view[4]. He further refers in this connection to Hali's view of poets in general in his book referred to above:

"It should be remembered that among the poets who have been considered masters, none will be found whose entire verse from A-Z will be of high quality in beauty and subtlety as that perfection can only be

---

[4]   Intekhab Kalam-e-Mir-Maulana Abdul Haq-Taraqqi-e-Anjuman-e-Urdu, New Delhi ; C-Mir on Mir's Poetry. (Self Acclaim in the context of his Personality)

an attribute of God. The high point of poet's accomplishment is that his ordinary verse be smooth and prosodically correct and at places revealing surprising perception which gets imprinted on the hearts of all, lay reader or the elite and this can be found only in a poet whose poetry is simple and natural

In the preceding section, I have given at some length the accolades pain to Mir by poets of yester years and of recent times. Her give Mir's own estimation of himself as a poet for none has written so much on the subject as Mir himself. While Whitman's 'Song of Myself' was a great mystical journey into the self, Mir sings of himself as a poet being aware of his own poetic excellence, both in style and content. No sense of false modesty prevents him from speaking of his own eloquence. No doubt he freed the hobbled horse of Urdu verse from roaming within the confines of romantic love expressed in trite terminology of Gul-o-Bulbul (rose and bulbul), Shamma-o-Parwana (lamp and moth). Writing about poetry of his times, Mir writes in his critique of Urdu poetry 'Nukat-ul-Shora (written by him Persian) that Urdu verse has been limited to the language of Gul-o-Bulbul whereas he has more meaningful subjects to write about. The poetry for him was a medium to mirror heartfelt feelings which very often amounted, in his case, to outpouring of pain and anguish. To put in his own words:

Mujkho shair na kaho Mir ke Sahib mein ne
Dard-e-gam kitne kiye jama to deewan kiya

Do not, Sir, call me a poet
I gathered so many pains and sorrows to create this book of Verse

Nevertheless, even though Mir's self-evaluation may be fully justified, it must be said that it is somewhat overdone for he reverts to the subject every now and then. Some of these self—laudatory verses are given below for reader's perusal:

Rekhta rutbay ko ponchchaya hua usika hai
Mutqad kaun nahin Mir ki ustadi ka

Urdu poetry was raised by him to this eminence
Who is there who does not believe in Mir's masterlines

Jane ka nahin shorsukhan ka mere hargaz
Te hashr jahan mein mere deewan rahay ga

Never will fade away the resource of my verse
My poetry will on till the judgement day

Saare aalam par hoon main chhaya hua
Mustnad hai mere farmaya hua

Al pervasive am I in the world
So authentic is what I say

Bulbul ghazal sarai aage hamare mat kar
Sab ham se seekhte hain andaz guftgo ka

Bulbul recite not ghazal to me
All learn the art of conversation from me

Yehan se dekhiye yak shair shorangreiz nikle hai
Qayamat ka sa hangama hai har ja mere deewan mein

See from any angle my poetry proclaims aloud
My book of verse has the turbulence as if of the judgement day

Kya janon dil ko khainche hain kyon shair Mir ke
Kutch aise tarz bhi nahin aayam bhi nahin

What do I know why Mir's verse captivates the heart
It has nothing special in style or subtlety of expression

Agarche gosha nashin hoon main shairon main Mir
Per mere shor ne rooye zameen tamam liya

Even I remain aloof among poets
But my voice is heard all over the land

Baatein hamari yaad rahen phir baatein aisi na suniye ga
Padhte kisi ko suniye to dair talak sir dhuniye ga

Remember what I say for such talk you will not hear again
When you hear someone reading it, repent you
will for ignoring it earlier

Rekhta kahe ko tha is rutbar-e-aala ko Mir
Jo zameen nikhli usay to aasman tak lay gaya

Where was the excellence of Urdu poetry earlier Mir?
It was you who raised it to skies whatever ground (subject) you touched

Dil kis tarah na khainche ashar rekhte ke
Behtar kiya hai main ne is aib ko hunr mein

Why shouldn't the heart be drawn to Urdu poetry?
For I have transformed an addiction into an art

Mir darya hai sune shair zubani uski
Allaha, Allaha re tabiat ki rawani uski

Mir is a river, listen to him reciting verse
God, what a natural flow he has

Padhte phirein ge gallion mein rakhton ko log
Muddat rehein gi yaad yeh baatein hamarian

People will go around reciting my Urdu verse
What I say will be remembered for long

Rakhta khub hi kehta hai jo insaf karo
Chahiey ahal-e-sukhan Mir ko ustad karein

He writes exquisite Urdu poetry, to be fair to him
Poet should adopt Mir as their mentor

Na rakho kaan nazm-e-shairan-e-hal par itne
Chalo tuk Mir ko sunne ke who moti proota hai

Do not lend ear to the poetry of poets of these days
Just go and listen to Mir who strings pearls for you

Khol kar deewan mera dekh kudrat muddai
Garcje hoon main naujawan per Shairon mein peer hoon

Open my book of verse, O, you demanding nature
Even though young I am grand old man among poets

There are many more verses in the same vein in his deewans acclaiming himself as a poet non-pareil. As to his command over Urdu language Mir rightly claims his mastery over it:

Guftgo rekhte mein ham se na kar
Yeh hamari zuban hai, piare

Talk not in Urdu to me
That is my language

Yes, Urdu was his language even though exclusive claim above may be just a poetic overstatement. Nevertheless, he never compromised over its correctness and exactitude. In fact, he was so fastidious about the language about the language that it was often taken as churlish arrogance on his part. An incident in his life as told by Mohd Hussain Azam in his book "Aab-e-Hyat" illustrates the point. When he left Delhi for Lucknow, Mir had, for financial constraints, to share the carriage with another man. When they had travelled some distance, his co-traveller tried to strike a conversation but Mir turned his back on him. The man again said something addressing Mir who replied with acerbic disdain. "Sir, you have paid carriage fare and are entitled to sit in the carriage but what has it to do with a conversation?" The man said "Sir what is the harm? It is a pastime for the journey and in conversation one remains amused." Mir was annoyed and said sharply, "For you, Sir, it is a pastime but my language gets corrupted?"

Two main incidents related by Mir himself in his autobiography, Zikr-e-Mir may be narrated here to show his meticulousness and sensitivity about his poetry and the language. Mir has described how he had broken with his patron. Nawab Ryayal Ali Khan on whom he was financially dependent because of the said Nawab asking him to give some of his verses to a street singer who could memorise it for singing. Mir protested that his poetry was not for singing. Although he reluctantly complied with the Nawab's wish but he left his employment as he could not reconcile to his poetry being put to such a banal use as to be sung in the streets. Similarly, he was finical about the language about which an incident has been related a little earlier. Another incident described by Mir in his autobiography would show that he had imbibed this particularity about the language from a very early age. When as a young boy Mir was searching for employment in Delhi, he met Nawab Sams-ul-Daula, King's minister-cum-royal paymaster through one Khawaja Basit. The Nawab out of regard for Mir's late father, ordered that the boy (Mir) may be given a daily scholarship of one rupee from his administration. What transpired thereafter may be described in Mir's own words:

"I requested Khawaja Basit that since Nawab Sahib was showing so much kindness, he may as well give a signed order so that his clerks do not put me off by raising objections. I took out an application which I had written beforehand from my pocket. The said Khawaja, however, observed "This is no time for penstand?" At this, I burst out into a loud laughter. Nawab looked at me and asked me the cause of my laughter. I said, "I could not understand the expression. Had he said the carrier of inkpot is not present, then it would be something or that it was no time for Nawab Sahib to sign. To say that it is no time for penstand is an unusual construction. Penstand is no more than a piece of wood. It does not know appropriate or inappropriate time. Whosoever is ordered will bring it." The Nawab started laughing and said "What he says is right". In short he did not reject my application and obliged me by signing it."

Mir was then a mere teenage boy. In addition to showing his meticulousness about the language, this incident also illustrates the point that in the matter of giving went to his thoughts and emotions. Mir was free from any inhibition. Mir has been reported by some writers to be of irascible temperament which aggravated with advancing years and with personal tragedies happening in quick succession in his old age. He went into seclusion and even ignored the summons of his benefactor Nawab Asaf-ul-Daula who was a nobleman of liberal nature.

To be fair to the poet, it may be mentioned her that Mir was not unaware of this edge to his personality which made others indifferent to him, if not hostile. He confesses:

Teri chaal taidi teri baat rokhi
Tujhe Mi samjha hai yank am kaso ne

Your manner convoluted, your speech blunt
Mir, you have hardly been understood by anyone here

Elsewhere Mir confesses to his tendency to give free expression to his feelings:

Kaha jiz se jo kutch hoga samne Mir kaha hoga
Baat na dil mein phir gai hogi munh per mere aai hoi

Whatever had to be said to someone Mir must have said to his face
Whatever came to his tongue could not have been restrained in his heart

This outspokenness shows that Mir, as already pointed out earlier was completely free from repression in giving expression to his thoughts and emotions. This trait seems to have arisen from dedication to truth born of early exposure to Sufi saints and Dervaishes.

Viewed from a different angle, this aspect of Mir reminds us of 'Nietzsches' observations about poets in general (even though these are somewhat of rigmarole). In 'Thus spake Zarathustra', Nietzsche writes:

"Truly, their spirit itself is peacock of all peacocks and a sea of vanity. The poet's spirit wants spectators even if they are buffaloes. But I have grown weary of this spirit; and I see a day coming when it will grow weary of itself. Already I have been the poets transformed. I have seen them direct their glances upon themselves. I have seen penitents of spirit appear; they grow out of poets."

Dr. Salim Akhtar in his essay on Mir makes a similar point of poets making mirror of their own narcissism, one of the reason for which is a bitter feeling of non-recognition.[5] It appears that narcissistic element in a poet, through a mysterious alchemy, gets transmuted into creativity, also sometimes transforming them in spirit. This element is not to be confused with pathological neurosis and is not to be equated with vanity but is tied up with the creative urge. In the specific case of Mir, there was none on the scene to match his poetic excellence. He was aware of it and was sensitive enough to feel piqued when appreciation did not come forth. Notwithstanding the need for a pat on the back, Mir did not, however, let himself be unduly weighed down for want of it and his poetry went on blossoming till the old age where he became both physically and mentally

---

[5]   Mir-Taqi-Mir—A critical and Investigative Evaluation (Essay in Urdu) published by Ghalib Academy, New Delhi

ill in Lucknow. More about this is written in the next section of this chapter relating to the poet's stay in Lucknow.

D—IN LUCKNOW PINING FOR DELHI

While narrating the life and times of Mir, (Chapter I), it was stated that driven by destitution in Delhi, Mir migrated to Lucknow at the invitation of Nawab Asaf-ul-Daula, the ruler of Avadh. It was also mentioned there that despite being comfortably placed there, thanks to the benevolent nature of the Nawab, Lucknow's lifestyle and culture being decorative and of glossy superficiality was hardly conducive to Mir who was of a serious temperament. He considered Lucknow's poetry as colourful and decorative arrangement of words sans thought—emotive content. He dismissed Jurat, one of the leading poets of the city, as a mere versifier of "kissing and smooching"; and told Soz, the teacher of Nawab Asaf-ul-Daula, "Aren't you ashamed of reading your poetry before me?"[6]

Apart from its garish culture and lifestyle, Lucknow had nothing more to offer to Mir beyond facile contentment and quietism alien to his sensitivity. For Mir life and its thought-emotive content were earnest matters to be mirrored intensely. No wonder fun loving Lucknow could not respond to and show appreciation of his poetry which had a perennial quality mirroring life, as it did, from sensitively feeling heart.

As already mentioned, being not able to reconcile himself to the shallow sybarite culture with its unabashed hedonism, Mir felt stifled in Lucknow and experienced an agonizing nostalgia for Delhi. He began to grow wild and gradually withdrew from the society and went into retreat. In the words of Dr. Farooqi, Lucknow was nothing short of a cultural trauma for Mir. Disgruntled with Lucknow, he expressed regret for having left Delhi, the intensity of nostalgia for that city increasing with the advancing years.

In his poetry too Mir has at places given vent to his discontent with Lucknow and its people and has expressed painful longings for Delhi. Some of these verses are given below for readers' perusal:

Khak-e-Dilli se juda ham ko kiya yekbargi
Aasman kotni kador at so nikala yun gubar

---

[6]   Aab-e-Hiyat-Mohd Hussain Azad

With suddenness was I separated from Delhi
Heavens were hostile, so poured their venom on me

Barson se Lucknow mein igamat hai mujhke leik
Yaan se chalne ka rakhta hoon azam-e-safar hanooz

For years I have lived in Lucknow
But to move away from here is still my firm resolve

Kharaba Dilli ka deh chand behtar Lucknow se tha
Wahi mein kash mar jata saraseema na aata yan

Ruin that was Delhi was ten times better than Lucknow
I wish I had died there instead of coming here in pani

Haft aqleem har gali hai kahin
Dilli se bhi diar hote hein

Are there seven continents in each street anywhere?
Yet they do exist in cities such as Delhi

Dilli thi talismat ke bar jagan Mir
In aankhon se ham ne kya kye dekha

Delhi was a magic house whose every corner, Mir
My eyes behold a lot of wonders

Dil-o-Dilli donon hain garche kharab
Pe kutch luft us ujde nagar main hai

Delhi and my heart both desolate
Even then there is still some fun in the ruined city

Koochay nahin Dilli ke auraq-e-mussavar the
To shakl nazar aai tasveer nazar aai

Streets of Delhi no streets but a painter's folio
Every face we saw was like a painting

Jawahar to kya kya dikhaya gaya
Khareedar koi na paya gaya
Matai-e-hunr pheer kar laic halo
Bahut Lucknow mein raho ghar chalo

In varied ways I showed my talent
But there was no taker
Carry back your talents' treasure
Enough have you lived in Lucknow, go back home

Rahi na-gufta mere dil mein dastan meri
Na is diar mein samjha koi zuban meri

My tale remained untold in my heart
For none in this city could understand my language

Barang-e-soorat-e-jaras tujh se door hoon anha
Khabr nahin hai tujhe, ah, caravan meri

Alone far off from you like the sound of a stray bell
Alas, O, caravan, you are unaware of me

Kis kis ada se rekhte main ne kahe wale
Samjha na koi meri zuban is diar mein

Versatile was the verse in Urdu recited
But none in this city understood my language

The poet like any other artist has a great urge to communicate and to get appropriate response. Sadly this urge in Mir was frustrated in Lucknow. Another thing that aggravated his allergy to that city was his disappointment with its aristocracy which consisted of puffed up men sans substance. Even though they did not understand him as a poet, they would invite him on occasions and even reward him. Mir, being a hypersensitive person, considered such meetings as a matter of "disgrace".

As already mentioned Mir's discontent with Lucknow was compounded by his protracted illness in old age. Added to it was the tragedy of three members of his family dying in quick succession—his daughter died, within a year his son passed away followed soon thereafter by Mir's wife. He went into seclusion and gave up the pursuit of his poetic efforts regretting thus:

Bas bahut waqt kiya shair ke fun mein zaya
Mir ab pir hoay tark-e-khiyalat karo

Stop you have wasted enough time in the art of poetry
Mir you have now grown old, time to drop thoughts

Kis ka dimag shair-e-sukhan zof mein hai Mir
Apna hi rahe hai ab to hamein beshtar khayal

Whose mind bothers about verse in the infirmity of old age
I am, most of the time, worried about myself

Luft-e-sukhan bhi peeri mein rehta nahin Mir
Ab shair ham padhe hain woh shad-o-mad Nahin

Poetry is no fun in old age
In the verse I recite now that verve is missing

CHAPTER 4

SELECT VERSE OF MIR
TRANSCREATION AND ELUCIDATION

Verse 1

Hoga kisi deewar ke saye ke talay Mir
Kya kaam Mohabbat se us aaram talab ko

Lazing under the shade of a wall might be Mir
What has that easy going idler got to do with love

Here is an irony. The love is called 'aaram talab', an easygoing idler when he has in fact given up everything to be near the beloved. In the words of the grand old man of Urdu literature, Maulana Abdul Haq, "the expression 'aaram talab', is the life of this verse. Keep this in mind and then reflect on it, only then you will enjoy the verse. A person who has abandoned all ease and comfort because of love and has given up his home, his friends and is lying aimlessly, despairingly in the shade of his beloved's walls, is being taunted as an easygoing idler who can have nothing to do with love. Just imagine what can then be the torture of love."

Verses 2-6

Ishaq bi ishq hai jahan dekho
Saare aalam mein bhar raha hai ishq
Ishq mashooq ishq aashaq hai
Yehni apna hi mubtala hai ishq
Kaun maqsad ko ishq bin pahuncha
Arzoo ishq muddaa hai ishq
Dard hi khud dwa hai ishq
Sheikh kya jaane kya hai ishq
Tu na howay to nazm kul uth jaye
Such hain shairan khuda hai shq

Wherever you see there is nothing but love
The world is filled with it
Love is the beloved and the lover as well
In short love is absorbed in its own fulfillment
Who reached his goal without love
Yearning is love, so is that it yearns for
Pain itself is love, soit is its cure
What can priest know what love is
If you (love) were not, the entire world would vanish
into thin air Poets are right, love is God

In short, Mir considers love to be all embracing:

Zahir baatin awwal aakhir, pain bala ishq hai sab
Noor zulmat, maani soorat, sab kutch aap hua hai ishq

Out-inner, first-last, below-above-all are love
Light-darkness, essence-form, all in themselves become love

Mir here is rendering into verses, his father's teaching on love in the poet's early childhood which has been reproduced earlier in Chapter 2 of this book. Briefly, it says that love is all and is the only raison de tre of our lives and the existence at large in this world which in the absence of love is a mere mirage and clinging to it is like tying water with a string.

These verses have a remarkable resemblance to what Khalil Gibran later gave expression to on the subject of Love both in substance and language.

For instance, Mir talks of love being absorbed in its own fulfillment, Gibran makes an identical statement in his book 'The Prophet' that "love has no other desire but to fulfill itself."

Mir as a poet of love has been dealt as length in the preceding chapter. It may, however, be mentioned here that sometimes suffering in the poet touches a high point with love becoming a torture worse than that of hell:

Ishq hai ashgon ke jalne ko
Yeh jahanamm me aazab kahan

Love is to scorch the lovers
The hell could not have worse torture

Kaya kahon tum se ke kya hai ishq
Jaan ka rog, bla hai ishq

What to tell you, what love is
An affliction it is, a misfortune

Ishtkhawan kaamp kaamp jalte hain
Ishq ne aag yeh lagai hai

Quiveringly burn the bones
Such is the fire ignited by love

Such a world of love is a barren wasteland:
Aalam-e-ishq kharaba hai, wan koi ghar sabad nahin

The world of love is a wasteland where no house is inhabited

Chasm-e-namnak-o-dil-e-pur, jigger sadpara
Daulat-e-ishq se ham pass bhi the kya kya kuch

Tearful eyes, heavy heart and innards torn hundredfold
Thanks to the wealth of love, we too had many things

Above few verses may suggest an ambivalence of sorts about love, but such a view will be fallacious as his love poetry is of multiple strands. For better appreciation of Mir's poetry of love, be it sensual (with or without basokht), mystical or just aesthetical (where he shows exquisite delicacy in describing beloved's beauty), we may consider the matter of love in some detail and how this subject has been viewed may consider the matter of love in some detail and how this subject has been viewed by different people, thinkers, philosophers, psychologists along with the general attitude on the subject in Urdu poetry as compared to the poetry of some of the other Indian languages.

"According to early Greek myth, Eros, the God of love emerged to create the earth. Before all was silent, bare and motionless. Now all was life, joy and motion. According to the later Greek myth, Eros was born to Aphrodite and Ares. He did not grow as other children do but remained a small, rubicund cherubic child with gauzy wings and rougish dimpled face. When his brother Anteros, god of passion was born, Eros grew into a slender handsome youth but when separated from his brother, he regressed into childish and mischievous habits."

(Extract from 'Love and Will" by Rollo May)

The Greek myth above draws a clear distinction between love, raw, mechanical and of immature capriciousness and a mature love guided by passion.

Later thinkers, philosophers and psychologists have also differentiated between different kinds of love keeping in view whether it be warped or authentic. C.S. Lewis talked of 'need love' and 'gift love'. Maslow gave their psychological counterpart as 'deficiency love' and 'being love' respectively. The existentialist Sarte gives the warped version of love placing it within the parameters of 'subject-object' duality, a view partly shared by Martin Buber whose view of love, however, is not that depressing. Within the subject-object paradigm Buber draws the distinction between 'I—it' love and 'I—thou' love. In the former there is usage, possession, exploitation and domination whereas in the latter there are no such contaminations for love is based on mutual respect. In his great poem, 'The Prophet', Khalil Gibran talks of 'Love possesses not, nor would it be possessed.'

'Need love' or 'deficiency love' means dependence, bondage and possessiveness which in extreme form may become pathological. In any case such a love is destined to give heart breaks. On the other hand, 'gift love' or being love' means that something you have you love sharing it, within the abundance of life and energy overflowing to others.

The existentialists viewed love and human relationships in the "subject-object" paradigm with 'subject' and 'object' ever changing places in a merry go-round (we may as well call it sorry go round) of one using the other. Thus, exploitation and struggle for domination becomes in-built into any relationship. Satre[7] asserts vehemently that woman a viscous reality symbolizes, "a sickly sweet feminine revenge of the being. The viscous is docile. Only at the very moment when I believe I possess it, behold by a reversal it possesses me . . . I want to get rid of the viscous and it sticks to me, it draws me, it sucks at me . . . Here, we can see the symbol which abruptly discloses itself, there exists a poisonous possession." Pain, anguish, cruelty is inherent in the situation.

The western mind goes into the subject of love also in a scientific manner, i.e. to collect facts, verify their veracity, analyse and classify. That is how west arrives at a tradition and according to the tradition arrived at, Rollo May lists four kinds of love in his book 'Love and Will':

1. Sexual, lust, libido
2. Eros—to love, procreate, create,
1. the urge towards higher forms of being and relationship.
3. Philia or friendship, brotherly or sisterly love.
4. Agape or caritas—devoted to welfare of other people—another prototype of which is love of God.

The blending all the four constitute an authentic love. In contrast to the western attitude, love is reflected in the poetry of some of the Indian languages such as Hindi, Bangla, Gujarati, Marathi, etc., is influenced by Vaishnavite Bhavas, viz., Shant (equipoise in relationship), Das (service), Vatsalya (love between parents and child), Sakha (friendship), Madhur (love between man and woman). Even in Madhur Bhava, the sensual part is imperceptible. The Madhur Bhava, the sensual part is imperceptible. The Madhur Bhavas is epitomized by love of Radha and Mira for Lord Krishna. Both of them are instances of combining all the five Bhavas which is a must for being one with one's divine ground.

Love in Urdu poetry follows the Persian paradigm of 'Ishaq-e-Majazi" (sensual love) and Ishq-e-Haqiqi (love of the divine). The former is eros-related and the latter covers Sufi Marfat (love for the divine expressed in

---

7   I 'being And Nothingness' Part III Three—"Being-for Others". Chapter Three—Concrete Relations with Others'

I—first Attitudes Towards Others; Love, Language, Masochism—Jean-Paul Sartre

2 'From Socrates to Sartre'—T.T. Lavine, The Philosophic Quest.

ordinary sensual terms). Sufi love culminates with the merger in the divine. Persian Sufi poet Jalal-uddin-Rumi proclaims:

> O, let me not exist, for non-existence proclaims
> To Him we shall return

These two types of love should not be taken to be mutually exclusive. On the other hand 'ishq-e-majazi' may be a means to 'ishq-e-haqiqi as observed by Maulana Zamir.

> Ganimat dan gar ishq-e-majazi ast
> Ke az behr-e-haqiqi kaar, sazi ast

> Consider sensual love a blessing
> For it may be means to the love of the Divine

Verse 7

> Hamare aage tera j ab kisi ne naam liya
> Diye-e-sitam zada ko ham tham tham liya

> When someone mentioned your name before me
> I, somehow managed to keep a hold on my afflicted heart

Here is some example of poetry in basokht tradition in which Mir complains of beloved's cruelty. Language of the verse is simple and suggestive. The very mention of beloved's name pangs into the poet's heart. The poet is also committed to keeping his emotions hidden for he does not want to compromise his beloved. So he keeps a hold of himself, somehow.

The poignancy of suffering in love is oft repeated theme in Mir's poetry. The mention of beloved's name evokes this agonizing response in Mir:

> Jab naam tera lijiye tab chashm bhar aaway
> Is tarha ke jeene ko kahan se jigar aaway

> When your name is mentioned my eyes are filled with tears
> From where do I get the heart to live such a life

In so far basokht of these verses is concerned, it is necessary to mention here that even though basokht is somewhat of hackneyed tradition, it does, nevertheless, deal with human inclination of the moods of female of the species which may at times be one of indifference or of caprice moving on to outright cruel

Verse 8-9

Nazki us lab ki kya kahaye
Pankhdi ek gulab ke si hai
Meer un neembaaz aaankhon mein
Sari masti sharab ki si hai

What to say of the delicacy of the lip
It is as if a rose petal
Mir, in those open eyes
The entire ecstasy is as if of wine

Mir has, in his poetry, used similes very sparingly. However, here he does so very effectively even though words and images are simple. Delicacy of lips and ecstasy mirrored in the almond eyes of the beloved are exquisitely expressed, the former in floral delicacy and the latter in bachnalian abandon. We see here the aesthetic sensibility of the poet

Verse 10

Aise ahoo-e-ram khurda ki wahshat khoni mushkal thi
Sahr kiya ejaz kiya jin logo no tum ko ram kiya

Hard was to control the wildness of runaway deer
Those one won you over performed a magic-a miracle

Here is another complaint against the beloved in basokht tradition to the effect that she is wild, difficult to catch like a runaway deer (in Western parlance playing difficult to get). So to her over is a daunting task tantamount to performing a magic or a miracle. The beloved's caprice is uncontrollable confronting the lover with almost an impossible situation for he is no messiah to perform such miracles and nothing short of miracle is needed to keep up with the wayward beloved.

Verse 11

Apne to hont bhi na hilay unke roo-broo
Ranjish ki wajah Mir who kya baat ho gai

I did not ever open my lips before her
What then has given her cause to the angry

In the tradition of the earlier verse, here the beloved is portrayed as an enigma, wanton in behaviour, taking offence either way. Even when the lover is tongue tied, being overwhelmed by her presence, she is pigued at being ignored. In a similar vein a modern Urdu poet, Faiz Ahmed Faiz writes:

Woh baat, sarey fasane mein jis ka zikar na tha
Woh baat unto bahut nagawar guzri hai

That something which found no mention in the entire story
It is that to which she has taken exception to

If we view these two verses from psychological angle, we have first to understand that the opposite of love is not hatred but indifference. Love and hate both imply emotional involvement but indifference is just indifference sans hope. Indifference may cause greater hurt and is hard to handle. Ghalib has this to say on the subject:

Laag ho to ham usey samjhain lagao
Jab na ho kutch bhi to dhoka khain kya

Even if there be enmity
I take it to be relatedness
But when there is indifference
There is nothing to hope for

For Ghalib any contact was better than no contact:

Qata keejey na taullaq ham se
Kutch nahin to adawat hi sahi

Snap not the contact with me
If nothing else, let us be at loggerheads
For then he will still be in touch with you and
will have the hope to win you over

Verse 12

Dag-e-firaq-o-hasrat-e-wasl, arzoo-e-shauq
Main saath zeer-e-khak thi hangama le gaya

Sorrow of separation, craving for the
beloved, yearning for love
I carried a tempest down to my grave

The great turmoil, the poet has taken to his grave, is his unfulfilled desires. In fact, in life too our desires ungratified, which fill us with turbulence, and in despair. On the other hand, gratified desire, as William Blake holds, "grows fruits of life and beauty there", whereas ungratified desire, according to him, "sows sand all over ruddy limbs and flaming hair."

In Buddhism, it is believed that consciousness does not die with the body but survives it. So desires are carried forward after death till one is reborn in another incarnation.

Like Mir who talks about our being caught up in our desires up to our graves, another poet puts in this last gasp plea:

Dafnana dekh bhal ke hasrat zada Ki naash
Lipti hoi kaffan se koi arzoo na ho

Bury carefully the body of the dead one stricken with craving
Lest there be still a desire sticking to the coffin

Mir has also said about desires elsewhere:
Hasrat uski jagah thi khwabida
Mir ka khol kar khafan dekha

His desire was aspleep in its place
When Mir's coffin was opened

Verse 13

(Sufi humanism)

Mat ranja kar kisi ko apne to aitequad
Dil dhaye ke jo kaaba banaya to kaya hua

Hurt no one that is my faith
What is kaaba if built on the ruins of a heart

This is the poet's religion, one of love and compassion. He believes that if you break human heart by word or deed, all your building of temples or mosques is of no consequence. This theme is common to Sufies for whom love is a mean to attain Godhead. Bulley Shah, a Punjabi Sufi poet has said the same thing as Mir is saying in his verse. He says in his usual vehement style, "Break if you must the mosque and the temple but never the human heart in which dwells the beloved (the lord). Says Kabir, "Benares is to the east, Mecca is to the west; but explore your heart for there are both Ram and Allaha."

For Sufies love transcends all boundaries of religious forms which sometime lead to indifference to human suffering. In some cases, it degenerates into 'me first' approach or uncaring quietism or desire for nirvana or moksha. Varanasi in such cases epitomizes the flowering of indifference to human suffering.

Verse 14

Aadam-e-khaki se aalam ko jila hai warna
Aaena tha to magr kabil-e-deedar na tha

It is the mortal man who lends glory to this world
Otherwise the mirror (existence) was not worth looking at

The verse reminds me of the prayer of my schooldays in which we used to praise God for creating this beautiful, wonderful world. Mir, here, says something contrary to that as he praises man for lending glory to this world which but for him, would not have been worth looking at. The poet elevates man to a place of pre-eminence in the universe. As we have seen in the preceding verse, the human heart for him was more sacred than Kaaba.

He shared that belief of Sufies of the east and mystics of the west. American mystic poet Walt Whitman (declares in the 'Song of Myself':

And I say to mankind
Be not curious about God
I see something of God each hour
of the twenty four hours and each moment then
In the faces of men and women, I see God
and in my own face in the mirror.

From the write up on this it will be seen that Mir has gone a step further than the English poet William Blake who holds that 'Where man is not, nature is barren'.

Verse 15

Haq to sab kutch hi hai tu nahaq na bol
Baat kehte sar kata Mansoor ka

God pervades all, blab not about it
For talking about it, Mansoor's head was chopped off

Mansoor used to go into a trance and declare 'Anal-Haq' which is identical with Vedantic statement. 'Aham Brahm Asmi'. I am Brahm, all pervading God. The poet questions the advisability of blabbing about it, even though it is the truth of all truths, like Mansoor who lost his life for talking about it. Mystical experiences of this type can hardly be conveyed in words. It is an experience of the kind about which Lao Tzu has said:

He who knows, does not speak
He who speaks, does not know

Reference in this verse is also to the danger inherent in talking out of turn about God on whom intolerant clergy is presumptuously having copyright claims. Ghalib too has dwelt on the subject:

Qatra apna bhi haqeeqat mein hai darya lekhin
Hamko taqleed-e-tunak zarfi-e-Mansoor nahin

Drop that I am is in fact too a river
But I would not subscribe to the impulsive
tattling about it like Mansoor

These verses of Mir and Ghalib may be viewed in the context of the very nature of mystical experience which according to William James ('The varieties of Religious Experience') has four attributes viz., ineffability neotic quality transience and passivity. Briefly, these may be states of directly experienced feeling defying expression and the insight into the depth of truth beyond the reach of discursive intellect. These states cannot be sustained for long (Ramakrishna, however, used to go into these states for a relatively long duration and at fairly regular intervals but his disciples invariably feared for his life at such occasions). In such a state, one's own will is in abeyance and one is connected with certain definite phenomena of secondary or alternative personality, be it prophetic speech, automatic writing or mediumistic trance as in the case of Mansoor. It is said that when Mansoor was warned by Jumaid, his mentor about the danger he was putting himself into by declaring 'I am God', as it may be construed heretical, Mansoor replied that he was helpless as at that time God spoke through him.

Kabir sings of God's immanence and non-dual nature of reality thus:

"Behold me in all things it is the
second that leads you astray."

However, western mystic Echart views reality differently: "More God is in all things, the more he is outside them. The more he is within, the more without."

What Mansoor said in a direct manner and what cost him his life was more subtly paid by another Muslim Sufi saint of bygone era, Bayazid of Bistami. Says he, "I went from God to God and until they cried in me, 'O, thou I'." When someone knocked on his door and asked, 'Is Bayazid here?" He answered "Is anybody here except God:"

Verse 16

Ab past-o-buland aik hain jun naqsh-e-kadam yan
Pamal hua khoob to hamwar hua main

High and low here are the same as footprints
More I was trodden, smoother I became

Mir's stance in this verse is identical with the attitude of ancient Chinese religion. Taoism which extols the virtue of humility says Lao Tzu, "He who humbles himself shall be preserved entire. He that bends shall be made straight. He that is empty shall be filled. He that has little shall succeed. He who has much shall go astray."

What this verse expresses and what Taoism in operation holds are contrary to the western attitude of striving, seeking eagerly earthly possessions, self-assertion, domination, individually, nationally and internationally. Lao Tzu describes operation of Tao, "Production without possession, action without self-assertion, development without domination."

In the materialistic world, the quality of 'having' drive in an individual is societally extolled whether it be the east or the west leading to a rat-race which is concomitant or rather the cause of not only peptic ulcers but also of mental disorders, hypertension and heart failures.Life remains misery amongst material plenty which acquires its own momentum and very often there are no brakes. Men with drive are driven by unseen hands over which they have no control. For drives to yield positive results at all levels, material mental, emotional and spiritual, one has to have an understanding of one's drives, developing in the process a self-control mechanism and at the same time not to live unidimensional life. Adding an extra dimension to oneself is one of the ways to secure you from evil consequences of your drives provided one does it with full awareness of one's motives in the thought—emotive processes as translated into action. Only then your drives will get integrated in the totality of life where different components of yourself will be in perfect equilibrium.

Verses 17-18

Kal paon aik kasa-e-sir par jo aa gaya
Yaksar woh astkhwan shikaston se choor tha
Kehne laga ke dekh ke chal rah bekhabr
Mein bhi kabhi kasu ka sir-e-pur garoor tha

When my feet tread on the cuplike head
Really it was a skull beaten into pieces
Walk verily, it said O, you careless one
I too was once someone's head full of pride

Care is the key to existence, particularly in relationship. The poet wants us to remain in an awake-state and to tread the earth carefully so as not even to trample a dead bone.

Mind is the seat of ego. Arrogance is one of the symptoms of what is called as ego's inflation. Heart which, stands for emotions and bhavas has to be in harmony with the mind. Only when the head and heart functions in tandem, there is a possibility of wisdom taking over from pride and raw emotion. Mind with its accumulated knowledge is ever proud that it knows too much whereas wisdom realized it has a lot to learn.

Philosophy contained in these verses of Mir is similar to that of Zen Buddhism. Let us reflect on this Zen story where head (intellect) has been equated with shoes we wear. Both have functions but neither is of any special importance:

"Nansen saw the monks of the eastern and western halls fighting over a cat. He seized the cat and told the monks that if any of you say a good word, you can save the cat. No one answered. So Nansen boldly cut the cat in two pieces. That evening Joshu returned and Nansen told him about this. Joshu removed his sandals put them on his head and walked away. Nansen said, "If you had been here, you could have saved the cat."

We have to remain alert and watchful of our heads lest they get swollen. For Joshu the head had no more importance than his footwear.

Verses 19-20

Shirkat-e-Sheikh-o-Brahmin se Mir
Kaaba-o-dair se bhi jaye ga
Apni daid eint ki judi masjid
Kisi weerane mein banaye ga

Once Sheikh and Brahmin join, Mir
you will lose both Kaaba (mosque) and temple
So, build your own tiny mosque
in a secluded waste land

This is what priesthood does to temples and mosques meant to be the places where you go to feel the presence of God while they become, with the participation of priests, not the house of the Lord but of the 'money changers'. They are lost to the genuinely religious people. For Mir, for that matter for any truly religious person, religion is a matter of individual's own experience of divinity which transcends collective identity of temples and mosques. Such an identity would entail conformity to outward forms which priesthood would lay stress on for the material benefits that accrue to them on that account. William Blake conveys the idea in answer to Parson's question:

The question: Why of the sheep do you not learn peace?

The Answer: Because I do not want you to sheer my fleece.

In the hands of priesthood, the religion gets progressively converted into an instrument of exploitation, creating inter-religious and intra-religious tensions and conflicts. Historically, as Aldous Huxley has pointed out, hardly any major crime through ages has been committed except in the name of religion.

What does the priest do to us at micro level? Nothing more than what William Blake says, "binding with briars my joy desires." And that suits him as joyous people have no need for him and thus not susceptible to exploitation by him. The priest cashes on our fears, superstitions which he instills in us invoking religious sanctions. In his essay "Why I am not a Christian", Bertrand Russel has observed "Religion is based, I think primarily and mainly on fear—Fear is the basis of the whole thing—fear of the mysterious, fear of defeat, fear of death. Fear is the parent of cruelty and therefore, it is no wonder if cruelty and religion have gone hand in hand.

Punjabi Sufi poet, Bulley Shah, castigates mosques and temples in the strongest of terms (reminding us of Jesus Christ overturning the tables of money changers saying "It is written, My house shall be called the house of prayer but ye have made it a den of thieves":

Dharamsal dhaarwal renhde
Thakurdwaray thug
Witch massete rahan kaseetey
Aashiq rahan alag

In the abode of pilgrims dwell dacoits
In the Lord's house live thugs
In mosques live evil doers Lovers live alone

Verse 21

Marg ek mandagi ka baqfa hai
Yaani aage chalein gay dam lay kar

Death be a respite from tiredness
To wit we will proceed further after resting

This life is not our final destination, says Mir, but only a path to an eternal journey on which we are on our way after a rest which we call death. For him life is not the final goal but a passage. At another place the poet says:

Jahan se tu rakhat-e-iqamat ko baandh
Yeh manzil nahin bekhabar rah lhai

Wind up your worldly affairs
This is no destination, O, you unaware it is a passage

In short, there is no arrival point in life's journey. We participate in the eternal now. Death becomes illusory. For the liberated, the embodiment and disembodiment become irrelevant. As Yoga Vasishtha puts it successfully:
"Troubled or still water is always water. What difference can embodiment and disembodiment make to the liberated? Whether calm or in tempest the sameness of ocean suffers no change."

Verse 22

Hai bekhabri mujhko tere dekhe se saqi
Har lahza meri jaan mujhe meri khabr kar

Seeing you I am lost to myself
My dear, wake me up to myself every moment

Saki, as a beloved in whom the poet loses himself, is put on a pedestal as a mentor, a Guru whom Mir beseeches to wake him up to himself from moment to moment. Here he seeks help to remain in a state of awareness. However, in the case of a Zen master, it is said that whenever he found himself in a state of lessened awareness, he would address himself by his own name, loudly questioning who he was and where he was, thus regaining the state of wakefulness.

In a similar vein, Mir says at another place:

> Bekhudi le gai kahan hamko
> Dair se intezar hai apna

> Where has self-abandon taken me
> I have been waiting for myself for long

Verse 23

> Elahi, kaise hote hain jinhein hai bandgi khwahish
> Hamein to sharam damangir hoti he khuda hotey

> O, Lord! What sort are they, desiring obeisance from others
> Playing God would make me hang my head in shame

The poet here speaks of the folly of seeking obedience from others, which he says, would put a decent man to shame. There is no need for any man to genuflect to another, not in any case to those who hunger for obedience. Mir's stress is on self-respect and dignity of an individual which is threatened by power oriented people.

Significantly, such obedience to the other has nothing to do with humility. On the contrary, the key to it is fear. J. Krishnamurti observes in his book 'Meeting Life', "Obedience is violence, and humility is not related to violence. Why should human beings have this fear, respect and disrespect? He is afraid of life with all its uncertainties and anxieties and he is afraid of gods of his own mind. It is the fear that leads to power and to aggression." Mir says at another place

> Sir kaso se fro nahi aata
> Haif bande hoay khuda na hoay

> This head bows to none
> Sorry you are just a man and not God

For Mir man is the focal point of the world from whom, it draws its glory. Mir says of man and the universes:

Aadm-e-khaki se aalam ko gila hai warna
Aaeina tha to magr qabal-e-deedar na tha

It is the mortal man who lends glory to this world
Otherwise the existence's mirror was not worth looking at

Those, who crave for obedience from others, are people responsible for a great deal of mischief in this world. And the greatest tragedy of this so-called civilized world is that these are the very people, who are glorified in history, such as, Alexanders and not Diogneses. The desire to exercise power over others, according to Adler, is to compensate for real and imagined deficiency in oneself. This desire for power over others is born of fear of others and depends, in its turn in instilling fear in others.

Fear is the key to cruelty. "Neither a man, nor a crowd, nor a nation", observes Bertrand Russel, can be trusted to act humanely or to think sanely under the influence of great fear. And for this reason poltroons are more prone to cruelty than brave men."

Mir, with his Dervaish temperament and outlook did not subscribe to kowtowing to the high and mighty:

Ho koi badshah ya koi Wazir ho
Apni bla se baith rahey jab fakir ho

When I sat down as a fakir
What do I care if someone be a king or his minister

The idea expressed by Mir here may be illustrated by a parable from Khalil Gibran in which he asks the scarecrow of the field whether he was not tired of standing alone and still in the field and the scarecrow replies that the pleasure of terrifying birds is so much that he is hardly conscious of how and when the time passes. Gibran says that that was his experience too for all those filled with grass and straw were familiar with his pleasure.

Verse 24

Sirhane Mir ke aahista bolo
Abhi tuk rote rote so gaya hai

Talk only in whispers over Mir's bedstead
He has just drifted to sleep after incessant weeping

This is a shining example of a simple verse in everyday language intimately communicating to us the plight of the poet. Sorrow could not have been expressed more tellingly in such simple words.

Commenting on this verse, Maulana Abdul Haq writes, "This verse is so simple. What can be more simple; ordinary, everyday language? But the style of expression is replete with anguish and from each word drips the longing and despair."

Sorrow lingers in the air as someone softly whispers in your ear to be quiet and to let sleep take care of the suffering and to give respite.

This verse fails in the category of his poetry which because of its pathos brought Mir, the sobriquet, among some of the leterati, as the poet of Ah (Sighing). In another verse, he expresses his despair, loneliness and hearts numbness thus:

Sham hi se bujha sa rehta hai
Dil hua hai chirag muflis ka

As the day dims, so does my heart
Like the lamp waning in poor man's hut

While we are on the subject, we may illustrate Mir's capacity to convey in a simple wistful manner a poignant idea by another of his verse:

Hamare aage jab tera kisi ne naam liya
Dil-e-sitamzada ko ham ne tham tham liya

When someone mentioned your name before me
I, somehow managed to keep a hold on my afflicted heart

In conclusion, we may keep in mind the fact that even though personal sorrow was one predominant theme of Mir's poetry, there is no trace of self-pity or bitterness which are inclined to creep in when we deal with personal sorrow. Mir, however, deals with the subject characteristically in a straight forward manner, in simple and gentle language.

Verse 25

Ab ke janoon mein fasla shaid na kuch rahe
Daman ke shaak aur garehaan ke chak mein

In madness now perhaps there be no distance left
between the seams of the collar and the lowest hemline

In love of Majnu paradigm, the lover roams in tattered clothes. Here in his extreme despair, the madness is so intense that the tearing of his apparel is complete from top to bottom and the lover goes about in shreds reflecting his miserable state.

Maulana Hali in his Muggadam Shair-o-Shairi (A Critique of Urdu poetry) has connected on his verse thus:

"Despite the triteness of the subject, Mir has treated it with extreme simplicity and in a unique, novel and scintillating style that nothing better can be imagined. It is simple, natural and in spite of that unique."

Another poet, Azurda, has termed it as verse non-pareil placing it at par with Koranic injunction, "God is one and the only."

In conclusion, it may be mentioned that it is above all, a perfect visual picture of the frenzy of passion conveyed in simple expression.

Verse 26

Wasl-o-hijran se jo do manzil hain rah-e-ishq mein
Dil-e-garib in mein khuda jane kahan mara gaya

The path of love has twin destinations
The nights the lovers meet and the nights of their separation
Poor heart, God knows where it perished in their midst

In the romantic love only two states are mentioned, the ecstatic state of union and the pangs of separation. Not in any way disregarding romantic love, Mir takes love to be ever transcendent state needing no dependence, being its own completeness, its own eternity, its own fruit. Love here goes beyond the suffering of the separation of the nights or the joy of togetherness salacious nights

Verse 27

Piar karne ka jo khuban ham pe rakhtey hein gunah
Un se bhi to poochey tum itne kyon piare hoay

The fair ones blame us for the folly of love
You might as well ask them why they became so lovable

The idea is simple. This is in fact Urdu version of Sheik Saadi's Persian Verse:

Dostan mana kunandam ke chira dil buto dadam
Bayaid awwal buto guftan ke cheen khub chirai

Friends warned me against falling in
in love with beautiful ones
They should in the first place ask the beautiful ones
why are they so beautiful

Mir's verse is, however, better in so far as expression is concerned. Hali in his Muggadama, referred to earlier, has observed that the use of the word 'khub'(beautiful) by Saadi is less appropriate than the word 'piare' (lovable) for the beloved may not necessarily be beautiful, but it is must that she be lovable.

What Hali has said above also holds good about another verse of Mir which too is translation of Sheikh Saadi, Persian verse:

Kehte the yun kehte agar woh aata
Sab kehne ki baatein hein kutch bhi na kaha jata

He said that he would say this or that if the beloved comes
All that is just talk; he would have remained tongue-tied

The Persian verse of Saadi reads:

> Gufta boodam choo beaey gham dil ba tu bigoyam
> Chih begoyan gham az baroday choon beaey

> I said I would relate to him my hearts sorrow
> But I could not say a word before him
> about my heart's affliction

The words "Sab kehne ki baatein hain" 'all that is just talk' has made Mir's verse read better than the original.

Verse 28

> Ashk aankhon main kab nahin aata
> Lahoo aata hai jab nahin aata

> When the tear flows not from the eye
> It is then the blood trickles down from it

It is sorrow beyond tears when even the weeping, which could have a cathartic effect is not available to the sufferer. The sorrow is experienced intensely. A sensitive man is inclined to experience every emotion passionately. A lukewarm response or indifference to experiencing life is more like death. This verse reminds us of Ghalib's oft quoted lines:

> Ragon mein daudte phirne ke ham nehin qaill
> Jab aankh hi se na tapka to phir lahoo kya hai

> I subscribe not to the coursing of blood in veins
> I care not for blood unless it drips from the eyes

Mir's experience of sorrow is intense. He says elsewhere:

> Musalsal rote hi rahiye to bujhe aatish-e-dil
> Aik do ansoo to aur aag laga jaate nahin

Weep on and on to quench heart's fire
For a few tears would only fan the fire

In similar vein he writes at another place:

Qtra qtra ashk bari ta kuja paishe-e-sahaab
Aik din to toot pad ai deeda-e-tar ho so ho

How long will you shed tears in droplets before the cloud
Four down in a burst one day, O, tearful eye whatever may happen

Verse 29

Dair-o-haram mein kyonke kadam rakh sake ga Mir
Idhar to is se but phire and khuda phira

How can Mir stay into the temple or mosque
Icons deserted the one and God left the other

This is a recurring theme in Mir which has already been discussed in an earlier part of this book. To recapitulate briefly, it may be stated that there can be no better description of the irreligiosity of the organized religions, the deities of the temple and mosque having deserted them. The religion in essence is the individual's experience of the divine reality and has to transcend narrow denominational walls put up by priests to further their own unholy ends. That is why Mir in a verse we have discussed earlier, speaks of building a separate tiny mosque for himself in a deserted place.

Verse 30

Juz martha-e-kul ko hasil kare hai aakhir
Yek qatra na dekha jo darya na hua hoga

Finally a part reaches up to become the whole
Not a drop is seen which did not become a river

That in short is the merger in the divine in the Sufi sense of Fana, which literally means dissolution but in Sufi language it is being one with the

divine transcending the separate personal ego. Lover is lost in the beloved (the Lord) and the two become one as Rumi proclaims:
"The beloved is all in all. The lover merely veils him. The beloved is all that lives; the lover is a mere dead thing."

Like Mir, Ghalib too spoke of Fana as merger of the part with the whole, but in more existential terms of pleasure and pain:

Isjrat-e-qtra hai darya mein fana ho jana
Dard ka had se guzrna hai dwa ho jana

The joy of the drop is to merge in the river
Pain crossing all limits itself becomes cure

Here too 'fana' is not used in the sense of death and dissolution but in the sense of Sufi merger losing one's separate ego identity and becoming one with the divine ending the painful separateness.

Like the Sufi experience of merger, Buddhas, when enlightned, lose their separateness from existence, an experience common to Taoism. Hui Neng says of Buddhas:

"When not enlightned, Buddhas are no other than ordinary beings; when enlightned ordinary beings at once turn into Buddha's."

In other words, a drop contains ocean within itself. It remains a drop so long it continues to cling to its separateness. The theme of merger with the divine, losing of individual identity in search of Him and our existence on the earth being veil which hides Him from us, is repeated by Mir in quite a few of his verses:

Hasti apni hai beech mein purdha
Ham na hovein to phir hijan kahan

My existence in veil in between (self and divine)
If I cease to be where then is the veil?

Bekhudi le gai kahan humko
Dair se intezar hai apna

Where has the self-abandon taken me
For long have I been waiting for Myself

Dikhai diye yun ke bekhud kiya
Hamein aap se bhi juda kar chale

Showed me a glimpse of Himself thus
Lost in Him I am separated from myself

Use dhoondte Mir khoy gaye
Koi dekhey is justjo ki tarf

Just look at this search
Mir is lost in the process

Mahav kar aap ko yun basti mein uski
Boond pani ki nahin aati nazr pani mein

Merge your existence thus into Him
Like a drop of water is not seen separately in water

This epitomizes the Sufi belief of Fana (non-existence) being road to
Baga (immortality, merger with Godhead). In words of Jalal-uddin-Rumi:

O, let me not exist! For non-existence Proclaims

"To Him we shall return."

Unlike Rumi and Mir, Ghalib has given expression to the idea of the
part and whole being mutually inclusive not in terms of Sufi experience of
the divine but in the framework of human consciousness and sagacity:

Qtra mein Dajla dikhaye na dai aur juz mein kul
Khel ladkon ka hua deeda-e-beena hua

If in the drop the river Dajla is not
seen and in the part the whole
It is children's play and not a discerning eye

Verse 31

Wasal mein rang urd gaya mera
Kya judai ko munh dikhaon ga

Meeting the loved one, I turned ashen
How on earth will I face separation?

Meeting the beloved is such an overwhelming experience for him that instead of bringing him happiness, the result is quite the contrary. Psychologically speaking, over-intention negates what it intends, for it brings in its wake anticipatory anxiety. Similar idea is conveyed in Ghalib's verse:

Khush hote hain par wasl mein yun mur nahin jate
Aayi Shab-e-hijran ki tammana mere aage

Happy meeting the beloved but dying thus of joy
The fruit that the longings of nights of separation brought me

Ghalib's and Mir's verses here talk of obsessive love and its fall out but elsewhere Mir moves from obsessive love to moderation:

Nahin hai chah bhali itni bhi dua kar, Mir
Ke ab jo dekhon usey mein bahut pyar na aaway

So much love too is not good, so pray Mir
I do not get besotted with excessive love when I see her

Verse 32

Sabaat Qasar-o-dar-o-baam khisht-o-gill kitna
Imarat-e-dil dervaish ki rakho buniyad

Now long will last the palaces, doors and roofs of mud and mortar
Lay, rather, the foundation of a heart of a dervaish

Existence is transient. Palaces too will crumble. There is a Sufi parable in which a Dervaish asks a king whether he could stay in his Serai (inn). The king felt insulted and asked angrily of the dervaish how he dare call his palace a Sarai? Dervaish replied that he had visited that place a few times and every time he found a new person living in it. So it can only be a Sarai.

The heart of a Dervaish is larger and grander than palaces of kings, being free from wordly desires and the only desire, for that matter an overwhelming desire, is to merge with the divine. Desire, Mir says, is the only impediment in the way of man reaching his empyrean heights:

Sarapa arzoo hone ne banda kar diya hamko
Wagarna ham khuda they gar dil-o-bemudda hote

Our being desire-incarnate has rendered us to be just human
Otherwise we were God if our hearts were free from desires

Verse 33

Rah-e-marg se kyon darate hain log
Bahut to us taraf ko j aate hain Log

Why do people frighten me of death
When so many people go that way

So, what is there to fear? The death is the nature culmination of life. Wde observe in nature that through death there is a continuous renewal. I can do no better than quote from my own poem. 'Nature Renews, Humans Pickle.'

Seed, sapling, tree, fruit
Back to seed
Life return in dewy freshness
Egg, larva, caterpillar, chrysalis, butterfly
Back to egg again
Ever renewing life restarts
All over again
—*From 'Abyss', 'A Collection of Poems' by the author*

Death also makes us sit back and think. Wordly ambitions, competitive drives, cravings for position, power and material possessions all fade away against the background of impending death. A slight brush with death might make us drop our pettiness. As someone has aptly put, "Death is the only wise adviser we have."

The question is not one of prolonging life, but improving its quality on which will also depend the quality of one's dying, i.e., whether to die gracefully or in mortal terror. Mir says elsewhere:

> Kaha main ne kitna hai gul ke Sabat
> Kali ne yeh sun kar tabassam kiya
>
> I said how long the flowers' life is
> Bud, hearing this blossomed.

So bemoan not the translence of life, but live it like a blossoming bud. This is the positive attitude. In the sphere of inevitability of death which we should accept gracefully instead of tossing in bed in restless fear of death, we need to go along with Ghalib:

> Maut ka ek din muayyan hai
> Neend kyon raat bhar nahin aati
>
> Fixed is the hour of death
> Still man tosses sleeplessly, night Long

The attitude that we find expressed by Mir and Ghalib is not of an austere stoic but of those who have found the insignificance of death in the light of abundance of life. Here I reproduce what a character in Kazantakis ways, "What is this fuss about death. When the death comes, I would turn my face to the well and die." He was the character who is painted as having lived his life abundantly, joyously. In short, it may be said that life cycle comes to a natural and with death. We must accept that inevitability and death, the final stage of the life cycle, must be entered into with a sense of integrity and not in despair.

Verse 34

> Uske firog-e-husn se jhamke hafsab main noor
> Shammay haram ho ya ke diya Somnath ka

His beauty's effulgence shimmers through all
Be it a lamp in a mosque or a taper in Somnath temple

As distinct from the trappings of all organized religion, Sufies and Saints have experienced God as effulgence. Earlier saints like Kabir, Guru Nanak and Sufi poet Bulley Shah had spoken of God and light. Light is light, why draw distinctions as a Persian poet says:

Parwana chirag-e-haram-o-dair na danad
Moth distinguishes not between the lamp of mosque and temple

Likewise, Mir is concerned here with the light and not where it emanates from. At another place he says:

Kis ko kehte hain nehin mein janta Islam O kufr[8]
Dair ho ya Kaaba, matlab mujh ko tere dar se hai

I know not what is Islam or Kufr (non-Muslim)
Be it temple or mosque I am only concerned with your door [9]

Verse 35

Aam hai yar ki tajjali, Mir
Khas Musa-o-koh-e-toor nahin

His efflugence is everywhere
And not confined to Moses and The mount of Sinai

On the mountain of Sinai, God is supposed to have revealed Himself to Moses who was so dazzled by the light as to become unconscious. Mir says that His effulgence is everywhere, then why go to mount of Sinai? As already mentioned in the write up on the previous verse, God as light has been experienced by a number of Saints and Sufies.

However, this experiencing is possible only through efforts to remove the impurities so as to have spiritual capacity to experience the divine within and without. If we are not ready we may suffer the fate of Astean of Greek

---

8   Here he means Hinduism
9   Here he means door to God.

mythology who was torn to pieces by Diana's dogs after the Goddess cursed him and transformed him into a doe for having set his eyes on her while she was bathing in a pond. Mir, in another verse, says that we have to ignite the fire (of love) in our hearts to experience the effulgence like that of Mount Sinai:

> Aatish blund dil ki na thi warna ai kaleem
> Yak shola barq khirman-e-sad koh-e-toor tha

> The fire was not inginted enough in the heart
> Othewise, O, prophet, one spark would have created
> effulgence hundredfold than that of Mount Sinai

Mir's contemporary Sauda has also given expression to the idea contained in the verse being commented on here:

> Har sang mein sharer hai tere zahoor ka
> Moosa nahin jo sair karon koh-e-toor ka

> Every stone contains spark of your presence
> I am no Moses to go searching Him to Mount Sinai

This experience of God in every phenomenon culminates in Sufi Sarmad, the mentor of Dara Sikhoh, (elder brother of Aurangzeb and the real claimant to Moghul throne). When the executioner sent by Aurangzeb to behead Sarmad arrived, Sarmad recognized God in him (the executioner) and welcomes him thus:

> Fidaye tu shawam, beaa! beaa! Ke har soorte
> Ke me aai man tura khoob shanasam

> I love you so, come, come for I recognize
> You easily in whatever form you come

Even in his killer, he saw manifestation of God. In short, to experience the radiance of the Divine by dispelling spiritual darkness within us is, according to Surfies, the aim and purpose of human life.

Verse 36

Kya chetne ka faida jo shaib mein cheta
Sone ka saman aaya to bedar hua mein

What is use of awakening if it comes in old age
I woke up when it was the time to go to sleep.

The verse contains a mixture of Persian and Hindi words. But the implication of the verse is far-reaching. It is a great irony that even the people who are serious minded get lost in collecting mess of pottages, living unexamined lives till the twilight years when death starts staring them in their faces. A few may experience what Jung calls individuation in the middle age which may set them on a journey into the self. However, in case of most of us what Freud says is true that the fear of disease, old age, death are all our spirituality is about. This implies that the time to lay foundation for awareness is while you are young and not in old age for in the process of growing old, we would have acquired granite hard habits and attitudes. The process has to start fairly early, even though not as early as that of Buddha, to give us a chance of becoming integrated.

Mir has hit the nail of the head when he calls the awareness of old age worthless for what he says. "It is time to sleep." The death is around the corner. The sun is setting, lay down the tools and be prepared to depart towards the unknown. In the words of Dag Dehlvi:

Hosh-o-hawas, tab-o-taban Dagh, kho chukey
Ab ham bhi jaane wale hain samaan to gaya

Gone, Dagh areconsciousness, senses and the strength
Baggage is gone; we too are ready to depart

Hindu, or for that matter the Buddhist, belief in 'Ant mata so gata' that the last moment consciousness gives you deliverance is a delusion, for consciousness is the product of your entire life and the possibility of a flash conversion is non-existent. The possibility of last minute awakening is nothing more that a priestly prop to keep you in a state of ignorance which suites his trade. The Hindu story of Ajamal getting Moksha (Deliverance) by calling by name his son named Narayan (God) at the last moment is one of the most absurd stories ever told.

In so far as the last moment consciousness is concerned what a Tibetan Buddhist teacher says sounds nearer the truth:

"How said it is that most of us only begin to appreciate our life when we are on the point of dying. I often think of the words of the great Buddhist master Padmasambhava: 'Those who believe they have plenty of time get ready only at the time of death. Then they are ravaged by regret. But isn't it too late?' What more chilling commentary . . . could there be than that most people die unprepared for death, as they have lived, unprespared for life."

—*Sogyal Rinpoche in "The Tibet Book of Living and Dead" (pp10-11)*

Verse 37

Bood-e-Adam namood-e-shabnam hai
Aik do dam main phir hawa hai yeh

Human existence is like appearance of dew drops
It vanishes into thin air in a moment or two

So transient is the human existence, it evaporates into thin air in the twinkling of an eye. If we keep this in mind, our consciousness has the chance to get transformed and death may lose its terror for us, brightening our chances of living and actualizing ourselves in the time available to us. Otherwise, we may advance towards old age and death in a state of stupor, decaying at all levels alongside the physical decay. Dard, a poet of Mir's times has bemoaned the transience of life thus:

Aai, Dard, jis ki aankh khuli is jahan mein
Shabnam ki tarah jaan ko apni who ro gaya

Dard, whosoever's eyes opened upon this world
Like dew he wept for his life

Even though the poet Dard is ruing here the transience of life, he is far from being overwhelmed by it. On the other hand, he believes in living life fully and joyously in spite of its evanescence:

Saqia yan lag raha hai chal chalao
Jab talak chal sake sagar chale

O, Saqi (wine server), we are all in transit
Let the wine flow so long it lasts

Here, the poet Dard is advocating living fully, ecstatically so long it lasts instead of being morbidly pre-occupied with death.

Returning to Mir, transience of life is one of the many recurring themes in his poetry. At other places he says:

Reh guzr sail-e-hawadars ka hai bebuniyad daihar
Is kharabe mein na kar fikr tum tameer ka

Earth is flood of travails sans foundation
Better not build in this ruin

Maujain Karen hai behr jahan mein abhi to tu
Jane ga baad marg ke aalam hubab tha

You are as yet creating waves in the ocean of existence
After death you would know that the world was a bubble of water

Verse 38

Dilli ke na the koochey aurag mussavar the
Jo shakal nazar aai tasveer nazar aai

Delhi streets were not mere streets but sheets from painter's folio
Whatever face we saw looked like a painting

This is one of the numbers of verses Mir wrote in Lucknow born of the poet's nostalgia for Delhi. Here is a romantic picture of Delhi, with its streets being the folio of a painter and its people as the paintings. This is quite in a contrast to the devastion of Delhi. Mir has so poignantly depicted in his autobiography, as already quoted earlier in this book.

Despite the misery he saw in Delhi and in spite of the fact that he was comfortably placed in Lucknow, he kept on experiencing agonizing nostalgia for Delhi. He went on painfully yearning to return to Delhi and repenting his coming to Lucknow where he never felt at home. His verses dwelling upon his state of mind in Lucknosw have been discussed earlier in this book in the Section dealing with the poet's life in Lucknow.

Verse 39

Patta Patta boota boota haal hamari jane hain
Jane na jane gul hi na jane Bagh to sara jane hai

Every leaf, every tree knows my plight
The entire garden knows, only knows not the rose

Here is a simply worded basokht (explained earlier at more than one place) yet conveyed through the imagery of the garden, leaves and rose. The entire world knows the sorry plight of the lover, the sole exception being his beloved who is totally indifferent. And indifference is worse the hatred. In the words of Mirza Ghalib:

Laag ho to ham use samjhein lagao
Jab na ho kutch bhi to dhokha khain kya

If there be hatred, I will take it related ness
And when there is nothing no illusion is left

Verse 40

Shikast-o-Fateh to bani hai duniya mein Mir
Muqabla to dil-e-natwan ne khoob kiya

Victory and defeat in the world be two Sides of the same coin
What matters is the stiff fight my weak heart gave

I am taking up this verse as it provides us a profound perception and deep insight into both existential and spiritual truth despite doubts expressed in some quarters about its being Mir's verse, being not in his style. Any struggle or striving will result either in success or failure. But preoccupation with the outcome will make the action fall short of one's potential. The extent to which it fails short will correspond to the intensity of pre-occupation. This will happen because of what Dr. Frankel calls 'over intention'[10] causing anticipatory anxiety that makes it hard for us to focus on

---

[10]   Man's Search for Meaning'-Dr. Victor Frankel

the task in hand. Its spiritual equivalent of it is found in the Gita where Lord Krishna tells Arjuna:

Karmannay va adhikar aste ma
phaleshu kada chana, ma karmaphala
hetur bhur, ma tai sangostv akarmaniy

Your right is confined to action and not to the fruit thereof. Act and make an offering of your action to Me (the Lord). Action motivated by desire for fruit is non-action. Thus, an action is pure spiritually only if it is totally detached from the fruit of the action even though it sounds existentially a larger than life-size ideal which it is better said than done. I wonder whether any one has ever lived up to this divine injunction.

Verse 41

Tujh ko masjid hai, mujhko maikhana
Waiza apni apni kismet hai

For you the mosque, to me the tavern
O, preacher, each one to his own fate

Maikhana, tavern symbolizes abandon, ecstasy, whereas mosque symbolizes rigid religious discipline. Two poles here are the Sufi and the Maulvi (the priest of the mosque). Mir commiserates with the priest for the destiny he has chosen for himself in which there can hardly be any joy in life, having forced himself into strict discipline imposed from without. There can be no spontaneity in life which is totally conditioned by his rigidly held beliefs.

For Mir, truly religious persons transcends the limitations of the priestly edicts for the religion is for him is the merger in divine through love. In so far as the religion preached by the priest is concerned, Mir would havd agreed with Nietzsche indictment, "Religion has not been able to transform man but has poisoned his joys."

Even about the puritanical discipline of the priest, Mir has elsewhere called it hypocrisy thus:

Kya kya dawain mange hain khilwat mein Sheikhji
Zahir jahan se haath uthaya to kya hua

What does not priest pray for in his privacy
What is the use if he overtly professes renunciation of the world

Verse 42

Jafe uski na pohnchi inteha ko
Draiga umr ne ki bewafai

Her cruelty could not reach the extreme
Alas! My life's ending let her down

This is another instance of basokht, paradigm of 'La Belle Dam Sans Merce', female fatale perfecting her malevolence towards the lover. Here the lover's death deprives her of her pursuit of tormenting the lover and thus preventing her from perfecting the art of cruelty.

Even though 'basokht' cannot be held to be a high tradition, as already stated in the write up under Verse 7, it does bring out human inclinations, dealing as it does with strange moods, giving us understanding of the human mind. The poet, in the verse discussed here, gives us a peep into female caprice which may culminate in wanton cruelty.

Verse 43

Tu hai bechara gada, Mir, tera kya mazkoor
Mil gaya khak mein yan Sahib afsar kitne

You a helpless beggar Mir, what to talk of you
How many high ups in power here have been done to dust

This is one of the many verses depicting his tragic times, both personally and collectively. Mir was a witness to the large scale murder, loot and destruction going around. His depiction of these turbulent times in his poetry has already been given in detail in this book. Here only a few verses throwing light on the plight of the then 'so-called' ruling class are given.

Dilli mein aaj bheek bhi bhi milti nahin unhein
Tha kal talak dimag jinhein takhat-o-taaj ka

They do not get even alms in streets of Delhi
Those who were proud of their thrones and crowns

There are a number of verses in similar vein in which, as already stated earlier, the suffering of the poet's dil (heart) gets intermingled with the anguish of Dilli. We cite a couple of these here. Referring to the two tragic events blinding of the King Ahmed Shah by his minister Imad-ul-Malik and Ghulam Qadir Rohilla's blinding of the King, Shah Alam, Mir writes:

Shahan ke kehle-e-jawahar thi khak pa jinki
Unhein ki aankhon mein phirti silaein dekhein

Kings, the dust of whose feet was precious collyrium
I saw their eyes being pierced by needles

In the face of these abomination, Mir too, like Webster in 'Duchess of Maifi' mentioned in the preceding part of this book, became painfully aware of the utter emptiness of glory and hankering after immortality in the sense of leaving your name behind. Says he:

Tha mulk jin ke zair-e-nageen saaf mit gaye
Tum is khayal mein ho ke nam-o-nishan rahe

Those who lorded over this country were cleaned wiped out
You are still toying with the idea of leaving your name behind

The poet reverts to the subject of horrendous times every now and then in his verse. He himself refers to this fact thus:

Darhami haai ki hai har so mere deewan mein
Sair kar tu bhi yeh mujhmooa pareshani ka

Everywhere in the collection of my verseis the talk of turbulent times
You too should visit this compendium of anarchy

Verse 44-45

Is butkade mein maaeni ka kis se karein sawal
Aadam nahin hai soora-e-aadam bahut hain yan
Aalam mein log milne goon ab nahein rahe
Harchand aisa waisa to aalam bahut hai yan

There is no man here even though many look like him
In the world now no people are left who be worth meeting
Even though a world of sorts is very much in existence

This is true of all ages. This is the fate, the serious-minded thinking people have shared in getting alienated from the mainstream of populace who are at home with exchanging inanities and indulging in frivolous activities. Even though surrounded by crows of people, they have an intense feeling of loneliness for meeting people and falking to them of everyday trifles to satisfy the gregarious instinct is, for them, a meaningless waste of time.

Creativity is, perhaps, the only outlet available to the people of reflective nature unless they choose the path of reclusive monkhood. They have, otherwise, to live with their own loneliness in a state of perpetual introversion for the chance of their experiencing serendipity to discover 'God of (or (in) Small Things' is rather remote.

PART II

ZIKR-E-MIR (THE STORY OF MIR)

INTRODUCTION

B oundless be the praise for the poet (of all poets) whose unique masterpiece became famous world over and countless be the compliments to the Creator who has woven the garland of pearls of meanings into poetry and prose. He is the lord of wise who is well-versed in the thousand fold modes of poetic expression. He is the teacher who bestows faculty of speech on those of poor expression. He is that Giver of life who is kind to all creatures of the world. He is that designer who transforms clay into a human being. He is that guardian without whom our safety is impossible. He is that artist whom no one can dare to copy. He is that knower whose circle of knowledge is all-comprehensive and transcends all limits. That is why it has been said that God has encircled all things. He is that wise one who knows all secrets; he is the eternal one; the existence is He and He is the existence. He is that provider who gives us livelihood. He is the lord who gives life. He is the merciful one who listens to the repentance of the sinners. He is that compassionate one who bestows bounties and overlooks our faults. The sun is a particle of His manifestation and the moon a small ray of His effulgence. Nothing is without His light. In short, "Allaha is the luminescence of the heavens and earth." Since in His volition He likes submissions to His will, he does not disappoint those who bow their heads to Him in prayer. He is the creator who has created in abundance. He sees all and sees through all that is hidden. Even though Heaven of twisted movements plays tricks on me, I hope it will not let me be humiliated. What tongue does not repeat the litany of His name and what living being does not sing hymns eulogizing His goodness.

He knows about all so much so He keeps track of everyone's state of affairs. To pick the flowers of His favours, surrender to him is required and to view His creativity of ever renewing freshness, a discerning eye is needed. He is that unique one whose uniqueness is celebrated. He is that one God who is known for being the only God. He is that exalted one in whose court even angels cannot enter. He is that listener who listens to the pleading of the humble. The pen and tongue do not have the capacity to narrate each and every attribute of his perfection. Yet if He chooses to praise himself, the very perfection of His narration will leave nothing further to be done.

Hymn

Boundless are my greetings for that erudite who has mastered the field of eloquence and countless are the greetings to that eloquent one who reached up to Godhood, but did not become arrogant as also to the king who is full of wisdom and glory, to that bright moon which dispels the heretical darkness; to that leader without whose leadership no hurdle can be easily crossed; to that guide without whose guidance no path can be found; to that ruler whose orders we obey from our hearts and minds; to that helping hand whom we follow according to our capacity; that morning whose early rays will bestow luminescence to the mirror of this world; to that beautiful one whose beauty is reflected on the face of mankind; that beloved, the dust of whose feet is the bloodline of lives; to that spring under whose green banner's shade time is flowing; to that helpful one who is looked up to on the day of judgement for absolution. In fact, both the worlds are carrying on due to His (God's) compassion. May God's mercy be on him (the prophet) and our greetings to him and his pure and virtuous heirs, every one of whom has been Imam (the chief priest) of Momins (believers) and the pleader for the absolution of sinners.

Author's request

After the eulogizing the one worshipped by all, who is the Lord, the Creator and besides conveying countless prayers and Salaams (greetings) to the glorified one, the Sahib of the earth (prophet Mohammad), fakir, Mir Mohammad Taqi whose non-de-plume is Mir, says that he was in these days unemployed and had retired to a secluded corner without any company.

He penned down his life story which also contained tragic incidents of his times. Besides his biography, he has also written some tales and traditions of those times and the book titled Zikr-e-Mir ends with a few tit bits. He hopes from friends that if they found any errors in it, they might, by way of kind indulgence, overlook it and rectify it.

My Ancestors

My ancestors, together with their hapless tribe, were so despondent that their mornings became as lugubrious as their evenings. They migrated from Hejaz[11] reaching the border of Deccan with their meagre travelling baggage. During the journey, they bore untold hardships and tried their hands at sundry vocations. Some of them left for Ahmedabad, Gujarat. Some were too tired to move further and settled down there (Deccan). Some of them picked up enough courage to move forward in search of livelihood. My great ancestors despite opposition to staying there, settled down in Akbarabad (Agra). But due to sudden exposure to a different climate, he fell ill and bid farewell to his earthly existence leaving behind a son who was my grandfather.

My Grandfather

Girding up his loins he (my grandfather) started in search of livelihood. After running here and there, he was appointed as Faujdar (Administrator) of the outskirts of Akbarabad (Agra). He lived a prudent life. When he reached the age of fifty, he started keeping indifferent health. He got treatment for a few days. He had hardly recovered when he had to go to Gwalior. The jolts of journey, which acted as poison on the one already enfeebled by illness, brought in the relapse. He fell ill again and died. He had two sons; the elder
one was not free from mental affliction. He died young and was forgotten. The younger one was my father. He discarded his worldly life and became a recluse to acquire the knowledge of the phenomenal world without which it is difficult to reach the essence of things. He gained the wealth of inner knowledge by following strict spiritual practices under the guidance of Shah Kalim-ula Akbarabadi who was one of the accomplished holy men.

---

[11]   Area where Mecca and Madina are located

Under the guidance of that wise old man, he exercised austerities and did sustained meditations and reached to the state of Dervaishhood.

Father's Faith

As a youngman, he (my father) was a righteous man committed to cult of love. The fire of love was burning in his heart. He was known by the respected title of Ali Mutaqqi. It may be noted here that one day he respectfully asked the Sheikh that he (Sheikh) knew that he (Mir's father) has corrected his beliefs but what had you to say about the ruler of Syria. Shah Sahib said, "I will let you know."

After sometime at dawn, he came to Mahram Khan Khwaji Sarai Shah Jehanis' mosque. My father's servants ran for fetching water for Sheikh's preprayer ablutions. My father got up taking the metal pot (to help Sheikh in his ablution) then Sheikh sprinkling water on his hands and face said, "Mian Ali Mutaqqi, all my life his (Syria's ruler) name never came on my tongue. I do not have enough words to thank Him (God) for that." My father used to say, "Thank God that I never uttered his name again."

Teaching of Love

He would remember God day and night. God too did not put him to shame. When he was in an ecstatic mood, he would say to me:

"My child, adopt the creed of love, for love is the residing deity of this world. If love is withdrawn from the universe, the cosmos would turn into chaos. Life without love is a barren weight. To lose your heart in love is a real gain and joy. Love is fire, love is light. The fire burnth the dross in man. Love is the source and spring of all we perceive. The world, my boy, is in a state of flux; we have no time to waste; utilize every minute of your time for self awakening. Ups and downs characterize the path of life. Chasing the pleasures of this world is like chasing a mirage or an attempt to bind water with a string. Be then a nightingale of a never fading rose. Dedicate yourself to God. Catch time by the forelock and try to know thyself."

Without love existence would perish. We cannot really live when love is not there. See prophet Kinanni (Yakub) too loved his son.

He would remain in a state of wonder during the day and remain awake at nights. His brow would remain bent in prayer. He would always be in a state of joy, drunk on the wine of love. His face was pure. His effulgent face would brighten up the congregation of devotees. He was a sun but he avoided even his own shadow. At times when he returned to his own self, he would say, "Son, world is nothing but a turmoil; you should renounce it and let not dust gather in your mind; embrace the cult of love for God; remember that we have to face the other world; one who knows is able to comprehend that this life is illusory. Building castle of hope on this illusion is tying up water with a chord. Getting caught up in details of daily activities is measuring moonlight in yards. Ah! do not remain unaware of the world being transitory, a merry-go-round of comings and goings. Take care of essentials for the journey so that you do not perish on the way. Look up to the one whose reflection this world is called. Surrender to Him whom you search in your heart. If seeking is sincere, you will certainly attain to the one sought. Even though His splendour manifests itself everywhere, we have to show reverence when giving an expression to it.

(Point) God has same relationship with man as soul has with the body. In short, your existence without Him and His manifestation without you cannot be. Before the creation of the universe, He was and after it He, the immutable one, is mirrored in his creation.

"The difficulty is that while every particle is His reflection
Even then it is not possible to particulise it"

He was a Dervaish and held other Dervaishes in high esteem. Of distressed heart, he was fond of living a Spartan life. Even then he was of a charitable disposition. He liked travelling within the land. Liberal in religious outlook, a complete fakir in temperament and like water he would dissolve in every colour. When he would pick me up on to his lap and casting a loving look on my dark complexion, he used to say, "O, treasure of my life, what fire is it that is hidden in your heart, what it that is scalding your life." I would laugh but he would keep on weeping. Alas! I did not value him in his lifetime. He was a human being immersed in his present surroundings. He would never become a burden on anyone.

One day after his morning prayer, he paid attention to me when he found me preoccupied with playing and said, "Son, the world is flux of time, very little of it is available. Do not remain indifferent to studies. Walk warily here for on the life's path there are many ups and downs.

Your footprints are blueprints of sum total of your life
Walk warily in this world counting your steps

What is this playing, an absurdity you are caught in. Attach yourself to the one to whose bewitching ways heaven is ever beholden. Surrender your heart to Him to whose glory the people have sacrificed. Be a bulbul of that rose which is everlasting spring. Fall in for the simple one ever in ecstasy. Heaven's ambivalence changes for none. Hurry and treat the time as a blessing and know thyself."

His blessed face amongst the world of sensate creatures was expressive enough to show the essence of his thinking. He was a serious man full of resolve and never let go the reins of his will from his hands. He was such a puritan that never strangers had set their eyes on his hands and feet. His character was laudable, his qualities likeable, his temperament firm against odds. He was kind at heart, his eyes lachrymose and conditions of his living precarious.

Passage to Lahore

It is said that that he came home one day with his mind clouded with worry. He told the old maid servant, "The old one, I am very hungry today. I can stand it no longer. If I can get a piece of bread, some life may return to me." The old maid replied, "There is nothing in the house." He repeated, "I am hungry." The old maid got up and brought flour and ghee from the Bania (trader) so as to cook roti (bread). Torn by hunger, he expressed his impatience. The old maid got annoyed and admonishing him said, "Mian (Mr), in fakiri there is no place for impetunousnes." My revered father said, Old one, take your own time in preparing roti (bread); I am going to Lahore to meet a fakir there. Saying this, he picked up his handkerchief which had become a ball of cotton from nightlong weeping. When the old maid became aware that he was leaving out of pique, she ran after him and caught him by the hem of his apparel and tearfully dissuaded him from leaving but he remained unmoved. Becoming helpless, she completed Shagun (the auspicious ritual) of pouring water on the mirror[12]. On the way wherever he would break his journey, God, of the merciful's glory, would provide for him. After a few days, he reached Lahore and saw the crooked Dervaish who used to sit on the banks of the river called Ravi and defrauded people. He was known by the name of Khafshan Namood. He had memorized a few words of Persian. The ignorant and gullible people who knew not their

---

[12]   *This is a Shagun (auspicious ritual) for a journey, of Iranian origin, not heard of in India

meaning would genuflect in surrender before him. He said, "I am supporting the religion preached by the prophet Hazrat Mohammad but ignorant people consider me as one who leads people astray." Listening to this, my father became furious. He said, "Oh you mean one, our prophet's religion does not need the likes of your. Take care while talking; the sword lies here it its sheath lest you be killed."

In short, the meeting from the beginning was unsavoury and my father returned in bitterness and spent the night in a fakir's abode. In the morning that fraudulent fakir came to apologize. My father told him, "There is no point in asking me for pardon now. Yesterday, I ticked you off; I would do the same today. After your crookedness has been exposed, where is the question of apology? Go away before you are humiliated before all." He felt genuinely ashamed and contrite. To a great extent, he mended his ways. Thus, ended the unsavoury meeting.

Return from Lahore

Suddenly that dear one (my father) tied up whatever little there was for the journey and after ten, twelve days reached Shahjehanabad, (Delhi). Here he stayed with Sheikh Abdul Aziz's son Qumar-ud-Din who was Dewan (Minister) of the province and a near relation of my father. There near ones in the city gathered around him and served him with great devotion. The man of God was drunk on the wine of love. When he sat, he sat in abandon; when he got, he got up in ecstatic state. He talked freely and ecstatically. Hisvery breathing would fill everyone with fire of love. Many touched his hand with their foreheads to get his blessings. Many would faint before his intense gaze. The water used by him for ablution was carried around with devotion and was given to the ailing to drink and whoever drank it was cured.

He used to weep so much as to lead to hiccoughs. He would wail into the skies. News had spread that such a Dervaish had arrived in the city. Nobles of the city requested for an audience, but he declined telling them that he was a fakir (poor) and they were rich, how could the twain meet? The nobleman Amir Samsaam-ul-Daula[13] pleaded his past privileges and requested that he be not deprived of the golden opportunity and that if he (Mir's father) condescended to see him, this sinner (the Amir) might see

---

[13]   He was the Nawab who gave the boy, Mir, a scholarship of Re. 1.00 per day later.

deliverance and join others who have received absolution. Hearing this, he (Mir's father) smiled and said commonality is a must for a meeting and he hoped that he would be excused (for not meeting him as he could not help it. When he got tired of the excessive crowd around, he got out of the city after midnight prayer. The people searched him everywhere, but he could not be found, norwas there any trace of him.

> When did the heaven treat the pure harshly
> Look how Christ got away from needles tip

After two, three days, he reached Beana, an old habitation of gentry near Agra and sat haplessly at the door of a mosque.

Meeting a Sayyad Born

(Story) There he saw a youth of lithe body, rosy cheeks, a Sayyad born. He looked at him and the youth came towards him as if bewitched. The proud fair Youngman got so affected that he fell down unconscious at the feet of the ecstatic one. The people around understood that the boy's disturbed state was because of Dervaish's glare into his eyes. They requested him to take pity on the youth. He called for water which he sanctified with a prayer and put it to his (the boy's mouth. As a few drops went down the boy's throat, he opened his eyes and sat reverentially on legs bent backward before him (Dervaish) and requested, "If you could be my quest for a few days and gave an opportunity to this devotee to serve you, it would be a great blessing for me although the world in which you live ego has no place for all his non-attachment." My father replied, "There is no harm (in accepting your offer) by way of friendship but I am the one with my feet in the spur and intend leaving tomorrow." Those present said, "We submit to your wishes and our insistence will be impertinence, but if you could go to boy's house and have something to eat, it will be an act of kindness." Since the request of those worthies of the city was acceptable, he said, "All right, I accept but fakir's heart is sometimes in joy and at times in sorrow, no one should interfere in the state in which I may be in anyway." The people said, "We dare not and then who can accept a situation in which by an exhibition of anything against the inclination of your reverend self we may turn our reverence to our misfortune." In short, the people took him to the boy's house and Dervaish partook something there.

Condemnation of Marriage

Coincidently, it was the night of that boy's marriage. After sometime at night, he (the boy) along with respectable people of the city presented himself and submitted, "If your reverence could grace the occasion of my marriage, it will be a matter of pride for us." He (my father) replied, "Congratulations, but I am sorry, marriage is inimical to God worship."

(Addition) O, dear one, you know not that word damaad (son-in-law) is combination of two syllables dam and aad. Iranian use the parallel, such as, abaad (settled) and naushad (happy). Thus, one who marries is in dam-e-bla (a net of troubles). I am a free man and I have broken out of the trap like lightening. These things do not concern me. Go, man is helpless in this matter. In the beginning of youth, I too was intoxicated by the sensual pleasures. Finally, I got nothing but a painful hangover. When one of the God's men gave me deliverance from this imprisonment, I created firmness of resolve and started burning like a lamp, by a single wick. Now, I am no more than a heap of ashes. That heart is no more where lust could be born. That mind is no more which could be attracted towards fun fare of this world. These lights carried alongside you are danger signals. Surprisingly, what kind of a beautiful dear one are you that cannot make good his escape. If your wits are intact, go to the heart of this point, "God alone is; the rest is lust."

In short that boy went to the bride's house and Dervaish, the non-attached one left that city. After a day and a half, he reached Akbarabad (Agra) and contentedly entered his home.

Young man's Sorrow

(Story of Seeking) When the Youngman of the rosy cheeks, of tall stature and lithe body came to know that the Dervaish, all knowing about heart's state, had gone, he brought his bride home, but he did not even partake water. In short, weeping, he with his feet staggering proceeded towards jungle in his (Dervaish's) search. He would enquire about the whereabouts of Dervaish from whomsoever he met on the way. He ran hither and thither but found no trace of his mentor. Disheartened, he raised a heart rending wail and said, "O, Khidr (guiding angel of travelers) I, the ignorant one is in despair without your leading me. Be kind to come to me and lift me up from the dust, lead me by the hand away from my misery. If I could see you in this desolation, it would be as if I came upon a precious treasure.

The hem of my wear which used to be filled with flowers is torn to pieces. The head which used to rest on a soft pillow is filled with dust. Have pity on me for my feet are no longer in a position to go on. Be kind to me for I am so lonely in my wanderings. It is the time for me to receive your munificence. You are the sun. Pass on your light to this humble particle. After what happened to me, repose deserted me and I fell into the hands of this rudderless wandering

Anxiety ridden am I about myself
Knowing not what happened to my heart

Madly I go whirling like an eddy. Perhaps you have forgotten all about me. Anyhow I get little for the pains I am going through. But even now I have not given up hope. In the desert I be wanderer and in the hills like Majnu. My cheeks, before which a rose wet with dew was ashamed, are burned ashen by the intense heat of sunrays. My eyes which were envy of a doe, have turned white. You are the sun, I am the shadow that falls. You are a rich rider in control of all and I am a footman. When dust arises, it looks as if you are coming. When you do not appear, in despair I cry myself hoarse. You are in every particle, in other words a perfect one, then why are you indifferent to the ignorant ones." The youngman went on weeping thus. He would stop and remain standing at times and then again start walking. Suddenly, a reverend old man appeared from behind and said politely in a kindly manner, "O, youngman who are looking for and what is it you are saying. Go on without worry. You will find Ali Mutaqqi in Akbarabad." Hearing this happy news, his restless heart found repose. He started walking with peace in his heart and thanked God. He entered the city of Akbarabad at midnight. He went in search and after making enquiries reached the desired destination, kissing the master's feet with devotion. The tears of joy trickled down his moon face. Sorrow of failure vanished with the joy of achieving his desired goal which was beyond his imagination. The heart piercing Dervaish looked at his handsome face and with his benign vision raised him to perfection. He treated him with so much love that it is beyond description. He embraced him with great love and said, "O, Mir Amaan Allaha, you went through a lot of hardship bearing hot and cold of this world. But now you will not be sad to miss your relatives. This is your home. I and my servants are yours. Rejoice for you have merged yourself like a canal merging with a strange river. Be grateful for like cypress you have escaped (earthly contamination). Centre yourself in the heart. Close the door, sit down and meditate centring in yourself for a few days so that you are able to pull God to yourself."

Advice to Sayyad Born

(Beneficial) "Listen, this is the ripe time to benefit from the word of wisdom. That apparel of yours called body is transient. The temporary clothing needs to be kept neat and clean. The soul that is essence of your being should not be entangled in everyday trifles:

Take care of your soul for body is unreliable
for the creature of clay is nothing more than a tomb

Go beyond your ego and look within. Be ever aware of God and repose your trust in Him. Create humility in yourself for prayer alone will not always stand by you. Create tenderness for without it heart is of no value. Pride is a sin. Leave all your affairs to God. Do not look down upon those more lowly placed than you. Arrogance is a great sin. Be warned and turn away from it. Make humility a habit so that you are able to get in touch with your heart. To the extent possible, avoid hassles of this world and do not unnecessarily saddle yourself with burdens. Cleanse your heart of the impurities acquired from others for unless your house is neat and clean, it would not be suitable for the guest. Try getting along with the suitable and the unsuitable for unless man builds character, he does not become human being. Treat everyone well. That is fakir's religion. Live here like an alien for you are to remain prepared to move on. This world is a house of wails. Staying long here is not the custom. The people of the world are in mourning. Stay here for a brief time for providing solace to them. This is a frightening jungle. Here even the snakes and ants tread warily. Take care to get the wherewithal for the journey for the caravan may suddenly be on its way. If you want to go away healthy from the place of sickness, drink the water of wisdom and eat the food of virtue.

(Point to ponder)

The fakir is the one who does not have even the things he needs. Rich is the one who has renounced the kingdom of the other world in favour of his near ones and strangers. We have our fakiri[14]. God is the only wealthy one, we are all poor. Remember, in this garden, there is only one fresh flower who shines as a thousand hues. The beloved is one but countless are his manifestations[15]

The truth is one but its manifestations are diversely expressed.
If you consider carefully
the beloved is the one only.
From manifestations manifold
One is happy seeing
the One in tune with one's inclination[16]
See only God in creation

Search for Him only
Call for Him only
Where is the duality
Only the cross eye sees two for one
Although between the two eyes
There is but one vision

"Go and eat something and go to sleep. You are tired from the travelling. Take rest and lie down for sometime for you have undergone a lot of hardship." He instructed a servant to look after his (Amaan-Allaha's) comfort carefully and not at any time neglect to serve him.

Death of Amaan-Allaha's Wife

In short that dear one lived in contentment and my father call him "Dear brother". Morning and evening he would present himself before the

---

[14]   A state of voluntary poverty, contentment, abstinence and denial of sensuality in the spiritual search, on the way to God.

[15]   This is identical to the Vedantic statement, Aikam Satya Vipra Bahuda Vedanti.

[16]   Unlike the theistic religions, such as Islam, Christianity and Judaism, in which God is a monotheistic reality both in existence as well as it manifestation, Sufism and Vedant hold that manifestations of reality are manifold. The very same thing said by Tulsi Das in Ramayan, 'Ja ki rahi bhawana jaisi Prabhu moorat tin dekhi taisi'. Whatever is thy inclination you will behold God accordingly.

Dervaish and do practice towards perfecting the self. He (Dervaish) would not for a moment neglect comforting him and daily open to him a new chapter in various stages of Dervaishhood. In short time he (Amaan-Allaha) himself became a Dervaish to perfection. So much so that a stage reached when in a twinkling of an eye he would show strange things and with a shaking of his sleeves a miracle would come to pass. When his relatives heard the news, they rushed from their homes in great zeal. His wife died after a few days of consumption.

In short when his Dervaishhood gained currency in public, the devotees started gathering in large numbers. He did not see any merit in meeting people and went into seclusion. When a year had elapsed, my father sent him a message that now he should open the door of his benevolence to the people. When he came out of his secluded place of worship which could be an envy of the angels, he greeted the Dervaish (Mir's father) and fell at his feet. The Dervaish said, "O, Sayyad, you are a good man. You have made your mark. Lust drives man crazy with restlessness like a cat on a hot tin roof and sex is an uncontrolled trouble maker. By tying the store of contentment to your stomach, you bridled your desire.

> What you have done
> has rarely been done by men

At that time, I (Mir) was seven years of age[17]. He (Amaan-Allaha) affectionately gathered me on to his lap. He would not leave me with my parents. He adopted me as his son. He would not let me be separated from him even for a moment and would nurture me with a lot of love and care. Thus I used to be with him day and night and under his guidance studied the Koran.

LOVE (Infatuation)

One Friday he went for a stroll in the bazar when he saw the son of an oil merchant who was a rich Youngman. He (in love for him) lost his heart. All the firmness of resolve he had was forgotten. In short he could not bear it and was beside himself. When the boy did not reciprocate his affection, he

---

[17]   These reflections in retrospect would indicate that either Mir was an exceptionally precocious and perspicacious as a child or many of the reflections may be wisdom of the hindsight.

returned heartbroken. He made every effort to keep hold on himself, but his heart's restlessness remained unbridled. He could step out and walk on the ground only with a support, his hand resting on the servant's shoulder. He would tell his heart, "O, dear, does anyone play this ridiculous game that you have played with me to disrepute in streets and bazars. Whereas I was in state of self-possession with a firmness of resolve now reduced to this helpless state. The mischievous act of yours even a child will not indulge in. The path you have adopted, even the blind will not step on it. Heart is a precious object which you have showered on a cheap boy. Your heart has burnt for someone who had never stepped out of his house in the afternoon sun. You are mad about someone who had never taken a single step on the heart's way. These eyes are shedding more tears as if these are waiting to burst. The heart is all the more in anguish as if waiting for an excuse that as soon the eyes met, it will start torturing itself. How far can I watch my eyes and how long take care of my heart. Never in my youth did I care for love at sight, now in old age these goose pimples have come on. If I take hold of myself, my heart is in turmoil driving me to despair. If I try patience, tears flood my eyes. Lost I am, knowing not what to do. What should I do to untie the knot? There is no way out unless Pir-O-Murshid (Mir's father) could attend to my problem. So I go and seek refuge in his benign self."

In this shattered state, tears in his eyes, sighs on his lips, he came before the Dervaish around the evening prayer with support of a servant. The congregation paid its respect. Dervaish gestured to him and gave him a place of prominence. My father said, "O, brother, where were you? After a very long time, you have shown your face today." He submitted, "I had gone for a stroll in the bazaar on Friday." My father put in, "You have not perhaps heard:

> One in bondage of love alone knows
> Looking on (with love) the boys of the bazaar
> (cheap)
> brings about madness and humiliation

Go and do not come out of your cell for eight days and nights. Do not at any time remember this incident. God is merciful. He may send the boy to you and vindicate your honour."

Notable was the coincidence. Hardly a week passed that one evening the boy with the face of full moon came out of his house and sat down restless in his shop. One brother, who was standing, inquired, "What is the matter?"

The colour of your face looks faded tonight. You look very perturbed." The boy replied, "How should I tell what I am going through. I can hardly bring it upon my lips. But since I consider you as a friend, there is no harm in telling you. Today is the sixth day, a Dervaish passed this way. He looked at my beauty and for some time he stood there lost. I, in my arrogance, treated him with indifference. Helplessly he sighed from his singed heart and left. But now his face is haunting me. I cannot shake him off my heart. Sleeping, awake his face follows my imagination. What should I do? What do I do to pacify my heart? From whom to ask his name? From where to get his address? Where to do? To whom to relate my misery? The broker replied, "O, he is a well known Dervaish. He is sans ego. The people bow at his doorsteps. Many are his disciples. He is the younger brother of Ali Mutaqqi. He is known all around. He is unique under the blue skies. From his abode, from the door of which the people carry dust considering it to be holy is outside the city near Idgah. Come with me and shake off the shackles of sorrow." In short that humble man brought that Youngman to my father. He related to him the entire episode. He (my father) said, "After all the love non-attached has had its revenge on indifference." He gestured to a servant to inform his dear brother that the one he sought was now seeking him. When this summons, this good news reached the heart torn recluse, he came out of his humble corner with open arms and tired feet. He bowed first at the feet of his mentor. Then with great goodwill he extended his arms to embrace the boy. In short in accordance with his hearts' desire he hugged the boy. He reaped the fruit of his heartsdesire in keeping with innermost yearning. The Pir permitted them to talk to each other in seclusion. When the talks proceeded, the story came out. Dervaish (Mir Amaan Allaha said, "O, beautiful youth, I am fakir, my heart is non-attached. I am not the one to be taken in by external beauty. God knows where my heart is stuck and what is this life seeking whole heartedly? So beware, do not feel proud and coquettish lest you have to repent. Dervaishes are outside the circle of capricious skies (in other words are different from common people), but they also cannot be left in a single state. In short, our state of affairs is different. All right, go, you might have always suffered much."

The boy replied, "Even though I went through suffering but I found a treasure. I know the blessings of sweeping these doorsteps. I hope you will not deprive me of that privilege and will not turn the away from your kindness and compassion." He would come and sit before him (Dervaish) every morning and serve him whole heartedly.

One day the Dervaish (Mir Amaan Allaha) was sitting in a heightened state, when the youth came. He addressed him as 'the dear young one' and made him sit by his side. He bestowed such a look on him that the young man reached the blessed state according to his heart's desire and he came to be known in the world by the title conferred on him by the Dervaish. He came to be respected by the people of the city. Other disciples used to envy him. Finally, he reached a stage when in the spiritual path he had no parallel. How true when Dervaish's eye affected men, it transforms the humble dust to gold.

Ahsan Allaha

(Story) The reverent Dervaish, viz., my respected uncle (Mir Amaan Allaha) used to go once a week to meet a fakir named Ahsan Allaha who was a free soul. His house was surrounded by large plastered four walls whose door would remain closed, its walls were high. It was known as fakir's takia (abode). On the doors of that singed heart was written in golden letters this verse—

If you want to have
a contended heart
Keep the door closed
for open door means
your apparel would remain torn[18]

If someone knocked on his door and asked for him, he would come to the door and say, "Ahsan Allaha is not at home, go away, this house is empty." Once my uncle decided to meet him and he also took me along. When we reached the door, we got the same answer, that is, Ahsan Allaha is not at home. My uncle replied, "If Ahsan Allaha is not, Amaan Allaha is." He laughed and opened the door. What do I see? A taut muscled man riding thesun on whose brow was shining God's glory. His body was wrapped in a thin Iranian sheet with a lungi (a sheet worn around waist) around his waist. He had imposing red eyes as if a lion had gone to sleep in the love of God. They shook hands at the door. They sat in the shade of a berry tree. After enquiring after each other's welfare, he (Ahsan Allaha

---

[18]   The verse means that you should remain a recluse for by meeting people you would become dispersed

said, "Mian Mir Amaan Allaha; I became a recluse for one hardly meets a man worth meeting. But I like you from my heart. Had you not come, I would have been brooding and by the way whose child is this?" My uncle said, "He is the son of Ali Mutaqqi but he has been brought up by me as an adopted son." He said, "He is budding even now. If he goes on like this (with proper training), in one leap, he will cross the clouds. Tell this child to adopt the meeting Dervaishes as a regular habit for the company of fakirs can bestow great bounties." Then he gave me a dry piece of bread after dipping it in water. I never tasted anything so delicious so much so that its taste lingers in my memory. That taste has been a matter of pleasure up to this day.

Teaching of Dervaish

(Point) He went on, "O, dear friend, knowing God is like the pursuit of a wild dear in this dustful desert. Soul is the rider and the body the horse. If the hunt succeeds, one need not bother if the horse is done to dust in its pursuit. But if the horse is dead and hunted one too escapes, suffering one goes through is so intense as to surpass the wretchedness of the grave.

(Advice) Let me shun pride and lust. Sex is a greedy dog. If you give up the path under its influence, you will ruin yourself. If you strive and transcend your ego, take it that you have reached the acme of human destiny. The ignorant one does not understand the evil inherent in his bad deeds but a wise man does not create his own gallows' rope to hang himself with.

(Point) This sky (universe) is phantasmagorical curtain on which strange images appear and disappear. These comings and goings are not in the hands of any visible body but its strings are being pulled by some other (invisible) hands. Do not get involved in this world which is a shameless hooker. When the father leaves her, the son sleeps with her. The good-natured and self-respecting people do not pay any attention to her.

(Mystical talk) The evil people out of self love take pride in living life of illusion. The four walls of the material world which should be quickly broken through, they instead take their stay within them as if the world would last forever and sit around completely idle. They might apparently look smart but they are unaware of reality of existence. They feel confused in aloneness which is of pure nature. What is the need of being in their company? The worthy company is of a quiet Dervaish who is not even obliged to sit in the shade of a tree or of a naked fakir who, in his contentment praises the Lord or a wrestler in loincloth who wages a holy war against sex or those holy Dervaishes who are not attached to either the self or friends and whose foreheads are smeared with dust and whose hearts are pure like running water. They are the lions of the forest of fakiri who drink their heart's blood. They are a quiet sea and a silent storm. They roam the streets of love. In the desert of their holy madness, they are the igniters of holy fire. They are the people who are ever connected with God. They live away from others but remain centred in the heart. They crave for the vision of the beloved while lying down in dust under the shades of beloved walls. They are the swimmers in the ocean of reality and guides in the forest of faith. They are the travelers who have reached their destination from whose shadow the sun rises. They are the dwellers of earth who have hooked on to heaven. They are recluses but their names are known all over. They are the flowers of the garden of modesty asleep on the pillow of hard stone and their dress would suggest madness. They tie stones to their stomach (means they go around hungry) but not a word of complaint. They are not avaricious. They are not attracted to tasty victuals. They are content with simple fare of dry bread.

They are strange pale-faced people long afflicted with love. Proud by nature so much so that one whom they are dying to see may only get from them a fleeting glimpse. They are self-respecting and unless the sharp eye of the beloved orders them to sit, they themselves won't. They are in harmony with the real beloved whom they seek with great zeal and love. They are fighters who have made peace with many better sects. They are such alchemists as to have transformed a thousand times lowly dust into gold. Dervaishes are in control of life's environment. They are what they are. Whatever you wish they can grant by raising their hands in prayer. They can grant the essence of both the worlds. Remember such Dervaishes and consider asking them for courage. If you can, be the one like them so that you yourself is known as Dervaish. The reality is a vast river, the path of which is blocked and the key to which are the words of Dervaishes. Sprinkling prayer on water and walking freely is their grandness—behoves Dervaishes' dignity.

When the dusk came, he said, "O, friend it is time now for the evening prayer. Although I am reluctant to part with you but before sunrise and sunset it is time to prepare our hearts to pray in humility. You should not stay now. Go and convey my respectful greetings to Ali Mutaqqi."

Bidding us farewell, he closed the door. My uncle conveyed fakir's greetings to my father. The latter raised both his hands in token of acknowledging the greetings and said, "Meeting Ahsan Allaha may be considered as God's blessings. Keep on going and conveying my regards to him."

On the fourth day my uncle again went to his (Ahsan Allaha's) house. He also took me along with him. He got the same reply, "I am not home." My uncle said, "If you are not, then who is there who is squatting in my friend's house." Ahsan Allaha laughed and opened the door. We received from him rare wealth of goodness, utmost joy from his stimulating talk. He bestowed on us limitless kindness and compassion.

He said, "My dear, love has brought me to this state and imprinted itself firmly on my heart that I have no eyes for the things of this world and this world itself has absolutely no attraction for me. I practice aloneness. I am without fear. Even if the entire world becomes topsy-turvy, it will hardly make any difference to my centredness. Even if heaven was to crumble on earth, my heart will not possibly deviate from the path. When I close my eyes, I see the face of my heart which is more delicate than sunflower which cannot withstand heat of the eyes. When I look within I become witness to the beloved whose manifestation is thousand fold sharper than the lightening. Thus, it does not tarry with me even for a fleeting moment. If my beloved came in His full speed, this world will disintegrate. If the highest of the high stands upright, this world will go topsy-turvy. Render yourself as dust of His dwelling so that you become crown for heads to wear. Grind yourself for him so as to become collyrium of the eyes of the discerning. Make the heart which may be to His liking. Make the life that is stitched to him. Seek the guidance of one better than you since that is the way you will reach to the difficult destination. Beware of idleness for sitting crippled leads to a downward path."

(Point) "O, dear friend, death is a strange mutation which is bound to come. Do not ignore virtue. Thus look on yourself with the eye of an enemy for that will be real friendship with yourself. Be awake to all states after giving up identity with the body like the ecstasy of the one who has shunned love for a particular person. Since there is no exemplary newness in the world over a long time when the inebriation born of attachment to the world wans, then suddenly you get the bliss of togetherness with the beloved. Woe to the ignorant one who even after he has renounced the world, has not been able to get connected with the other world. He would remain in a state of sorrow and these two states (sorrow and bliss) are called by the awakened one as heaven and hell."

(**Advice**) "O, dear friend, better it is if your heart is acquainted with pain. Sorrow that makes the heart tender is refined. Dervaish seeks sad heart and not happily refined one. They want life of alleviating other's pain rather seeking cure for their own. Turn your prayer towards the transcendent one. Leave all the affairs to Him who runs the world. Live in seclusion and have faith in God. Centre in the self. If sufficient prayer is born in you, it would be the bird Anqa[19]. If your heart becomes tender, it is panacea; a precious metal:

> Precious is our goal, the path of our long
> Search
> This is why, fellow seeker, to inescapable it
> is life in seclusion

(**Point to ponder**) "O, dear friend incomparably apparelled beloved manifests itself in many hues of His choice, sometimes a flower, at other times colours, at places a red ruby and at others just a stone. Some people are happy with flowers, others are enamoured of colours.

One class considers ruby as of pre-eminence, others believe stone to be God. Beware here, there is a fear of a pitfall. We need an eye which opens not on His otherness and the heart which is not attracted to towards anything other than Him. All friends and enemies are from Him. He possesses our hearts. Guidance and misguidance are His expressions. One in abandon and the one who is awake are both on the way to Him. Arch is born of His eyebrows and wine tavern appears from his eyes. The puritans earn the rewards of their prayers and submission. They pour down the wine cups of the tavern. Enter the arch with a bent head. Come to the wine tavern as if inebriated. Thus enter every moment with openness and show respect where it is due."

(**Point to ponder**) "O dear friend, existence proper is in no need of argument or proof:

> One who talks of God giving arguments
> He, in short, is searching for the sun with
> a lamp in hand

---

[19]   Anqa is a mythical bird. It is believed that over whose head it flies becomes the king.

Sun rises and the day spread. If the Lord was not there, heavens would fall and mountain would not be standing. Sun would not give heat, nor moon go around; neither fire will burn nor wind last; neither the clouds will rain, nor lightning's flicker; neither the grass will grow, nor flowers blossom; garden will not rejoice; neither the fruit be born, nor trees grow.

God is called the compassionate one. But under the influence of this attribute, we should not neglect paying obeisance to Him for He is the master of all and when He blesses the dust, it is raised to the status of man and when His benevolence is withdrawn, man is reduced to dust. Our prophet the chosen one of God, thus eulogized by God (If you were not I would not have made heavens), would pray the whole night. He would sit so still that his feet would get swollen. Those who saw this would ask him, "O, prophet of God, why do you pray so much. You have delivered the entire world from sorrow." The kind one would smile and say unto them, "What to do? I am His Servant. So, dear, the relationship of one who obeys and the one obeyed is very delicate. Create obedience in yourself so that you are not afraid when you go before the Master."

When his discourse reached this stage, the herald of City's Subedar (Governor) came and after making Salaam (greetings) said that Nusrat Yaar Khan (the Subedar) was coming to pay his respects to him. Dervaish said, "All right, even though he does not deserve to meet fakirs but I feel a bit sorry for him as he has been sent back without meeting a number of times. If he goes empty handed now, God knows if at all he gets an opportunity of meeting. When he (the Subedar) came to the door, got down from the elephant, he bowed at Dervaish's feet and offered him five Ashrafies (gold coins). Ahsan Allaha said, "Welcome, may you be happy." The Subedar submitted, "My good luck that I was admitted to your service and that I could get a glimpse of your holy self according to my heart's desire." When he found Dervaish affectionate, he requested, "Sometimes bestow your blessings on this sinner." Dervaish said, "Be of firm heart. Confidence has been reposed in you. God in His grace and greatness has bestowed power on you. Make sure that you go before Him with your hands clean. In gratitude for this blessing of God, bestow your kindness and charity on the needy and helpless. Do not be indifferent to their plight. Do not humiliate them. Be God-fearing. Do not be arrogant. Do not hesitate to help the poor and do not leave it to others. Turn not away from the despairing lest you have no face to show to the Creator on the day of judgement. Now you go because this dear friend (pointing to Mir Amaan Allaha) is a mirror holder of light and is of a sensitive nature, I cannot help being partial to him." Subedar in great humility and in token of obedience rubbed is face with the dust from fakir's feet and after kissing fakir's doorsteps with great devotion, departed.

Death of Ahsan Allaha

In the meantime a boy minstrel with a kinky hair, bookish face, ebony complexioned carrying a single stringed musical instrument (Tamboora), wearing golden earrings came to pass that way. Fakir saw him and became fascinated. He asked my uncle to call the boy and ask him to sit with them. That boy came and sat down. Then on his own started singing Umdy Qiblan's Verse in Bhairavi which is a Ragni (tune) which is sung at anytime:

Come beloved for my dear life is spent in
search of you
My life departed in my desire for you
but not the memory of you from
my heart

Dervaish went into a trance and became ecstatic. He said to the boy, "My dear, stay for the night and whatever you know sing to me on you own."

The boy agreeing said, "This is an opportunity to be of service to you for which I am obliged."

Since it was growing dark, Dervaish bid us goodbye and closed the door. He sat down to meditate on God. Then we heard that when fakir got up to say evening prayers, he put the gold coins under the pillow. The evil boy saw it. After sometimes, he went to the bazar, brought a cup of milk, mixing poison in it. He made the Dervaish drink it. As soon as he drank it Darvaish started feeling ill. He started losing control over his body as poison was having its effect. The cruel devil escaped with gold coins. At midnight the people woke up to Dervaish's heartrending agony. When they ran to help, they found him breathing his last. Some people searched for the evil one, but he had vanished into the darkness of the night. When the night was far advanced, the Dervaish closed his eyes on the world. Such a bitter end it was for the life so sweet. The prominent people of the city joined the funeral in a state of extreme sorrow and in accordance with his wishes; he was buried in his own dwelling place which is to-date a place pilgrimage for those to whom he was dear.

Heavens have shed blood of many
God's good people have suffered at its hands

Impulsive heaven acts wantonly and strange are its designs. Often it causes suffering to the humble. Every night it is up to a new mischief. Some, it makes them fall prey to lethal poison and others are done to dust with the sword. The people immersed in love should not ignore its vagaries so that they do not undergo (unexpected) hardship and nor stray away from the path.

Bayazeed (Story)

My uncle was fond of meeting Dervaishes and liked the company of these extremely saintly elders. He heard from someone that a fakir named Bayazeed was staying in a room of a building near Serai Geelani which had been washed away by floods and it (the room) was like lovers heart having a thousand holes and that he was worth a pilgrimage. When he had traced the whereabouts of a fakir, his desire to visit him intensified itself and he started becoming indifferent to things around him. Leaving me he hastened towards the fakir. He saw a young man, tall and imposing, totally withdrawn as if an angel had landed in this world. Nay, this earthly life had no significance for him. He had a stone for a pillow, a bed of dust, dying every moment. Broken hearted, broad faced, burnt out life, matted hair, liberal of heart, he was immersed in God lying down on bare earth. Indifferent he was to earthly desires. If someone with lovely eyes passed before him, he would not give even a fleeting look to that person. He would not meet anyone and lived an indigent life with eyes closed lost in meditation of God. He would avoid eating not even partaking water. He was a stoic and was very incisive in his thinking. He wore very incisive in his thinking. He wore a dress of qalandari fakir (a sect of fakirs of bohemian nature). He asked my uncle, "What is your name? Where are you from? You look compassionate and of lover's sect." My uncle replied, "I live in this city. I am known by the name of Amaan Allaha." He said, "Sit down, let us for sometime entertain each other by talking." When they started talking, Bayazeed said, "O, dear, I have strived at this and that. I have been through a lot of sorrow. I have run around and gone down various streets. I have gathered myself like a cloud and struck at places like lightening. Over a long time I have been unhappy and for long my heart has been clouded with anxiety. For some days I went about with my eyes full of tears. Like a vagabond I tramped around in jungles and habitations. For nights I would not sleep. For days I talked to no one. Sometimes I sought the hems of the rich and at other times I bowed my head at the fakir's dwelling. Only after all that His flippant eye got tender towards me and He acknowledged my state of destitution:

If you want to be counted among those who bear hardship on this path, bring the heart to be of steel and innards to be of stone."

(Stranger's Utterances) "O, dear, if that immaculate looking one is before your eyes, it is eternal paradise but if He is not visible to you, then you, the hopeless lover, is confronted with hell. Remember reality has no other shore, meaning we know nothing. Who knows what the puritanical worshippers have in mind and those ecstatic ones, what do they know? One class remains tangled in desires, the other opt for voluntary poverty. Those who seek reality are free from hope and disappointment. Those dear ones have surrendered to God and bowed to His will. Lovers have, no doubt, to go through privations. But they are made of such a mettle that they can, in short, live in joy even then. Bear with the sorrow so that you can be at ease with yourself. Live with hardship so that you can pass through this world easily. Better it is to detach yourself from the world. What is wrong with it even if you do not get to the mystique of reality? The world's structure is about to collapse. Its foundation is based on illusion. This blue-tomed sky would fall poised as it is precariously on the wind. If you want to reach your goal, make a way to someone's heart and for the sake of God be of service to others to the extent possible. You are a swimmer in the river. If you cannot reach the shore, then remain on the river's bank. In other words, if you are not inclined to risk your life, you should remain prepared to die when the death is indicated. Save yourself from the prisons of mosque and temple and in short be a man of Gods and go everywhere.

(Of Benefit) Awakened ones have two groups, the people of one group are symbolized by wall; they thus remain silent. In short they are wonderstruck by God's creativity and renewing freshness. What they have seen and understood, they have seen and understood. The people of other category have, like almond a brainy tongue and they discern, in short, the hints of the expressive eye of the beloved (God). They show the subtle moods of His eye. They describe it in variety of colours and in hundreds of ways they relate the fluttering manner of His eyes. As countless are the miracles of the ecstatic one, it is beyond words available with this unawakened one (me)."

It was the first meeting. It shortly came to an end. It was not considered appropriate to put the fakir to too much bother. My uncle came to my father and narrated the entire episode.

He (my father) said," Every flower is of a different colour and fragrance. Such co-religionist Dervaishes are rare. Go often to see him."

Second Meeting

One day after evening prayer he (my uncle) went to meet him. He took me along. Dervaish called me affectionately and made me sit opposite him decorously. I was of tender age. He addressed my uncle and inquired about me. The uncle told him, "He is the son of Ali Mutaqqi." He observed, "Oh! What is there to inquire from you? The father of the child is a great preceptor of life's mysteries. He is the sun of skies of Dervaishi, well known in the world, in fact a lifeline of Dervaishi. He is such a river whose bed yields pearls. What do we poor fakirs have in comparison? The son of the great one, convey my Salaam (to your father) and tell him it is not for the want of intensity of desire (that I have not presented myself into his service) but the broken state of my feet makes it impossible for me to come out. My luck is also too obdurate to let me come out of this desolate place. You (Mir's father) are a great and complete qalandar (liberated one) and I am at a much lower state as compared to you. Please pray for this helpless one whenever the time be favourable."

Then he changed the subject and addressed my venerable uncle, "O, dear, give your full attention and pay heed to what fakirs say."

(Point to ponder) Our worship is for ourselves to which kingdom of God is indifferent. Our worship of him should not inflate our ego and believing in God, we should not forget that if our prayers were accepted, it was only His grace for which we should be ever beholden. We are his servants. If we are ignored, we can say nothing more than that we are sorry. These senses which are leading your astray into believing that you are something, is mere close-fistedness and when you will know well your own reality, there is a mere emptiness.

His grandeur is absorbed in His own ecstasy and His holy lights manifest themselves or remain hidden in thousands of ways. What have you understood; what have you concluded; what have you thought? Whom have you lost your heart to? At times He would raise some trouble for you and at other times he will bring you honour. Never ever hurt any ones feelings.

Never be cruel in your behaviour. Heart is known as heaven as it is a special place for that Moon (God).

I see to it that I hurt no one from the fear that one may be your (God's) abode."

(Point) "O, dear, that beloved one is a loving one and takes lovers to His heart. Despite his detachment, He is always aware of lover's plight. When they are in meditation, He manifests Himself in their heart. When they close their eyes, He is there before them. Whenever they want Him, He is there. In whatever manifestation they seek Him, He shows them accordingly. Happiness and sorrow are reflections of their (lovers) own state of mind. If they are happy, the garden is freed (to bloom). If they are sad, not even a single bud will bloom. Their ways are far removed from the ways of the world. Even when the beloved sits by their side, still they have no joy in their hearts, searching they are at times and lost in thought at other times. Not at rest, not content, God knows what they want from Him. Even when they are sans desire yet they are in ferment.

(Parable) Have you not heard that at the time of Moses, there was famine in the land and many people started dying? The people said, "O, Moses, supplicate God as rains are not coming and His creation can no longer bear so much hardship. In vain the people are being killed. In vain they are losing their lives. Moses went to the mount of Sinai and made the request to God. He got the reply, "In that particular dunghill lies the one drunk with love for me. But for some days he has not looked towards heaven and does not talk the way he used to. Rain depends on his talking."

When he heard God's command, he rushed towards that place and found the man in rags lying on a bed made of lumps of clay. Around his body was wrapped a black blanket. Love incarnate was he, drowned in the river of God's love, a rare lyric in the poetry book of a cloistered man was he, non pareil among the men of seclusion. Seeing Moses, the prophet, he said, "O, Moses, how come you are visiting this cave? What possessed your heart that you came here?" Moses said, "There has been no rain. No amount of prayer has yielded any result. People are unable to live. I made a submission in His (God's) court but I was told that you had gone into silence. That is why there is a stoppage. Unless you talked as you did in the past, wind will not bring clouds and His mercy will not come by way of rains. For God's sake, look skyward and lift the curse."

The one lost in God said, "O, Moses, you have not understood that Deceiver and like me you have not lost your heart in His love. That Cunning One is very subtle and His hints can sink the heart at hundred places. I beg

God's mercy that I will not be misled by Him. Nevertheless, if I do not respect the words of His prophet, I will be an infidel. That is why it is said:

Be mad for God and be alert to His Prophet

In short one completely caught up in love and lost in the wonders of His glory lifted his face to the sky and murmured as was his wont, "Ye, the deception incarnate, the enemy of the poise, earlier, clouds, wind, rain, were all subject to your will and now they have become obedient to me. That I will tell them only then wind will blow; rain will come as if you have no control over them. Am I the one running this world? Leave this deception and have mercy on your creation." Twice or thrice he might have blabbed this mock self-glory that suddenly wind started blowing, thick clouds spread across the sky and they burst into heavy rain.

O, dear, what beloved can have so much respect for the lover? Pity if we do not get connected with Him and do not perish in seeking the treasure of life. If your heart turns to blood in His search, it is good for you. If you give up your life pining for Him, it is good for you. Get drenched in His hue so much so you become Him. Get lost in Him in the way that you are not seen again. Rubai (four line verse):

Lose not your heart to the memory of a face
or lock of hair
Nor lose your life lusting for colours and
fragrance

What value has life and heart here
Surrender completely to Him in love

In the meantime, it was time for evening prayer[20]. After the prayer we sat with our faces towards the east and he (Dervaish) said, "O, Mir Amaan Allaha I have today eaten something which I had not had ever before and such a tasty food had not come my way." My uncle who had become very informal with him said, "Shah Sahib, this is an extreme exaggeration and formalism. Your body is bent with the burden of starvation. On your belly is tied the store of contentment with a little you get to eat. Even a draught

---

[20]   In the start of this section, Second Meeting, it is said that they went after the evening prayer.

of water you hardly get. You live in extreme poverty. Everyday death draws near and in such a precarious state you stay in this desolation. In the circumstances what is the tasty food you talk of. Do not indulge in make believe." The Dervaish said, "God be my witness, am I a boaster or given to make believe. Where there is untruth I will not even peep there. Listen since morning I had been going through pangs of hunger. The mean desire (for food) brought about restlessness of a cat on a hot tin roof. I craved to go to the city to beg food from any one—rich or poor. But I lingered on with my head on a stone, to subdue my craving heart to save my self-respect. And suddenly a rat brought a piece of dried bread in its mouth and came into my cell which is more dilapidated than a lover's shattered heart. Externally I am a humble cat broken down by starvation but inside I am a tiger. I am not so (broken down). The rat saw me and ran away leaving the piece of bread. I was somewhat glad and picked up that piece. But there was no water to wash it to make it clean. I sat down waiting for some angel of mercy to come to my rescue. After a short time I heard the voice of a water carrier. I went out with a handless cup and brought the water. I washed the piece of bread, dipped it in water and ate it. God is my witness; its taste reminded me of the joy of tasting heavenly dainties. My dear, fakir's talk has no make believe or exaggeration. They are not disciples of boastful heavens, nor creators of bottomless containers (builders of castles in the air). In their company to mock at them is to cause grievous injury to yourself. Keep your tongue bridled for even a minor annoyance of a Dervaish can cause death of the insolent ones."

My uncle was put to shame by these words and he apologized for his senseless outburst. After admonition he said with his usual kindness, "My dear, you are dearer to me than my life but this admonition was necessary for insolence in speech is contrary to the code of Dervaish. Thus talking the night came. We asked for his permission to leave. He said, "God be with you." We went from there to my father. We conveyed to him Dervaish's Salaam and his message. My father said, "It is so kind of him. When you next go along with your uncle, you must convey my Salaam to him."

Death of Bayazeed

(Third meeting) We went to see him. We found him ill and lying on one side in pain. When he saw my uncle, he uttered a cold sigh. He called him to his side and recited to him the verse of Shafai:

I have none around my pillow
to attend to me in my illness
Only the sigh helps me
to turn from one side to another

My uncle inquired, "What ails you that you are so sad." He replied that
my chest is burning as if someone is igniting fire inside. The raging fire
drives to this lamentation; it is the flash of its sparks convey my Salaam to
him."

I do not know whether sorrow
is burning my heart or innards
It is as if fire has landed somewhere
and is emitting smoke around

If death concedes my mercy petition, consider it to be heaven, otherwise
it is hell which may be considered torment for my misdeeds. Death now
would be victory because breathing in and out is a torture to my soul. I am
sleepless at night. I am restless during the day. What am I to do? Whom to
contemplate upon in my heart so that I may die and find repose:

In great torture I pass the day into night
Now with what hope can I pass night into
the day

When wind blows it fans this fire. Drink of water acts as oil. No
medicine suits. No effort is of any avail. If you take me to the garden I
would keep rubbing my hands in irritation. Alas, I wish my chest was torn
open and my heart and innards taken out or I may be taken out from here
and buried alive."

In short his suffering in body and mind continued till sunset. Sometimes
he would stand with the support of the wall and at times sit down and
stumble. Sometimes he would open his eyes, look on with despair, at times
writhe like fish out of water.

Suddenly I said, "It is time for afternoon prayer. The Dervaish offered
prayer with sincere humility. In genuflection he said, 'praise be to the great
Lord' and breathed his last in prayer:

The fire of love burnt up many

Not to the extent it did in this case

My uncle, the reverend elder, with the help of some servants arranged the funeral and the coffin and buried him in his cell which was as broken down as a lover's heart. Hearing about it, my father was filled with sorrow and said, "Such a human being is born after a long time. Alas! he left this world prematurely."

(Copy) The heart-torched deceased appeared in my uncle's dreams and said, "You saw the love igniting such a fire in me that it burnt me out. Now there was no way out except death. When he saw my restlessness, he put me in the vast ocean of his mercy and gave me the pearl I sought. In short I became at peace and found repose. According to my heart's desire I received the togetherness of the everlasting heavenly beauty of my beloved."

After that my uncle's heart went berserk. For long nothing was of any interest to him. He often said, "Bayazeed was a strange heart singed. I feel his absence a sore in my heart. This will not vanish as long as I live."

The story as it happened he related to father who said, "What is surprising? God is entirely compassionate. Have you not heard the story?"

Story of Bayazeed Bistami[21]

(Parable) The house of famous Bayazeed Bistami, the awakened one (May God's mercy be on him) was adjoining to the house of a fire worshipper (Parsi). He knew him for forty years. He (the Parsi) would worship every morning beating wooden planks. He (Bistami) would address him thus, "O, fire worshipper the door Like of the heaven above would not open by beating the wooden planks. If you desire deliverance, you better embrace Islam."

One day he thought that Bayazeed is not an eccentric. For forty years he had been inviting him to embrace Islam. This could not be without merit (thinking this); he came straight away to his meeting and said, "O, Sheikh, you say every morning that I should become a Muslim. Can you guarantee my deliverance?" The Sheikh was at time in a trance. He called from the

---

[21]   Bayazid of Bistami was a Sufi of the genre of Mansoor who too believed in immanence of God. Mansoor he too in a way said Anal-Haq (I am God). To quote him: "I went from God to God and until they cried from me in me, O, thou I." When someone knocked at his door and asked, "Is Bayazid here?" he answered, "Is anybody here except God?"

paper-maker for a piece of paper and wrote a note of guarantee thereon. He (the fire worshipper) went away and became a Muslim. It so happened that that he died the same week. His descendents buried him stitching Sheikh's guarantee to the collar of his coffin. When Sheikh came out of the trance, he became disturbed. When a disciple asked for the cause of his worry, he said, "In a state of trance I have done something for which I have no authority." The disciple said, "Yes Sir, your acquaintance, the fire worshipper, got your written guarantee for his deliverance. They say that he became a 'Muslim and died'. When the Sheikh heard this, he fell unconscious. Drops of water were sprinkled on his face, only then he regained consciousness. He said, "I was in doubt about my own deliverance. How did I become so reckless to assume the responsibility of others' deliverance? Staggeringly, he came to the grave of the newly converted Muslim and went into meditation on that matter. He saw the same paper on which was inscribed, "O, Bayazeed, your writing was of no use. Even before my showing this paper which I thought to be a missive of my deliverance, He, the compassionate one called me to Himself in such a manner that even surrounding angels were struck with wonder. Let your heart not worry. Come, here is your writing, you take it away with you."

When even sinners are recipient of compassion, that Dervaish (whom Amaan Allaha had seen in dreams) was one of the loved ones of this world. If he was not immersed in the river of His kindness, then this whole episode (Bayazeed's illness) would have been meaningless.

Father's Mystical Sayings

(Sayings Par Excellence)
"O, brother dear, as you know that He, the ever blooming rose of all seasons, appears in His myriad manifestations and this garden has been spruced up by him and these colours are His creation. If you look at them with full attention, whatever you do, you do it fully aware. Every atom of this existence is the reflection of that Sun (God). He who can recognize His ways, his heart is fulfilled. The one whose heart is alive and eyes discerning, he knows that a drop and a wave emerge from the river. The indifferent one is also right in his own way; for he, is in a state of indifference, what he will know of the river remaining on the bank? Come let us wade through (to the other shore) and it is probable we may perfect ourselves according to our life's desires. The season of youth has gone by. Fun of life is gone. At sixty years, old age has arrived. The back is bent. The strength has waned; the

brain is weakened. Gone is the quickness of comprehension. Eyes are losing sight and ears the capacity to hear. Enthusiasm is conspicuously wanting. Teeth are weak, so are the feet. Head is empty; hair white, heart hopeless. Remove the rust (impurity) and chains (bondages) from yourself. The time for decorating fakiri is past and put the chain of the head (mind) on the feet[†]. Days of decorating qalandri[22] have vanished into thin air.

(Point to ponder) Live up to your reputation (in other words, be what you are known for) Use your wisdom for your hereafter. Let your external be the same as your internal. Let your internal world be guided by wisdom. If the beloved is manifest in the mosque, it becomes an art to be a Muslim. The heart's yearnings are for Him whatever the door He comes from. If His effulgence manifests itself in a temple, then what harm is there in becoming an infidel[23]. Eyes seek Him wherever He may be or wherever He may be seen.

We go around to temple or Kaaba
What matters is our search
Irrespective of whether we find Him here or there

Uske farog-e-husn se jhamke hai sab mein noor
Shama-e-haram ho ya ke diya Somnat Ka

His beauty's effulgence shimmers in all
Be it a lamp of a mosque or taper in the temple
(of Somnath)

(Mystical Advice) You should remain in seclusion living alone for a few days. Put collyrium of invisibility in your eyes and vanish from the eyes of all. Do not be attached to anything. Look out for God and do not in any case meet anyone. You had enough of the company of greedy ones. Now the time has come when in a wink of the eye death can appear. How long would you keep on dozing? Discard your unconcern. If you catch the point, understand the meaning of this verse:

---

[22]   He means that now in old age one should confine oneself to removing impurities without moving from place to place like fakirs.

[23]   A sect of fakirs known for its free and unfettered living without caring for respectability.

I kept the colourful company of hundred of books
The only line I chose that of being alone

God knows what you are thinking of that your do not cure yourself. Banish the weight of your surroundings and desires. Lose your head in inebriation of remembering God. In respect for your own grey beard, give up deception and flattery. Do not cling to tatters of your habits. Do not keep your cows in God's barn. Claiming the Godhead is making your asininety known in the city. If unwillingly some miracle gets performed (through you), do not assume airs as pride brings about grief. Cockiness is considered a sin by Dervaishes and excessively proud man is not considered as human"

When uncle left he vowed in his heart not to go anywhere in future but come twice (in the service of Pir-O-Murshid) during the day.

One day my father said, "O, brother dear, brain is deteriorating, in short every day its capacity is dwindling. What if it is utilized to memorize Koran?" Uncle said, "It is good thing you have thought of." In a year and a half both of them committed to memory the entire holy book.

Coming of Asad Allah

(A strange narration)One day these two were sitting going through holy Koran when a Dervaish named Asad Allaha appeared wearing a blue dress and a woolen cap. When he came before my father, he (my father) said, "O, you, the one dressed in blue, you a well-to-do breakfast vendor, why did you travel so far letting yourself be flattened by journeying the deserted path of travails." That dear one came before my father and fell on his feet. My father embraced him and seated him by his side. Surprised by the warm welcome my uncle inquired, "Who is this old reverend." My father said, "He is an old friend of mine." At this my uncle was even more surprised and said, "Such fast friendship requires meeting often but before this date, I have never set eyes on him." My father said, "He and I are disciples of the same Pir. This man used to present himself before the Pir once in two years. One day I asked of the Pir-O-Murshid, what to do that I perceive symptoms of death beforehand so that I get busy preparing for the end and not remain involved in other things. I got the reply that when you again see this breakfast vendor in blue attire, take it that next year you will not be alive. Then you must believe that your life has only a short time left."

My respected uncle became very sad after hearing this and said, "God willing, I will not see this happen. That day I will not live to see another day in this cursed world and will not be able to bear this shock." When he started conversing with the newly appeared Dervaish, he (Asad Allaha) stated, "For sometime my shop was not doing any business. My breakfast fare had no takers. I would cook at night and throw it away in the morning. Whatever saving I had, were gone in covering losses. Disappointed, without hope, with dry lips and wet eyes, I was lying on the ground. Suddenly I dozed off (and went to sleep). I saw Pir-O-Murshid standing over the head of my bed and was saying, 'Asad Allaha, even though there are difficulties in travelling and distance is also considerable but it is essential that you meet Ali Mutaqqi. He and I have an understanding about an indication. As soon as you reach him, he will understand. You should depart immediately. Do not worry about want of customers for when you come back, your shop will be doing a roaring business.' I awoke, handed over my shop to my apprentice, took scanty dry bread for the journey and was on my way. After sometime reached from one world to another. In short in this blue attire I came to Agra and found you as my heart wished you to be. My going back depends on you. Whenever you permit, I would be on my way (home). My father smiled and said, "O, Asad Allaha, why do you ride a flying horse[24]. Your breakfast food would not be spoiled that you are so restless. You are tired after going through so much trouble. Even if you are not fond of fakirs like us, stay for some days for the sake of rest. What is the hurry? Time too will come for going back. He ordered a servant to make his (Asad Allaha's) bed in my uncle's room and to render him necessary service. In short my father would not remain away from him even from a brief period. He would take care to reassure him and entertain him with humour.

(Benefit/Of Importance) One day that dear guest raised a question, "I have a doubt about God's manifestation. There are two classes of Dervaishes, one thinks that one day we would see that pride of moons (God) manifest Himself like we see full moon. The other class believes that our eyes are incapable of seeing that sun." My father said, "We, fakirs have no doubt. We have come to realize that he is creation incarnate. Wherever we see, we see Him. We see His reflection is everything. If to the eyes His grace is available, His essence can be seen in every face." In short after a week, Asad Allaha departed and that too in a hurry.

---

[24]   Meaning, why are you in such a hurry.

Uncle's Death (A Tragic Story)

One the morning of Eid, my uncle put on new clothes and went for offering prayers. When he came back, he suffered from pain in his chest and the pain was so intense that his face turned pale and he lost poise. He called my father and told him that there was severe pain in his chest and that it looked like the end for there was such a constriction (in the chest) that he was getting suffocated. It looked as if his weak body had no life left. He asked to be stripped off his mantle as he felt uncomfortable in it and to remove his cap as it weighed on his head. That his body was weak and his illness was too much for him to bear. When the evening came, the pain became even worse and wails became louder. That man who was the 'feeling' incarnate started withering like a bud when he tried to control himself and started scattering like flower when he moaned from pain. When the seizer of the heart came, he would sigh with the intensity of fire that the smoke of his suffering heart would reach the skies[25]. If he spoke, he would recite this Rubayi:

> It is the time for life to suddenly depart
> For this pain is sans cure
> My heart afflicted with fatal illness named love
> Whose cure is nothing but death

When the night had advanced an hour or so, weakness touched its lowest ebb. He addressed Pir-O-Murshid (my father) thus, "Finally my heart bore this hardship and my eyes have turned stone from this suffering. You are the wise one who knows the secret of this tavern. If my life's cup has some lees left, give it to someone else for strong innards are required to drink it (lees). I consider the bitterness of death preferable to the sweetness of living. Please favour me with your attention so that I might die in peace. Be merciful so that I may have rest." When the night had advanced somewhat, he gave me his night cap and closed his eyes oppressed by weakness. When the night had passed and the dawn came his suffering soul came to his lips. As the priest called for prayer with Allaha-ho-Akbar, the ailing one went to sleep. In short he put his hand on his heart and gave us his life unto the Creator.

---

[25]   Hyperbolic description of the intensity of suffering

His Pir-O-Murshid (my father) threw down his turban on the ground, tore off his collar and in anguish started beating his chest. His disciples with dust on their heads and sores in their heart performed the last rites in sorrow and prepared the coffin for the funeral of the compassionate one.

> Love is suffering sans cure
> Ever troublesome for life and heart

When the people stood up for offering funeral prayer, many collapsed on to the floor. My father said, "O, you who was not acquainted with the regard for intimacy, late did I realize that you did not keep faith and departed in such a hurry scorching my heart. Friends do not depart thus. Those who share sorrows do not show such indifference:

> What happened to the promise
> to stand by each other
> What did I say to you
> And what did you say to me

The respected elders put their shoulders to the bier. In short they picked it up with respect. Pir-O-Murshid's (my father's) sighing was preceding the funeral procession like the deceased's banner. The disciples of the uncle were carrying the bier shedding bitter tears and after burying him in a corner of a garden showered flowers and said prayer for the departed. They suffered this terrible loss but could not help but bear it.

The third day when the people of the city gathered for offering prayers for the departed, my father said, "One whose such a dear one has died, it will not be inappropriate to call him 'dear, dead one'. From today onward I should be called, 'dear, dead one'. Accordingly he came to be known as such in the city. He would weep a hundred times during the day and would live as if he was dead. I whom he (my uncle) had brought up and whose all needs were met by him and who used to eat and sleep with him, I would remember him all day and grieve for him all night. Dervaish 'dear, dead one' (my father) would console me and would not let me be sad. Sometimes he would say, "Son, I love you very much but I am consumed by the grief that I too am about to depart." At other times he would say, "My moon, you are not now a small child to be nursed. Thank God, you are now ten years old. Why torture your heart? After all you are a son of a Dervaish. Straighten your heart. Give yourself up to God. Be happy. Consider me the one who will cater to your every caprice. My dear, you are not a suckling infant that keep on weeping all the time. Do not be sorry for yourself. God will be your protector. Those gone will never come back. Those who have passed away won't show up. Son, this world is nothing but comings and goings on. Everyone is on the move. Do not take this world to be place of lasting stay. This is a delusion created by this gathering which is in flow. Those present have departed. Those living here have gone. Do not trouble your heart. Smile like a flower. The spring is about to depart from this garden. Do not bring sorrow into your heart. This world is such a gambling den where many have gambled away their heart. Never traverse the paths of this world till you know its ways. There is a saying among the players of gambling games, 'go on the gambling way only if you know how to'. In other words if you are a novice, do not play." He would talk like that every day and was bringing me up with fondness.

Ahmed Beg (Narration)

One day in a bitter mood, we were performing the ritual of distributing halwa (pudding) on uncle's death when a tall fair complexioned youth named Ahmed Beg appeared and gave offering of a few western grapes and said that he came from abroad and intended to go on Haj (holy pilgrimage to Mecca) and that when he came to the city he heard the fame of his (my father's) Dervaishi. Out of fondness he came in the service of his (my father's) sublime self. Father said, "You have not perhaps heard:

O, then bound Kaabawards
Why don't you bow to your own feet
Thou art that
being shown to you
from a distance
(Kaaba is your self
Know thine own reality)

First find yourself, then go to Kaaba. Kaaba is another name for broken hearts of Dervaishes. The goal of tattered hearts of the bearded ones is to perfect themselves. If you get to their hearts you will reach your Goal of Kaaba without an effort. That is why it has been said,

I am coming from Kaaba

But I envy those
spattered with blood
who came back from pilgrimage
of the wounded hearts

Strange is the place called the heart of a Dervaish. This desolate place has pleasant breeze. Heart the moon is the destination. At this door they seek reality. One pilgrim had gone to visit Kaaba but in that house he found none. He came back disappointed with heart's desire unfulfilled. In that state, he said:

What you say, the knower of Kaaba says the same thing. Whom you are seeking Kaaba is searching for Him:

When I saw Kaaba
My heart melted
with the anguish of loneliness
The host which called us
was himself guest of someone else

Whoever I saw
Like me wandering in search
Kaaba too I found
Busy seeking (Him) in the desert

I asked Kaaba
Who be friend
in this house
He whispered to me
who is a stranger here either?

Go around the hearts. That is what going around Kaaba amounts to. Be a seeker of yourself. That alone is the good purpose. The other does not exist. None exists except Him pity your youth for you are in for a lot of sorrow and even then you will not reach the goal. Listen to Dervaishes with full attention. Stay for some days here and do not go away from here." When he found Dervaish, he did not disobey him but stayed there. He became busy with strict practices. He had a good brain. He strove and in seven months he reached the stage of perfection. This lovable youth became a Pir of such merit that he could bestow great blessings on others. He became a young man of great faith and a Pir with a discerning eye as was seldom seen by the world and rarely heard by it. Day and night they lived in great closeness and harmony. He (the youth) was not prepared to leave the Pir (my father) even for a moment and he came to be known by sobriquet, 'Youth, the dear one.' It so happened that Pir (my father) got some money in offering from somewhere. He told the young man, "Use this money and go on a journey to Hejaz[26]. After the morning prayer, he (Pir) performed the turban ceremony and gave him (the young man) the prayer mat and bid him farewell.

Father's Death

One day in the scorching sun, Dervaish, 'Dear, dead one' went to inquire about the health of Mohd Baais, the nephew of his dear brother (Mir Amaan Allaha) who was a learned scholar and a mystic who lived in Alam Ganj which, was a well known locality of Agra. When dusk came, he came back home. He prayed in his mosque combining two prayers (of west and evening). When he went to bed to sleep and I presented myself he said, "Son, the heat of the sun has affected me adversely. My head is aching and symptoms indicate that I will have fever." He did not have dinner and went to sleep. When he got up in the morning he had high fever. Abu-ul Fateh who was his old physician came and gave him cooling drink but there was no improvement. Purgatives were also given in plenty but of no avail. The fever of Dervaish lingered on. In short he would have fever in the evening and it would be there throughout the night. Countless measures were taken but this complicated knot could not be untied. After a month it was diagnosed that fever had affected the heart and had settled in his bones. The weak Dervaish who was no more than a skeleton was suffering from tuberculosis.

(One day) He told me, "My son, my life is devoted prayer and my body is decaying. I have no inclination towards food. When I eat I feel heaviness. The medicine the physician gives me in the mornings remains settled as it is in the stomach till the next morning. I want to give up eating till death. Bring five six bouquets of narcissus so that I may sometimes smell life." Accordingly I procured these and would keep them before him. He would take a bouquet in hand whenever he opened his eyes. He would

---

[26]   Mecca Medina

smell it and say, "Thank God I am fulfilled." When he gave up food, we, the helpless ones, despaired for his life. His strength started waning and extreme weakness set in. He would speak very little and prayed only in signs. When the physician, as usual, brought the cooling drink, Dervaish frowned on it and declined to drink it. He said after throwing the medicine cup on the ground, "The effectiveness of medicine shows itself from the first day. I had been drinking (the medicine) out of respect for you. Alas! you did not understand (even this small thing). Go away, leave me alone. Non-comprehension of what is wrong is itself a disease which is sans any cure."

Mohd Hassan

Then he sent for Hafiz Mohd Hassan who was my stepbrother and told him, "I am a fakir, I have nothing. Nevertheless I have three hundred books, bring these to me and distribute among brothers." He (Mohd Hassan) replied, "I am a student and I am keenly absorbed in this work (studies). Both the younger brothers have no interest in books. They will tear up pages from the books. One will convert them into kites and the other into paper boats and float them in water. If your leave them in my custody, well and good otherwise you are the master." My father knew about his perverse temperament. He reprimanded him and said, "Even though you have renunciated the dress but not discarded the edges of yourself[27]. You want to deceive these children and as soon as I close my eyes to harm them. Remember, God is self respect incarnate and likes the people who are self-respecting. It is possible that Mir Mohd Taqi may not depend on you. If you treat him badly you will be exposed and you will not get even a semblance of respect from this child. If he reaches his goal, you will see that in exchange of one copy of book he will tear skin off your body. You, of little wisdom, do not deserve to be trusted. Miserliness and jealousy are the evidence of meanness. All right, you can take the books and keep them." Then he turned to me and said, "I owe three hundred rupees to the bania (trader) of the bazar. You will not perform my funeral rites unless you have paid him as I have been a righteous man and have not deceived any one in my entire life. I submitted that I did not see any property besides these books which you handed over to the elder brother. How would I pay off the

---

[27]   *He means though you have changed outwardly but inside you remain contaminated

debt? With tears in his eyes he said, "Do not lose heart. God is kind. Hundi (cheque) is on the way and is about to arrive. Wish I could live till it arrives but life's span is short. It is impossible to stay." He prayed for me and gave me unto God's care. A few moments later he breathed his last.[28]

Brother's Indifference

When Dervaish was no more, the world became dark before my eyes. This was a big blow as if heavens fell on my head. I shed copious tears. Peace and patience were gone. I would strike my head against the stone. I would roll on the ground. There was a great turmoil as if the day of doom had arrived. My brother (Mohd Hassan) put humanity on the shelf and turned away his eyes (meaning he became indifferent). When he saw that father was poor and died destitute and the creditors would be after him, he washed his hands off saying, "Those whom he gave his love, it is for them to do whatever is to be done. I was never a part of my father's life. I was not given the trust as a son. Good luck to the successors' of Dervaish who are beating heads and tearing at their faces, they would do whatever be required by times." I had to bear fresh shock of helplessness. When I heard his cadish talk, I was both sad and angry but I did not make any plea before him. I took courage in my hands and waited with faith in God. Banias of the bazar brought another two hundred rupees and imploring me a lot to accept but in deference to the last wish of the Dervaish, I declined. I kept them involved in evasive talk. In other words, I did not hurt them. In the meantime, the servant of Syed Mukkamal Khan who was a disciple of my respected uncle came with a Hundi (cheque) for five hundred rupees in current currency and joined me in my sorrow. After paying three hundred rupees I got the promissory note discharged and spent a hundred rupees on the funeral rites of the fakir and buried him by the side of his Pir's tomb.

My Story

(After the death of my father) Heavens turned hostile to me. I went through travails. Nay, how were the heavens and the world to be blamed? I was under the influence of an evil star as such sun's shadow was removed from over my head. Whatever was done was done by my destiny. No hand

---

[28]   Belonging to a totally male oriented society and unrelenting segregation of sixes Mir, no wonder, has nowhere talked of his mother or sisters.

patted my head except my own.[29] None spread cooling shade over me. Whatever material resource I had I spent guarding my self-respect and never knocked at any door for help, nor my lips knew how to plead for help. I never looked up to anyone, I neither asked anyone to help, nor did anyone come to my aid. In short merciful God did not put me in anyone's obligation and did not leave me at the mercy of my stepbrother who was hostile to me. I distributed ritually sanctified food in the memory of Dervaish and left the rest to God. I left my younger brother in charge and started in search of livelihood all around length and breadth of the city but to no avail. In short there was nothing for me in my own land. I had no alternative but to seek livelihood elsewhere and took on myself the hardship of journeying and after undergoing travails I reached Shah Jahan Abad (Delhi). Here too I wandered around but found no one sympathetic.

In Delhi

Khawaja Mohd Basit who was the nephew of the pre-eminent Amir, Samsam-ul-Daula taking pity on my state of affairs, took me to the Nawab (Samsam-ul-Daula). The Nawab, when he saw me, inquired, "Whose son is he? Khawaja Mohd Basit replied, "Mir Mohd Ali." He, (the Nawab Samsam-ul-Daula) observed, "His (mine) coming here implies that he (my father) is no longer alive." After expressing his condolences he said, "He (Ali Muttaqi) has a lot of claims on me. Give this boy one rupee a day from my government."

I requested Khawaja Basit that since the Nawab Sahib was showing so much kindness, he might as well give me the signed order so that his clerks did not put me off by raising objections. I took out an application, which I had written before hand, from my pocket. The said Khawaja observed, "This is no time for the pen stand." Hearing this, I laughed loudly. The Nawab Sahib looked at me and asked the cause for the laughter. I submitted, "I could not understand the sentence. Had he said the carrier of the inkpot

---

[29]   This finds expression in one of Mir's Verses

> Apna he haath sar pe raha apne yaan sada
> Mushafaq koi nahin koi meharban nahin

> My own hand alone ever patted my own head
> None was affectionate one nor was any kind one

is not present, then it was something or that it was not the time for the Nawab to sign—To say that 'this is no time for the pen stand' is an unusual construction. The pen stand is no more than a piece of wood. It does not know the appropriate or inappropriate time. Whosoever is ordered to do so, will bring it."

The Nawab started laughing and said, "What he says is right." In short, he did not reject my application; he called for the pen stand and obliged me by signing my application as requested. That was the day of the King's court. He got ready for the court and very kindly bid me goodbye.

From that date till Nadir Shah's invasion[30] of Mohd Shah who is now known by the sobriquet of 'Heaven, the haven of rest' in which the said Nawab was killed in the forefront of the battle, I had been receiving this stipend which was my only source of sustenance.

In Delhi Again

After that turbulence (Nadir's invasion), cruel times again tortured me. The people who in the lifetime of Dervaish used to treat the dust of my feet as collyrium, now looked down on me. Again I came to Delhi and bore the heavy load of obligation of my step-uncle, Siraj-Ud-Din Ali Khan Arzoo who was the uncle of my elder brother. In short I stayed with him for some time and read some books borrowed from friends in the city.

When I became capable of conversing correctly with someone, a letter came from my brother to his uncle that "Mohd Taqi was a troublemaker. On no account should he be brought up and in the guise of friendship be finished off." That dear one (Arzoo) was strictly a man of the world. Taking note of his nephew's enmity towards me, he started wishing me ill. If I went to him, he would scold me and if I avoided him, he would abuse me. His eyes always followed me. He often treated me with hostility. What to say

---

[30]   Nadir Shah invaded Delhi in March 1939. For seventy-four hours Afghan army, on his orders, indulged in wholesale massacre in the city in which more than thirty thousand people were killed. The treasures of eight Moghul nobles fell into his hands. He left on 05th May 1939 carrying with him estimated wealth to the tune of 70-80 crore rupees on ten thousand camels, equal number of horses and three thousand war elephants. For details see Frazer—'Nadir Shah'; Sarkar—Fall of the Moghul Empire Volume-I. We may also add here that besides the large-scale wealth, Nadir Shah also carried away with him fabulous Peacock throne of Shah Jehan studded with world famous Koh-e-Noor diamond.

what I got from him? In any case I would keep my tongue tied. Even in dire need I would not ask him even for a rupee but he did not refrain from ticking me off. If I have to narrate in detail, the story of his enmity, it would require another volume. My anguished heart was even more wounded.[31]

Madness

And I became mad. My depressed heart had become even more depressed. I went wild. I would close the door of the cell in which I lived and would go into seclusion surrounded by hordes of misery. When the moon rose, the doom will land on my head. If at a time, the maid servant helping me wash my face said, 'moon, moon', I would look towards the sky and see the moon, I would go crazy to such an extent and wildness would increase so much that the people would shut the door of my cell and would run away from my company.

(Narration of the offering) On a moonlit night a figure of beauty both of face and body would descend with elegance towards me from moon's circumference and drove me beyond myself. Whatever direction I looked, I saw that envy of a fairy. Whichever direction I saw, that pride of houries wasin view as if the door, roof and courtyard of my house were sheets of paintings. In other words in all six directions that wonderful face was seen. Sometimes she would appear before me like full moon. Sometime my heart was the place destined for her to stroll around. If I looked at moon, my my restless self would get singed. Every night I had her company and every morning without her I would remain in a wild state. When the dawn's dim light came, she would sigh with a tortured heart. In short with a sigh she would return to the moon. I would go crazy throughout the day and would torture my heart in her memory. Like a madman and one in a trance I would go around with a stone in my hand. I would stagger around and the people avoided me. For four months that shining appearance of the night played havoc with me in a variety of ways and tortured me with her strident mischief. Suddenly the spring came, the wounds of madness further

---

[31]   Mohd Hussain Azad in his book 'Aab-e-Hyat'—History of Urdu Poetry and biographical sketches of Urdu Poets, attributes the falling out of Mir Taqi Mir and Khan Arzoo to their religious differences (the said Khan being Sunny and Mir being a Shia) and Mir's hypersensitive nature. Khan Arzoo is depicted by Azad as a scholar who took fatherly interest in teaching talented young students ('Aab-e-Hyat'—pp 115 and 194).

burgeoned. In other words I went completely mad and become totally worthless, lost as I was in the delusionary face and her fragrant tresses. I became ripe for being segregated, in other words to be confined and in chains.

Fakhur-ul-Din's wife who was a disciple of the Dervaish (my father) and was a near relation spent a lot of money on my treatment. The exorcists used charms and spells to cure me. The physicians bled me. The physicians efforts proved helpful. Autumn came and spring departed; my madness waned. The delusionary imprint was erased from the heart's page. The lesson learned in madness was forgotten. Tongue became acquainted with silence. Thus ravings of the disturbed mind departed. With the massage of the head sleep also came. Lost strength was regained. Thus I became normal. Sleep was no longer disturbed and that moon face vanished from the sight. After the lapse of sometime I was completely cured and started reading Tarsul (a primer containing rhymes/prose to acquaint children with different letters of the alphabet).

Mir Jaffar (Narration)

One day I was sitting in the bazar with a portion of a book in my hand that a young man named Mir Jaffer happened to pass that way. When he noticed me, he came and after a brief pause said, "O, dear, it seems you are fond of reading. I too am a bookworm but there is no one to converse with. If you are interested, may I come occasionally?" I said, "I do not have the capacity to be of service to you but if for the sake of God you take the trouble of coming, it will be a benign act on your part." He said, "The only thing is that I do not step out of the house unless I get a little bit of breakfast." I replied, "This difficulty will also be made easy by God, the merciful one though I too have nothing." He arranged the pages of dispersed document in order of their page numbers, gave it to me and left. After that I often met that man with a human face and angelic nature. He would teach me. He would make mental efforts to educate me. I too would serve him to the extent I could. Whatever became available I would spend on him. Suddenly he got a letter from his native place, Azeemabad and he was constrained to go away.

Syed Saadat Ali

Sometimes thereafter I met a Syed named Saadat Ali who was from Amroha. That dear man took the trouble to put me on to writing poetry in Urdu medium, the verse which resembled Persian poetry. Urdu was the language of Hindustan by the authority of the king and presently it was gaining currency. I worked at it very hard and practiced this art to such a degree that I came to be acknowledged by the literati of the city. My verse became well known in the city and reached the ears of the young and the old.

In the Employment of Ryayat Khan[32]

One day my uncle invited me to a meal. I heard him saying something bitter to me. It was something so unsavoury that I got up without touching the food. Since being with him was doing no good to me, I left his house in the evening and proceeded towards Jama Masjid (great mosque).

It so happened, that I lost my way and reached Hauz Qazi. There is a small canal near the house of the King's minister Itmad-ul-Daula. There I drank some water. At that place, a person named Aleem Allaha came to me and inquired, "Are you Mir Mohd Taqi Mir?" I asked him, "How do you know?" He said, "Your eccentric ways are well known. Ryayat Khan who is the son of Azeem Allaha Khan and the nephew of Itmad-ul-Daula Qumar-ul-Din Khan is eager to meet you ever since he has heard about your efforts at thought provoking verse. If you accompany me and meet him, I will also get an opportunity to benefit from his company." I met him. He treated me humanely and took me into his friendship. I benefited from it (entering his employment) and was freed from the prison of poverty.

Invasion of Durrani[33]

When (Ahmed Shah) Durrani came to Lahore, Zakaria Khan's son Shah Nawaz Khan who was the governor there ran away. Then the minister (Qumar-ul-Din Khan) and Safdar Jung and Raja Jai Singh who was a big

---

32   The son of Subedar of Malwa who himself later became its Subedar.
33   Ahmed Shah Durani came for the first time to India along with Nadir Shah's army in 1739 and he saw with his own eyes scenario of decay and decline of the Moghul Empire.

landlord and his own son Ishar Singh accompanied Prince Ahmed Shah. Now the governor of Panjab Shah Nawaz Khan wrote to him that if he invaded India, the said Khan would help him provided the ministership of Delhi Darbar was given to him. Ahmed Shah receiving this invitation started in 1748. In the meantime Nawab Qamar-ul-Din started the fight (against Abdali). But the minister (Nawab Qumar-ul-Din Khan) was hit by a mortar in the outskirts of Sirhand and the said landlord (Ishar Singh) lost his footing. Moin-ul-Malik who was the son of the martyred minister and Safdar Jang with the Prince Ahmed Shah being put on a horse attacked the Afghans. In that campaign I was with the said Ryayat Khan and was maternal uncle of Shah Nawaz Khan coming to know of his dangerous intent (of his nephew) persuaded him to give up the idea (of helping Ahmed Shah Abdali/ Durrani). Durrani tried again to smoothen Shah Nawaz Khan but in vain. But he kept on the pressure and on January 10th, 1948 he crossed Ravi with his army and pitched his tents in Shalimar Gardens. Next day the armies clashed. Shah Nawaz Khan ran away. When the news of the fall of Lahore reached the ailing Mohd Shah (the King), he sent army of two lakhs under prince Ahmed Shah, Nawab Qamar-ul-Din and Ishar Singh son of Raja Jai Singh of Jaipur which reached Sirhind on 25th February 1948. They had advanced from this side only slightly when Durrani coming via Ludhiana route, captured Sirhind and started the killing and lootings. On 22nd March 1948 Qamar-ul-Din was in prayer in his tent when a mortar suddenly hit him from which he died instantaneously.

Moin-ul-Malik suppressed this news and he himself performing my duties as his employee. When Afghan army was badly defeated and fled, Moin-ul-Malik became the governor of Lahore and the said Khan (Ryayat Khan) giving up his (Moin-ul-Malik's) friendship like a discarded part of the body, left for Delhi along with Safdar Jung.

Death of Mohd Shah

Near Panipat which is a famous city situated at a distance of about forty Kos (equivalent of about 100 kms) from Delhi, news reached that Mohd Shah (the king) had died. The news created a stir. Safdar Jung proudly offered the crown riding Nawab Qamar-ul-Din's elephant came to fight. Durrani's arsenal incidentally caught fire and the elephants of his army ran helter skelter. One thousand of his soldiers were burnt alive. Durrani was constrained to retreat from the battlefield and royal army won.

On 9th April 1948 Mohd Shah's order came calling back the army and appointing Moin-ul-Malik as governor of Lahore. Moin-ul-Malik remained as such till his death on 3rd November 1753. After that his wife Mughalani Begum assumed the governorship of the province. But Imad-ul-Malik (the minister of the king), dismissing her, appointed Aadina Beg Khan in her place. She wrote to Abdali to come to India tempting him with wealth and booty.and throne to Ahmed Shah and made him the King. He entered the city in great splendour. On that occasion Javed Khan who was the Daroga (Palace Captain) of late King was awarded the title of Nawab and was entrusted with the authority of administering the kingdom.[34]

Ministership of Safdar Jung

When Nizam-ul-Malik Asaf Jah died in Deccan, Safdar Jung got the ministership and Saadat Khan Zulfikar Jung was made the commander-in-ministership and Saadat Khan Zulfikar Jung was made the commander-in-chief/Royal Paymaster. The minister lived in a grand style. So much splendour was not available even to the King. The new Royal Paymaster (Saadat Khan) sent Raja Bakhat Singh who was an experienced big and well known, landlord and his elder brother Abhay Singh, the ruler of Jodhpur State, after gifting them Ajmer, to fight against his brother (Safdar Jung). The said Raja took Ryayat Khan with him as the commander of his army. The two armies met at Sambhar, a township twenty Kos (around 50 kms) from Ajmer and artillery battle ensured. But both the sides remained evasive about fighting and like those untrue to their salt (perfidious people), not even for a day they fought with their hearats in the battle. Perforce Abhhey Singh entered into peace treaty with the mediation of Malhar, Marahatta Chieftain. After peace treaty I went to the holy shrine of the reverend Khawaja to get his blessings and after perambulating areas around Ajmer, I came back.

Here erupted a quarrel on some matter. Raja Bakht Singh was annoyed and fell out with Ryayat Khan. Sattar quli Khan Kashmiri who was a multifaced person castigated him and (the two) became enemies. The Khan (Ryayat) sensing that the time was not appropriate for him (to go) sent me (to the Raja) to apologize for the misconduct. I went and gave a solemn promise that no such thing would happen in future but he (the Raja) did not

---

[34]   Rights (of governance) keep on changing hands Perhaps wealth too is a fakir which is regularly found standing at someone's or others' door

relent and he gave no respite. He disbanded the army after paying it off and bid farewell to that place. Somehow it passed off well. Khan too relinquished his charge and came back to Delhi and stayed at home for sometimes.

My Senselessness

One moonlit night, the son of a ministrel sitting on the obelisk (for viewing moon) was singing to the Khan (Ryayat Khan). When the Khan saw me he said, "Mir Sahib, give a few verses of yours' to him to memorize. He will sing them after setting them to tune of a Raga." I replied, "I am not a singable man.[35] He said, you vow by my head." (i.e. that you will do it). Since it was a question of livelihood, I carried out his order hesitatingly and reluctantly. I got him (the singer boy) to memorize five of my Urdu verses.

But this thing weighed heavily on my sensitive nature. For two and three days I remained confined to my room. He, the Khan cajoled me in everyway but I did not go to him and left his job. But that man of personal goodwill could not bear the plight of this fakir. Out of affection for me, he employed my younger brother giving him a horse. After sometime had passed I went to meet him. He was all apologies. I said, "Goodbye to the bygone."

Nawab Bahadur

After the passage of sometime I found employment with Nawab Bahadur and came into his service. Asad Yaar Khan who was the commander-in-chief of his army acquainted him with my state of affairs, thereby getting me exempted from horse riding and rigours of service. He (Nawab Bahadur) was extremely partial to me. He used to keep on helping me and showing favours to me. May God bless him!

Journey to Farrukhabad

When Qaim Khan son of Mohd Khan Bangish got killed fighting Rohillas, Safdar Jung set out to forfeit his house. I too went, on that occasion, with Ishaq Khan Najum-ul-Daula for a walk to that side. Since there was a fierce fight with Ahmed Khan, the younger brother of quaim Khan, the minister (Safdar Jung) was squarely defeated and Ishaq Khan was

---

35   He means as a poet

killed. With great difficulty I returned to the city (Delhi) with the defeated army. The minister again set out on a military campaign and after defeating the Afghans victoriously presented himself to the King.

Ghazi-ud-Din Feroze Jung

When Zulfiqar Jung who was the commander-in-chief of the army was dismissed because of the enmity of the Nawab (The minister), Ghazi Feroze Jung the son of Asaf Jah was elevated to the high position of the Chief Amir. He (Zulfikar Jung) left to take over the administration of Deccan province but he died on the way. His son Imad-ul-Malik was crowned commander-in-chief/Royal Paymaster of the army. I stopped meeting people and got busy in extensive studies.

In the Employment of the Minister Mahanarain

When Safdar Jung got Nawab Bahadur (Javed Khan) killed treacherously, my world became topsy-turvy. I was again unemployed. The Dewan (chief executive) of the minister, Mahanarain sent something for me with his Daroga (the police captain). Mir Najam-ul-Din Ali Salam who was the son of Mir Sharif-ul-Din Ali Payam and invited in earnestness. I came under his protection and a few months were spent in comfort.

Even before the controversy about murder of the poor victim, the Daroga of the palace (Javed Khan) was over; the times blew in another trouble. In short the minister had some suspicions and he rebelled against the King. Every effort was made to bring about reconciliation. But in his arrogance of Amirhood, he did not bend. Perforce the King decided to punish him. At last he (Safdar Jung) left the city bent upon waging war against his benefactor Lord (King Ahmed Shah). On this side Imad-ul-Malik who was the grandson of Asaf Jah and was commander-in-chief of the army, his maternal uncle and Intezam-ul-Daula son of martyred Itmad-ul-Daula (Qumar-ul-Din Khan) and other chiefs of the royal army defended the city. The old city got looted. The battle went on for six months. Even though they did not have the capacity to fight him (Safdar Jung), the fighters of the royal army fought desperately and won the battle and the rebel minister was routed. In his helplessness he sent an appeal for peace. The king heaved a sigh of relief having defeated him (the minister) and sent him to Avadh province as its administrator. Intaezam-ul-Daula became the minister.

In the Haveli (Mansion) of Amir Khan

At that time harassed by unhelpful world, I left the neighbourhood of my maternal uncle (Siraj-ul-Din Ali Khan Arzoo) thinking that he would look down upon me. I came to live in the haveli (mansion) of late Amir Khan (who was an Amir in Mohd Shah's period) who had influence over the governance of Allahabad and over the kingdom. His pen name was Anjam. He was talked about among the people for his good manners and eloquence. He had a hand in victory over Mohd Ali Rohilla. It was at his instance that King attacked him (the Rohilla) and took him as a prisoner. Finally he (Amir Khan) was killed at the entry to Dewan-e-Khas (Special Court of the King) by one of his own employees. Shifting to the haveli I lived there undisturbed without hesitation.

Imad-ul-Malik collected a force in a short span of time and with the help of Maharatta chiefs invaded Suraj Mal who was a powerful landlord for the crime of his having sided with Safdar Jung. Securing a place for himself, he surrounded the fort and started harassing him (Suraj Mal). Malhar Rao's son was killed. The said landlord (Suraj Mal) and the minister (Safdar Jung) were corresponding secretly and that very fact caused ill-will between them (Imad-ul-Malik and Suraj Mal). The king also left the city and camped near Secundrabad twenty miles beyond Jamuna. One evening the news came that Maharatta chiefs and Imad-ul-Malik have joined hands with Suraj Mal and they had started fully armed and were about to arrive to loot the royal army. The King at the instance of Samsaam-ul-Daula, Mir Aatish and some other treacherous people who had already conspired with employees of the army command, ran away in panic dishonourably leaving behind royal wives and their ladies. In the morning the Deccani army (Maharattas) arrived and completely looted the army (of king's). Then they came in pursuit and pitched their tents on the other side of Jamuna.

Alamgir, The Second

The orders were given (by Imad-ul-Malik) that no man of the Royal family should remain in the fort (Red Fort) even though those perfidious ones had already fled from there. After settling this Imad-ul-Malik came and assumed the duties of Ministership. The idiotic minister (Intezam-ul-Daula) retreated to some hole out of cowardice. The King (Ahmed Shah) proceeded towards the garden in a state of panic. After sometimes his (Imad-ul-Malik's) treacherous companions caught him through deception. He was blinded with hot iron rods and Bahadur Shah's grandson Alamgir, the Second, was crowned as the King. The people of little consequence came to power. Whatever happened was unfortunate. Samsam-ul-Daula who was sans any sense became Amir-ul-Umra (chief executive of the minister). In this horrible happening I was with Ahmed Shah.[36] Coming back I retired to a secluded corner.

Maternal Uncle Journey to Lucknow

In those days Safdar Jung died and the state of Oudh passed on to his son Shujah-ul-Daula. My maternal uncle (Khan Arzoo) proceeded there (to Lucknow) tempted by greed. He had hoped that by joining Shujah-ul-Daula's army he would receive favours from the brother of martyred Ishaq Khan in view of the past obligations. But he got nothing. After being tossed about by fate he died there. His dead body was brought from there and consigned to earth in his own haveli (mansion).

Mir has written about the second blinding towards the end of his autobiography under the heading 'Atrocities of Ghulam Qadir Khan'. The Rohilla first blinded the King and then in a show of horrible brutality carved out his eyeballs. He not only committed heinous crimes of extreme cruelty against the members of royal family but also against those serving them. That part of the history reads like a horror book.

Raja Jugal Kishore

After two three months, Raja Jugal Kishore who at the time of Mohd Shah was the counselor for Bengal and now lived in a grand style, took me to his house and asked me to correct and improve his verse. I saw no scope for improvement and often crossed out his writings.

---

[36]   Referring to this blinding and subsequent blinding of King Shah Alam by Ghulam Qadir Rohilla, Mir writes:

Shahan ke kehl-e-jawahar thi khak-e-pa jinki
Unhein ki aankhon mein phirti salein dekhein

Kings, the dust of whose feet was precious collyrium
I saw their eyes being pierced by hot needles

Raja Nagar Mal

In those days Raja Nagar Mal who in the days of the Heaven of Eternal Rest (Mohd Shah) was Dewan (Minister) for managing government land became Deputy Minister. He got the title of Maharaja and Umda-ul-Mulk (Grand man of the land). Since he used to give refuge to the oppressed and attend to their pleas for justice, many people became his enemies. If he went to the court, he himself would proceed with caution and in full splendour fully armed and his army would be on the alert. Thus he would not be taken in by his ill-wishers. He would live with his head held high. In those days the current army chief Samsam-ul-Daula died after suffering from pleurisy and his inconsequential son was appointed to the post in his place.

Invasions of Abdali

In the meantime Shah Durrani (Abdali) who had gone back after being defeated at Sirhind and who was obsessed with the idea of (invading) Hindustan, came to Lahore with a large army. What atrocities the common man and gentry there did not bear? What cruelty they did not put up with? There was none to stop him for Moin-ul-Daula had abjectly surrendered and after a few days he died of fall from his horse.

From there he (Abdali) proceeded to the city (Delhi). Hearing of his coming the people began to panic. The king and the minister could do nothing. They went to welcome him and got imprisoned. Raja Nagar Mal along with other nobles like Saed-ul-Din Khan, Khan Samaan etc., went away to Suraj Mal's fort for their safety. Nearly for a month's essential provisions were scarce in the city. Abdali handing over the kingdom to Alamgir, the Second, proceeded towards Agra taking the minister Imad-ul-Malik with him. His army started the carnage and looting. Mathura which is a populous and a buzzing city eighteen Kos (around 50 kms) from Agra was subjected to brutal killings. When the atmosphere there became fetid, Abdali becoming scared of plague departed leaving the matter of Suraj Mal for another time and marrying Mohd Shah's daughter quietly went back. Imad-ul-Malik remained around Agra. Najib-ul-Daula who became the employee of the minister at the time of war with Safdar Jung had a meteoric rise becoming Army Chief and Regent of the Kingdom.[37]

---

[37]   When Moin-ul-Malik, died, his wife Mughali Begum took over the administration of the province (Panjab). But Imad-ul-Malik dismissing her

Abdali starting from Kandhar reached Lahore on 20ᵗʰ December 1756 and 10ᵗʰ January 1757 crossing Sutluj without any opposition entered Delhi on 28ᵗʰ January. Here his army indulged in looting and atrocities on a scale of which Mir has not even written one hundredth part in this book.

Skirmish with Najib-ul-Daula

Here Raja Nagar Mal joined hands with the Maharattas. He took the minister Imad-ul-Malik, Ahmed Khan and these Maharattas to invade Najib-ul-Daula who got bottled up in the city. The artillery battle broke out. There were some chieftains who were autonomous and who would think of looting the city whenever a little opportunity presented itself.

After the carnage, the looting of its residents and the rape of the womenfolk of the gentry of womenfolk of the gentry of Delhi, his army proceeded to Mathura where countless Hindus and Muslims were massacred and bazaars were looted. All the houses were burnt. For weeks the corpses were lying undisposed in a state of decay and stink. The atmosphere became fetid and the water was polluted. Cholera broke out in his army and on an average 150 of his soldiers started dying every day. Perforce he had to come back. He decided to leave Hindustan. But before leaving he forceably married the late king Mohadmad Shah's daughter. When his caravan set out for Kandhhar, his loot was carried on twenty eight thousand camels, elephents, mules and bullock carts.³⁸ In Delhi, animal of any sort was not

---

appointed Adina Beg Khan as the Governor. In March 1756 Mughlani Begum wrote to Abdali (to raid) tempting him with wealth and booty.

³⁸　To come back to Mughlani Begum, her role in this carnage and loot and her relation with Abdali, Sarkar observes:

"Gorged with the plunder of Delhi, Mathura and Agra, Ahmad Shah set out from Delhi at the beginning of April, on his return homewards. During his stay in India Mughlani Begum had risen to his highest favour. She had been chosen by Delhi Emperor and his wazir as their mediator with Abdali; she had divulged to the invaders the secrets of all nobles of Delhi, telling Afghans of hiding place of every noble's treasure and the exact amount of wealth that could be squeezed out of each; and she had been Ahmed Shah's agent in procuring virgin tribute for him from the imperial family. She presented him with costly jewels on her own behalf. There was nothing that Afghan King could refuse to her. In high delight he cried out, "Hitherto I had styled you my daughter; but from today I call you

to be seen for Abdali did not leave even a cavaderous donkey behind. His entire army had to march back on foot for animals and carriages were all loaded with loot. The Minister restrained them (the chieftains) from looting, telling them that their looting the city would be an inappropriate and a stupid act and that our prestige will be done to dust by Deccan army. That they (these chieftains) were an inexperienced lot and they should take care lest the city be destroyed and we became infamous for it. Let us make peace with the Rohillas and take them out of encirclement and ensure the safety of the city. He entered into an agreement with Najib-ul-Daula and brought him out of the city. He (Najib-ul-Daula) went away toSaharanpur which was in his military control. The minister and his men entered the city. They bid farewell to Deccani army. The Raja's son (Bahadur Singh) was made Daroga (captain/ commander) of artillery and Ahmed Shah became the army chief.

Raja Jugal Kishore

One day I complained to Raja Jugal Kishore about my plight being with no means of livelihood. That dear man, blushed from shame, said, "I am myself poor. If I had anything, I would not have hesitated (to share)." One day he rode to Raja Nagar Mal's place. Introducing me (in absentia), he sent for me. Through him I met Raja Nagar Mal who received me with pleasure and kindness. He said, "You are welcome to poor man's feast. You will keep on getting your share." I got reassured and came away. Next day when I got an occasion to recite my verse he said, "Mir's each verse is a garland of pearls. I like the style of this young man." Thus I kept going there for some days but got nothing. Since the knife had reached the bone (poverty and starvation had gone beyond bearing), anxiety increased a good deal. One day after the morning prayer, I went to his door, the chief herald named Jai Singh came to me and said, "What time is this for the court?" I told him, "I am in a helpless state. He said, "The people call you a Dervaish, you have not perhaps heard that not even a particle moves without the will of God. Here no one bothers for anyone being preoccupied with matter of the State. You should remain patient and content. Everything happens in its own time. Here it would be difficult for you to have an access. However, you can meet

---

my son and give the title of Sultan Mirza." He presented to her the very cap, aigretle, coat and other vestments he was then wearing; there could be no more exalted khilat (gifts) than these."

—Fall of the Moghul Empire Vol-II p 45.

his elder son." Thoroughly ashamed I came back. One night, as suggested by that guard I went to see the Raja's son. The Durban (gate keeper) stopped me saying, "It is impossible to meet him now." Helpless I came back. After the night's prayer I went again. I inquired, "Where has the guard gone?" The people said, "Today he had such a severe headache that he could hardly sit." I thought that in this, God's help was at hand. I entered and met the Raja's son. I got the opportunity to recite my poetry. Khawaja Ghalib who was a powerful Young man having influence and who knew me narrated my state of affairs in detail and got something settled on me which I kept on receiving for a year. One night I presented myself before the Raja when he said after giving me one year's salary, 'Keep on meeting me often.' From that day after the night's prayer I would attend on him in his garden like an employee and would remain there till midnight. As an outcome of this service I led a contented and comfortable life.

Now my long winded pen deviating in narration would describe something else.

(An Event) The chiefs of Deccan (Maharattas) considered this country to be theirs and were planning to go to war with Abdali. When they heard that Shah Durrani's son, Taimur and his army chief were only with a few of their men, they, ignoring the consequences (or the strength in the backyard), invaded Lahore. The ruling army which was small in number could not bear the brunt, ran away and Maharattas conquered the area up to the river Attock. They left for Deccan after leaving a chieftain named Sahiba in charge for administering the area.

Some Other Events

Since I wanted to write about these events in brief, that is why many minor events I had not penned in detail for in this brief book there was no place for such details. [39]

Mischief of Marathas

Even before all these troubles were over, the wayward heavens brought in another calamity. The panic spread. In short, a chief name Jankoo came

---

[39]   Here Mir has listed sketchily minor happenings of the time which are too abstruse; hence omitted, being of no material consequence historically or biographically.

from Deccan with a large army. His army proceeded towards the city (Delhi) from different directions. Many people got frightened and there was a hue and cry. The rich nobility paled out of fear. The king and the minister entered into a pact with them. Joining hands with the chief named Datta who was the minister of this brave and hardened chief (Janko) they invaded Najib-ul-Daula who was dug in on banks of the Ganga and its adjoining areas. A fierce battle broke out. They gathered at the minister's house for parleys about the situation. It was felt that if the large army on its return attacked them, there would be large scale destruction and would reduce everything to rubble leading to the annihilation of the city. If possible they should join forces to kill Najib-ul-Daula or otherwise they should negotiate peace with him.

Murder of Alamgir, the Second and Intezam-ul-Daula

When this was decided, the minister (Imad-ul-Malik) came out and encamped on the other side of the Jamuna. Then he invited the King to join him. He (the King) excused himself on the pretext of illness. Since these people were distrustful of the King, they proposed to go to the city to finish him off and also not leave Intezam-ul-Daula alive. The same night Raja Nagar went away across the river. By morning these blackguards came to the city and took vows before the king that they were not happy with the minister but for convenience only keeping up pretence overtly. An opportunity has arisen from which His Majesty could benefit.

The gullible King was taken in by these worthless people. He asked, "What is it?" They said, "One Sahib-e-Kamal (an accomplished soul) a renunciate fakir has appeared in Feroze Shah Kotla during the last two or three days. He will leave tomorrow. If you could meet him, with the blessing of this reverend wise old man we might escape this calamity and overcome the minister." The King was unaware of the hypocrisy of these people consumed with worldly ambition. He promised, "I will definitely meet him." They took him in a carriage but when he reached Kotla, that innocent one was knifed to death and his dead body was thrown over the wall. After the evening when they had finished this, Khan Khana (Intezam-ul-Daula) who was in prayer was garroted and killed brutally and his corpse was secretly carried away and thrown into the river. The King's corpse remained lying on the ground in ignominy. Whosoever saw it cursed the perpetrators of this brutal act. His descendants buried him with heavy hearts during the night and did not even mourn the dead from fear of reprisals from these cruel people.

Next day these brutes entered the fort and crowned a youth named Shah Jahan as the King and offered him tributes. The reign of Alamgir, the Second, lasted seven years. When these few brutal people got the time after killing the King and Intezam-ul-Daula, they departed along with the minister. Travelling in great hurry they joined the Maharatta army to become their partners in the war. Even a week had not passed when the news reached that Shahi army (of Abdali) had crossed Attock and had defeated Sahiba.

The Maharattas giving up their war with Najib-ul-Daula, rushed restlessly to stop the advance (of Abdali's) army. They landed near Panipat crossing river Jaun. During their march, the people on their way suffered a whole lot of atrocities at their hands. Then indulging in large scale destruction, they pitched their tents in Karnal which is a famous city where exists the shrine of Hazrat Shah Sharaf Ali qalandar. In the evening it was heard that the Shahi army (Abdali's) was gathering towards the river; these people also readied their army and under a chieftain about eight thousand soldiers, other supporting personnel and riders were sent. When they faced the army (Abdali's), in the first assault, most of them took to their heels. The well-built hard-hearted brave men harassed them (Marathas) and uprooted the boastful lot (Marathas). The blood thirsty army (of Afghans) attacked so fiercely that in no time there were heaps of dead bodies.

This side the Maratha army got defeated and their young men were shaken by fear. Had that group (of Abdali) attacked the army gathering (of Moghuls around Delhi), there would have been large scale carnage and none of us would be alive in the city (Delhi). These people (Marathas) returned crest fallen and Durrani saddled with his loot, crossed over the river. When the King pitched his tents in Doaba (between the two rivers) and Najib-ul-Daula joined him, the Deccanis (Maharattas) entrusted administration of the city and the army to the minister and they themselves came along the bank of river and pitched their tents at six Kos (about 15 kms). Here the minister organized the city devolving powers on his subordinates and entrusting Dara Shikoh's heveli (mansion), which is situated on the banks of the river, to the Raja, he himself joined the new King Shah Jahan, the Second.

After four days Shah Abdali's and Najib-ul-Daula's forces advanced towards the river. The feudal chiefs and riding warriors were bent on fighting the Marathas. The Rohilla infantry led the attack and commenced the battle. They fought desperately taking on a lot of casualties. On the other side,

Datta who was the chief of Deccan's army came to reinforce the Maratha fighting force and confronted that formidable army. In the very first volley, an arrow hit Datta piercing him from the side. His (Datta's) dead body was taken to the river bank. They (Abdali's army) attached from the river's side. The Maharattas ran away defeated. [40]

Looting in Delhi

In the evening the Raja came out of the city and proceeded towards Suraj Mal's fort and safely reached there. I remained in the city to protect

---

[40]   Mir's reference here is to the battle of Bararighat where Jamuna forked into two channels leaving a broad island opposite Barari. Sarkar describes this battle thus:

"Najib crossed the river unperceived . . . his own Rohilas leading and Durrani's support bringing up the rear . . . Sabaji immediately engaged the army, but was driven back by the pressure of numbers and the dominance of musketry fire over the sword and spear, across the Barari side, with heavy slaughter. He had waged this losing combat for an hour when reinforcements came up from the rear, three miles away under Dattaji himself to restore the battle . . . He was too good a target to miss by Ruhela sharpshooters lying concealed among the jhau bushes with loaded muskets. As his horse was ploughing its way up the loose sand on to the further bank of the nala, the Afghan Jizails rang out at point blank range and Dattaji fell down with a bullet through his eye. With him fell many of his brave companions. At this psychological moment, Najib charged with fresh troops into the mingled mass of Afghan infantry. Once again the tide of battle turned against the Deccanies, they fled away giving up their chieftain's body to crows and jackals; Sabaji's entire contingent was destroyed, though he escaped. As Dattaji lay on the ground, Mian Qutb Shah cut off his head and took it to Abdali.
The houses were burnt after taking away the possessions. In the morning the hell broke loose. The entire Durrani army and Rohillas fell on the city and started the massacre. The city's gates were broken. The people put in prison. Many were burnt to death or were beheaded. The carnage was perpetrated all round and this continued for three days and nights.

The Maratha army now totally broke and fled towards Delhi; the enemy gave chase and there was heavy slaughter. Imad left Delhi for Bharatpur on hearing of the ruin of his ally."

—Fall of Moghul Empire Vol-II pp 155-56

honour of womenfolk. After the evening there was a public announcement that Shah had given reprieve and the public should have no worry. But when the night advanced only an hour or so, then marauders recommenced their atrocities. The city was put to the torch. They did not leave anything to eat and anything to wear. The roofs were destroyed, walls demolished. The chest and innards of the people pierced. Those evil doers were on every roof and the gentry were being subjected to extreme humiliation. The select of the city were in a precarious state. The people in high positions were thirsting for a draught of

water. Those having houses became shelterless and Nawabs became beggars.[41] The prominent personalities and gentry were reduced to nudity. The householder became homeless. The most of people got afflicted, their women and sons held prisoners. The marauders were crowding the city and carnage was rampant. Many were holding on to life by their teeth. The marauders would stab, abuse and snatch money and say nasty things. Whomsoever they came across, even his pyjama was snatched from him. A world perished bearing their atrocities. The people's dignity was done in. The new city was destroyed and raised to the ground. The third day one Arza-ula-Khan was appointed to bring about order. He deprived people of even their caps or whatever little cloth was still left on the people's semi-naked bodies. After the officials appointed by the royal court to bring about order got the city cleared of these marauders and started enforcing security arrangements, these brutes fell on the old the officials appointed by the royal court to bring about order got the city cleared of these marauders and started enforcing security arrangements, these brutes fell on the old city where they murdered lots of people. The trouble went on seven to eight days. Not a day's food and clothing was left in anyone's house. Men had no headgear, women were without scarves. Since all paths were cut

---

[41]   A number of Mir's verses depict the tragedy of those days. He writes about rulers becoming paupers:

> Dilli mein aaj bheek bhi milti nahi unhain
> Tha kal talak dimag jinhein takhat-o-taj ka

> Empty goes their begging bowls for none gives
> them alms even
> Those who were proud wearers of the crowns on
> their thrones

off, people died of their wounds and some were frozen to death by severe cold. Brazenly they assaulted the citizens subjecting them to humiliation. Foodstuffs were seized forcibly and sold to the poor under threats. Those suffering peoples' cries for justice were reaching the seventh heaven but the King who considered himself to be a fakir was too self-absorbed to listen. Thousands of destitutes bearing wounds of this ranging fire leaving their homeland proceeded towards the jungle but were extinguished on the way like the morning lamp. Many helpless people were taken to the army camp compounds, tied to their spurs like prisoners. These brutes were ruling the roost. They were high handed. On the strength of their sword they looted, collected wealth and raped women. With swords in their hands, they appropriated to themselves material goods. The citizens were too demoralized to do anything. Some were too anxiety ridden, the others stunned. Their ill-will spread to every house and every street was a site for murder. Torture and arrests were common. There was bloodshed in all directions and the people were being punished everywhere. They were pinched and slapped. The poor people were terrified. These looters were on rampage. Houses were burnt, localities became barren. Hundreds left for they could not bear the beatings with sticks. No one was there to listen to their cries for justice. A whole lot was done to death by their brutally. Nobody dared to breathe a word (against it). The area of the old city, which was called "the world of freshness' because of its bustle and greenery; was like a picture of a fallen wall. In short, wherever you could see, you saw the heads, hands, feet and the chest of those killed. The houses of those tortured ones were burning reminding one of the fireplaces. Wherever the eye could see there was nothing to be seen except gloom. The oppressed one who died found rest in short, and the one who came within their reach had no escape. I who was already a fakir became poorer. Poverty and deprivation made my condition even worse. My house on the road was done to dust. In short, those brutal people carried away the city (its wealth) and many of the city's residents died after bearing insults and humiliation.

Marathas Arrive Again

They had hardly stopped this loot and murder when the news came that Maratha's defeated army which had run away had joined their other army concentration which was in Mewat and now they were up to no good. Hearing this Shah (Abdali) proceeded towards them from the city after disposing of Shah Jahan, the Second who was guilty of misrule of a few months and imprisoning him in Salimgarh fort and making Ali Gauhar's son Jawan Bakht, the heir apparent. Imad-ul-Malik leaving the company of Maratha chieftains sought refuge in Suraj Mal's forts. When Shah (Abdali) came near Mewat, Marathas saw that their attack not succeeding and their army getting demoralized, they resorted to, as per their tradition to guerrilla warfare and they came up to Delhi and crossed the river.

The Shah came in their pursuit and after spending the night in the suburbs of the city crossed over (the river) through a footpath. When the army pitched itself on the other side of the river, the chief of his army Jahan Khan moved forward and attacked the army of Malhar (Malhar Rao Holker), as has already been narrated, near Sikanderabad. In a couple of hours the Shah (Abdali) also joined him with three thousand soldiers. The chief Malhar could not withstand the attack and after appointing one of chiefs to officiate in his place, slipped away.

That Maharatta chief fought bravely and was killed while fighting. His army became helpless faced by brave soldiers of the royal (Abdali's) army and ran away in confusion. Shah (Abdali) went after them in pursuit up to Kaul which is a famous township. Those fugitives found refuge in Suraj Mal's forts and after two or three days proceeded ahead. The royal army surrounded one of these forts which was on their side of the river Jaun and harassed these people. Suraj Mal, finding it beyond his capacity to help these people, became indifferent. These helpless people finding an opportunity escaped during the night and after sending an ambassador entered into a peace treaty.

(An Event) Even when the army was between the two rivers, news spread that a large army of Marathas had arrived around Akbarabad (Agra) and that any time it would reach here. Najib-ul-Dauala brought chieftains of the east like Shujah-ul-Daula, Ahmed khan Bangish and Hafiz Rahmat Khan (Rohilla) into the service of the King and each of them was promised territory to rule and was given precious gifts and they were persuaded to fight the Maharattas.

In the meantime, Bhau (Sada Shiv Rao) the chief of all chiefs of the Marathas passed with his army through the territory of Suraj Mal and he inveigled the minister, Imad-ul-Malik and the Raja of the land (Suraj Mal) to join him and captured the city (Delhi). Yakub Ali Khan who was related to Shah Durrani's (Abdali's) minister Shad Ali Khan haughtily engaged the Marathas in the fort in the hope that that Shah Abdali's forces were present on the other side of the river and they would not hesitate to come to his aid. The Deccani army surrounded the fort and captured the artillery. The Royal houses which were unparalleled in their beauty were razed to the ground.

As it was difficult for Abdali to cross the river due to rainy season; the said Khan (Yakub Ali Khan) made peace with the Raja and abandoned the fort. Because of this agreement no one interfered with these events.[42]

My Departure from Delhi

In those days I went to the Raja and submitted to him that I was under a great strain because of the times. That I wished to leave the city and go wherever I could find some respite and that I might, possibly, have luck to see better days. He was considerate to me and he bid me farewell. I, along with my family, proceeded on foot with no specific destination in mind. With faith in God I went on travelling. In a day we could cover hardly eight to nine Kos (about 25 kms). The night was spent under a tree of an inn. The next morning the wife of Raja Jugal Kishore (who has already been written about) passed that way and helped us in our destitution. She took us to Barsana, which is a place of pilgrimage for Hindus and is a town situated at a distance of eight Kos (about 25 km) from the forts of Raja Suraj Mal. In various ways she reassured us.

Barsana

On the last day of Haj[43], she went to Kaman which is three Kos (about 8 kms) from this place (Barsana) and falls in the boundary of the state of Raja Jai Singh (the ruler of Jaipur). I along with my family stayed on there (Barsana) during the fasting days[44] after Haj. The day next to the last fasting

---

[42]   This quick capture of Delhi by Bhau was more than one way contributed to the horrendous tragedy that was to overtake Marathas later at Panipat.

"Sada Shiv Rao's (Bhau's) capture of Delhi forms a turning point in his career. Its immediate effect was to restore the prestige of Maratha arms which had been ruined by the fall of Dattaji and rout of Malhar early in this year. Abdali's partners were now dismayed and began to waver . . . This far resounding success secured with the loss of less than a score of men and after a week of exertion blinded the Bhau to the realities of the situation."
—Sir JN Sarkar's 'Fall of the Moghul Empire', Vol-II p 181

[43]   Holy pilgrimage of Muslims to Mecca

[44]   Ten days

day (11th Moharram) I left the place and reached Kumhair (11th August 1761).

Kumhair

Here one Bahadur Singh son of lala Radha Kishen who was formerly the cashier of Safdarjung and was then with the Raja came to our aid and treated us humanely. I am particularly grateful to him for I had no claim on him beyond being a mere acquaintance. Thus a few days were spent in ease and comfort.

(**A Story**) One day I was sitting worried over the lack of provisions for food, it occurred to me that if I met Azam Khan, (son of Azam Khan the elder who was Amir of six thousand category in the times of Heaven of eternal rest (Mohd Shah) and was an extremely kind person, he might help and a few days might be spent in comfort. Thus I went and met him in Suraj Mal's stable which had become a sanctuary for the ruined ones of Delhi. that dear man, may God be merciful to him, inquired about my well-being. I told him of my miserable plight. Those who listened were numbed. When Kahwa (cocoa) and Hucka (hubble-bubble) were brought this (verse) came spontaneously to my lips:

When Urfi and I came across each other
We looked at each other, wept and departed

I recited a few such verses and shed a few tears. After a few moments I saw Khan to be worried. I said, "What thoughts are you occupied with?" He replied, "Nothing." I said, "There must be something." He said, "When you used to come in the city (Delhi), we used to send for various kinds of sweets and different types of halwa (pudding) which we both used to partake. Now what a coincidence that even raw sugar is not available that I may make for you a cup of Sharbat (syrup)." I replied, "I am not unaware of all this. That used to happen then by way of entertaining treat. You are aware that I am not a greedy person. Times change. That was the time of Sharbat (syrup) and sweetness, now is the weather of bitterness to be borne."

While this was being talked about, a woman with a food container on her head entered and said, "Said-ul-Din Khan Saman's sister sends her compliments to you and some pudding delicacy and sweet candies. The Khan lifted the cloth covering the container and was overjoyed to see the pudding and said, "This sinner knows his worth. For long time he has been undergoing starvation. What to talk of pudding and sweet candies, never a piece of bread or sip of water came from anywhere. You are my dear guest. All this is yours. Give me my share and send the rest to your home." I said, "This is too much. What will I do with that much?" He said, "Your son Mair Faiz will use it." In short that good man insisted and sent the plate of pudding and the container of sweets to my house and joyfully bid me farewell. For two days we lived on those sweats. The third day Raja's younger son (Bishan Singh) sent for me and after inquiring about my state of affairs, he said, "Till the arrival of the Raja, you stay with me." I said, "The means of livelihood have vanished." He said, "Rest assured, you will get every thing here." The new rose in the garden of kindness, may God keep him prosperous and happy, joyfully kept on sending necessary provisions to me.

Battle of Panipat (An Event)

It was heard in the city (Delhi) that there was widespread rumour that the army chief of Sirhind Samad Khan along with some zamindar (landlords) and a large army was coming and intended to fight the royal army. The chief of Deccan's army Bhau was an arrogant young man and never thought anyone to be worth anything before him.[45] After leaving the necessary equipment he moved towards the opposing side in keeping with his sharp temperament. In his heart it was ingrained that Wazir (Minister) had a lot of jewels and Suraj Mal was a great landlord and, if given the opportunity in time he would cozen[46] something out of them. Raja Nagar Mal had come to know of it because of his meeting with (Bhau's) Chiefs.

---

[45]   Mir here is stating commonly held belief about Bhau but omits the fact of his too easy a conquest of Moghul capital. Sarkar in his 'Fall of the Moghul Empire' questions the common belief on the basis of Bhau daily correspondence. Contrary to common belief he holds that "it could not have been so before his capture of Delhi . . ."

[46]   Bhau was in a desperate state financially for the "Maratha acquisition of the Moghul capital was in truth a barren spectacular success. It actually aggravated Bhau's difficulties in two ways. His residence in the dry sterile north western suburbs of Delhi (Shalimar Gardens) for away from the fertile old base in the Jat country, caused the drought oxen of his guns and munition tumbrils to die of famine and sickness. The stoppage of food from the Daob by reason of Abadali's occupation of the track immediately east of Delhi and flood in Jamuna caused his soldiers and horses to starve. And the occupation of the

One day he (Bhau) sent a message to the Raja that he (Bhau) would leave the administration of the conquered territories to him. That dear person after careful consideration replied that that he had been with the Minister for a long time and it was not appropriate that (the Minister) should fail and that he (the Raja) ground his own axe. It would be appropriate that he be appointed an emissary to Bharatpur so that he and Suraj Mal could pursue the matter of abandoning him (the Minister) and act according to his (Bhau's) instructions. Thus he smoothed him by sweet talk and flattery. On the eve of departure of Deccan army, he and Suraj Mal left on that pretext their army (Marathas) boldy along with non-com[47]batant supporters and came to and settled down in the strong fort of Ballamgarh, which is 12 kos (nearly 25 km) from the city(Delhi).

They sent away the Minister along with his tents and provisions. The advocates of Deccan's army made every effort to cajole them (to join Bhau's fight against Abdali) but they paid no heed and joined the king. The chief of Deccan's army was really a gutsy person and before his large army and huge equipment and armaments, he thought poorly of others (opposing him). When he heard this he became furious and said, "What are they? Their government's lamp needs only a single blow of breath to be extinguished. I have not come from Deccan depending on them. I will crush them with a snap of my fingers." He postponed the revenge for some other time and went and captured Nijabat Khan Rohilla's Fort and in time killed Samad Khan and dispersed his gathering. With the dispersal of this army, the Marathas were encouraged. Turning from there, they entrenched themselves near Panipat and became ready to fight an open war with the king's army. When the water of Jaun receded, Shah Abdali along with the eastern chief crossed the river with great enthusiasm and launched an attack on them. A few days before the regular war broke out, news reached that Govind Pandit was coming with a large army, intending to join the Maratha army. One of the chief's (of Abdali army) went quietly and surrounded and killed him; looted the provisions and his (Govind Pandit's) army was dispersed. In those days Raja (Nagar Mal) came to Kumhair which is Suraj Mal's fort. As luck would have it, I was then there. I presented myself to him and submitted, "I was waiting for your arrival. Give me permission to leave for I have no

imperial capital brought him no gain but actually increased his expenses by one lakh a month . . ."

—'Fall of the Moghul Empire' Vol-II, pp 183

47   He means Ballabhgarh

strength left to face adverse condition." The Raja, who was kind to me in the condition I was in, said, "It seems you were intent to perish in the desert but that will only if I let you go." He sent on that day something (cash) for my expenses and favoured me by sanctioning me scholarship with an antedated signature. That respected elder (The Raja) was settled here for now because Shah Jahanabad was no more than a desolate ruin and the people were uprooted twice a year. After all how long could one remain a nomad? In a way this place was a safe corner, the ruling class here was rich and not haughty. Under the shadows of these walls we made our haven and remained there.

(An Event) Now listen to the realities of two armies. Had the Marathas fought according to their traditional style of guerilla warfare, in all probability, they would have won.[48] But they settled for artillery concentration and Abdali's army ensured that their provisions did not reach them. When food supplies did not reach them, their worries increased precipitating the Martha chief to fight it out, and his fellow chiefs leaving

---

[48]   This is only a part of the story. Apart from this, historians attribute their defeat to Bhau's arrogance which alienated not only his potential allies but also his own generals. A foreign visitor as also gazetteers of those times, have recorded other causes of Abdali's victory. French Captain Jean Law who visited Delhi in 1758 gives convincingly the cause of Durrani's victory in his 'Memoire' thus:

"Nothing like it (viz., disorderly conditions of Indian troops) is to be seen in the army of Abdali; everything there is real, the men as well as the horses and the arms. His army is divided into squadrons of a thousand horsemen. Each squadron is distinguished by a cap of a different colour and under the command of a chief who invariably make his report to Abdali himself twice a day . . . The review of the troops is made rigorously all the month and—what merits attention—they are punished at least as often as they are rewarded.". "Each time this prince enters a campaign he keeps apart 12 or 15 of these squadrons. It is his reserve corps, destined for decisive strokes and of which the Marathas have felt the weight so often."
According to Sheikh Ghulam Hassan Samin (Indian Antiquary—Translated by W. Irvine), Abdali said that elephants were admirable means of baggage transport; but a mount the control of which is not in the hands of the rider and which can carry him wither it wills, should not be resorted to. While a litter (palki) is only suitable for a sick man.

their fortifications and dug in positions, came out for battle.[49] The fighters of Abdali army strove hard to harass them. His brave soliders retreated, regrouped and launched an organized attack and these brave ones unitedly sending showers of arrows. The trained ones manned the guns and took up positions to fight. The opposing forces (The Maratha) attacked with swords. It was a bloody battle between two warriors determined to fight to the finish. Front line started infantry fighting and sacrificed themselves to the battle. Young men got badly wounded and many were killed. Brave soldiers on both sides fought fiercely attacking. The chief of the Deccan's Army came to the battle field boldly and drove away many battalions of of the royal army. But victory was destined for Shah Abdali. Nothing came out of these efforts (of the army of Deccani chief's fight). They attacked with gunfire but there was no effect on the opposing side, many of their valuable soldiers were injured in the firing of the ordinary soldiers of the Shah's (Abdali) army. In short in the very first shower of arrows itself, Vishwas Rao who was heir apparent to the Martha kingdom was hit and fell to the ground (died). It is said that Bhau was a very proud man and fighting very bravely. When he saw this (Vishwas Rao falling to the ground in the first shower of arrows) happen he said that now he had[50] no face to return to Deccan. With do-or-die spirit he attacked the Abdali's army. In other words he deliberately pushed

---

[49]   The Panjab had been firmly under control of Abdali. He cut off Maratha army supply line even from the east and the south, the east being held by Rohillas of Najib-ul-Daula, a staunch ally of Abdali and the south by virtue of Abdali crossing over Jamuna at Baghpat and arriving at Sonepat even before Bhau had reached Panipat. The blocking of supplies led to a situation, "There was no food and no firewood for men and no grass for horses. The stench of carcasses of men and beasts lying uncremated and unburied, and the effluvia of the evacuation of four lakhs of living creatures made the confines of entrenchment a living hell for human beings." Starving Maratha army decided on fighting one desperate battle. "Finally on the 13th January 1761, the life became utterly intolerable to beleaguered Maratha army." The soldiers and officers told Bhau, "Do not let us perish in this misery. Let us make a valiant struggle against the enemy, then what Fate has ordained will happen." "The discussion went on till midnight, when it was resolved that whole army should march out an hour before day break and attack the enemy in a pitched battle."
           —'Fall of the Moghul Empire' Vol-II, pp 228-229

[50]   In the ensuring battle, Vishwas Rao, aged 17, who was the heir apparent to Maratha Kingdom got killed. After that Bhau could not show his face at Puna after having lost the precious charge entrusted to him. He fought on fiercely to

himself to death's door. Malhar Rao, a wily fox, ran away with two to three thousand riders while they rest of the army was annihilated. Those chiefs who remained alive were roaming in semi-nude conditions. Arms and horses of thousands were snatched by tenfold group of landlords around the city (Panipat). Thousands of naked soldiers, whatever they went weeping were a lesson to the people. Villagers distributed among them a fistful of grams each and thanked god when they compared their own condition with the miserable state these (soldiers) were in.[51] Such an exemplary end (defeat) had rarely been witnessed. Many died of starvation, many frozen to death by cold. The army they had left in the fort (Delhi) ran away from fear of loot and carnage. Materials worth crores of rupees fell in the hand of Abdali and eastern chiefs which they distributed among themselves with joy. Then justly apart from cash and goods artillery and other armaments, elephants, horses, camels were appropriated by Sujah-ul-daula. Durranies (soldiers)

---

the last moment. "Death had lost all its bitterness because life had no longer any meaning for him."

—'Fall of the Moghul Empire' Vol-II, p 246

[51] Suffering of the Maratha Fugitives".

"For the fugitives from Panipat, the open road to Deccan lay through west and south-west of Delhi, i.e., Hariana country or the modern districts of Hissar and Rohtak. Here the Marathas reaped as they had sown in the past. Almost every year since 1754 they had crossed and recrossed the tract pillaging or blackmailing the peasants and landlords alike with insane greed. Payment of the fixed revenue or tribute to one Maratha officer had not saved the village headman from exacting by another. The tenants of the local chief who had joined the Maratha banners had been robbed by Deccani troops and appeals for redress even to their highest general had only produced the comfortless reply."They are soldiers, they always do it."—(Malhar's speech to Imad-ul-Mulk, 31st May 1754).

It was only when the fugitives now at their last gasp from 200 miles of flight without food or rest through hostile population reached the Jat Kingdom that they found a haven of refuge. Suraj Mal received them with every mark of kindness and hospitality . . . Thus fifty thousand men and women, the sole survivors of Bhau's camp at Panipat were saved . . . Not a single man among them could have returned to Deccan if Suraj Mal had wished otherwise, as father Xavier Wendal justly claims (Fugitive Molested—Nur-ud-Din).

—'Fall of the Moghul Empire' Vol-II, pp 253-255

who were mere paupers became rich, every village unit (of tribe men) got a hundred camelload of goods and every one of their servants two donkeyload full. Much wealth fell into their hands; everyone was beside himself with joy. Shah Abdali after such a glorious victory as no past king has ever had, entered the city (Delhi) in great splendor and sent messages to chiefs around to come and join his service.

Nagar Mal—Deputy Ministership

Raja (Nagar Mal) got a written message that Shah (Abdali) had become the King of India and now he would not return leaving this fertile land. As he (Raja) had in any case to seek employment (in the royal court), he went. Najib-ul-Daula took him along and he (Raja) obtained his employment with the Shah through his minister Shad Ali Khan. This meeting was pleasant. The Shah bestowed his Stamp of Authority and made him Deputy Minister. Thereby he became mainstay of the well-being of prominent nobles.

Explanation from Shujah-ul-Daula and My Journey

The Minister (Shad Ali Khan) one day said (to the Raja) that Shujah-ul-Daula's father had a good deal of goodwill for him (the Raja) and he (Shujah) was still a child and knew nothing apart from being arrogant and pretentious. He did not realize that Abdali was the king and on even a slight impertinence, he would raze the world to ground. One should be careful. This type of boasting irritated him. Out of friendship he (Abdali) was overlooking but he (Shujah) should not forget himself:

Kings and the Virtuous (Dervaishes) are of
strange genre
For they submitted to none nor they will

It would be better if he (the Raja) and Najib-ul-Daula went and made him realize his position otherwise if something untoward happens, he (Shad Ali Khan) would not be responsible for it. Thus both of them went and brought him after persuading him to apologise and obtain the minister's permission (to meet him). Luckily this meeting turned out to be pleasant and ill feelings were removed. In this journey I was with him (Raja Nagar Mal).

Delhi Looted Again

(**Narration**) One day I went for a walk and went through newly devastated areas. I wept at every step and I learnt a bitter lesson. As I went along my surprise increased. I could not recognize the houses, none of them left intact and no building had any trace, nor was there any trace of residents:

About whosoever I inquired
I got the same reply
He wasn't there
About whosoever's address I inquired
The people had the same reply
That they had no idea

House after house had been destroyed. Walls had been broken. Holy shrines were without Sufis, taverns sans drinkers. From here to there was one bleak and barren wasteland:

When I saw a brick lying in some ruin
It looked like a page from a householder's
Story

There no longer were bazars which I could describe. Nor were there bazar's handsome youth. There no longer was the beauty which I used to worship. Where had the loving friends gone? The handsome youngmen had vanished. Gone were the puritanical elders. Big and grand palaces were devastated. Streets had disappeared. Everywhere chaos was prevailing. Love was still born. I remembered a Rubayi of a master:

I passed through the ruins
Of the city of Toos
I saw an owl
Perched in the place of a bird
I asked him to relate
the condition of that ruin
He said that I know only this
Alas, Alas

Suddenly I found myself arriving in the street in which I used to live, organize meetings, recite verses, live life of love, weep at nights, love the lovables, praise their beauty, live with the beloved of long tresses and worship the beautiful women. If I was separated from them, I became restless. I used to organize mehfils (gathering) to which I invited the beautiful ones whom I entertained. I used to live colourful life. Now no known face appeared with whom I could exchange a couple of words to cheer my heart. Nor did I meet any worthwhile person in whose company I could sit. Then leaving the crazy place I stood back in a corner and looked on the signs of destruction. I was anguished and vowed that I would not come there again and so long I remained around, I would not come in the direction of the city.[52]

Abdali's Going Back

When it was decided that Shad Ali Khan along with the Raja would go to annex more areas, Abdali's army which had struck rich with the booty started agitating gathering en bloc at the fort gate. They demanded to go back to their homes and that it was up to Abdali to stay back if he so wished. They said that they had been away from home for long and they had no news of the welfare of their families. The Shah (Abdali) thought that in the alien land it would be impossible to stay without his army.[53]

---

[52] His poetry too contains reference to those times. To quote a few examples

Dilli mein ab keaa kay yaaron ko na dekha
Kutch woh gai shatabi kutch ham badair aaye

This time around we did not see our friends
For some departed soon or maybe we came late

Manzil na kar jahan ko ki ham ne safar
se aa
Jis ka kiya surag suna woh guzar gaye

Make not the world your destination for
returning from travel

[53] Although Maratha's rout at Panipat was complete, Abdali's victory as Dr HR Gupta observes in his 'The History of Sikhs' turned out to be a pyrrhic one for it destroyed both the victor and the vanquished. No wonder there was near rebellion by his war weary soldiers who wanted to go back to their homes in

Tu hai bechara gada Mir tera kya mazkoor
Mil gaye khak mein yaan Sahib Afsar kitne

You hapless beggar Mir what to talk of you
How many sahibs, officers were done to dust here

Dilli mein aaj bhik bhi milti nahin unhain
Tha kal talak damage jinhein takt-o-taj ka
They do not get even alms in Delhi today
Those who heads, till yesterday, were held
high with their crowns and throne

He was constrained to decide to go back to his capital Kandhar. The minister who had sent his tents ahead (for annexing campaign) had tocall them back and he had to bear the shame of feeling small before the chieftain (for deserting them.) Two days before his departure he bid farewell to Raja Nagar Mal and Shujah-ul-Daula and appointed Prince Jawan Bakht as vice-regent of Shah Alam and entrusted the administration of the city to Najib-ul-Daula and departed. On the way he made an Afghan tribes man, named Rais Khan, (a tribes man) the governor of Sirhind and he himself reached Lahore.

As his tribe's arrogance had crossed all limits, God's ire fell on them through the Sikhs at whose hands they met with humiliation. The Sikhs were gatherings (in and around areas of the Panjab) of non-descript people, homeless nomads, weavers, cotton ginners, cloth merchants, middlemen (agents), Banias (retailers of groceries), carpenters, dacoits, peasants, the poor people, the barbarian, the bushmen, merchants, menials and the deprived[54].

Afghanistan. On their way back home they were badly mauled by Sikh Missals (bands). With the battle of Panipat began the swift end to Abdali's long rule in the north. Sikhs promptly seized Sirhind and then pursuing Afghan army captured Lahore.

[54]   The description of Sikhs is more of a poetic exaggeration than accurate, giving an erroneous impression of Sikhs as a motly crowd including decoits, menials, barbarians and non-descript people.Overwhelming recorded historical evidence supports the common knowledge that the sect was mostly recruited from sturdy Jat peasantry with a large addition in the form of converts from other castes. They carried to perfection the work which Suraj Mal Jat had

About forty to fifty thousand Sikhs gathered to fight this huge army. They made Abdali's soldiers panic to such an extent that they were forced to resort to thousand-fold methods to escape and thus save their lives. Sometimes, they (Sikhs) would appear openly, attack the army and fight pitched battles. At times they would invade the city (Sirhind) and played havoc with it. They would come with their flowing hairs or hairs tied at the top, attack the army and throughout the night there would be much hue and cry. During the day voices of wailing for mercy and mourning were heard. Their foot soldiers (Sikhs) would attack riders with swords and drench the saddles with blood. So much so that even their menials would capture archers (of Abdali) and torture them.

In short these non—descript paupers humiliated these hapless demoralized lot to such an extent that when the chief around heard of it they looked down with contempt on them (Afghan army). They had no strength to match (attackers) and found it expedient to run away to save their lives. They (Afghans) handed over the administration of Sirhind to a Hindu and were on their way. This gathering of Sikh army pursued them, looted them and went thumpingly up to river Attock to punish them. Then they captured that province (Sirhind) which had annual revenue of two

---

begun on the same ethnic basis but which had been undone by his worthless descendants. The Sikhs owed their success to their religion of full brotherhood and the democratic organization of their society, while the Jats of Bharatpur were caste-ridden Hindus living under oligarchy of the heads of family groups. The strength of the Sikh army before it was Europeanized by Ranjit Singh lay in its predominance of cavalry and preference for offensive tactics, while the Jat soldiery was mostly infantry excelling in defence of fortified positions. Sometimes they would come face-to-face and even when injured would not retreat. At times they would split,spread, encircle and carry away one to two hundred of Abdali's soldiers and put them to the sword. They would vanish in the morning but every evening they would fiercely attack from all four sides.

The Panjab is a vast breeding ground of the best horses found in India and blood of their Scythian ancestors made the Sikh horsemen the best skirmishers and guerrilla fighters after the Turks. A Swiss officer wrote after observing them in May 1776, 'Five hundred of Najaf Khan's horse riders dare not encounter fifty Sikh horsemen'.

—'Fall of the Moghul Empire' Vol-III, pp 101-102
(based on Sikhs—Asiatic Annual Register; Misc Tracts—G Forester;
Calcutta Review Vol 60 1875 Shah Alam by Franklin)

crores. After some days they killed the ill-fated Hindu who was then living in Lahore and they became lords and rulers. At that time as no claimant of the country was there to stop them, they crudely divided the areas among themselves and started distributing largesse among the public. Whatever fistful peasants gave them, they accepted considering it to be free. When the news reached Abdali, he came with his ministers. "The Durani force in two divisions, one under the Shah (Abdali) and the other led by his Wazir (Zain Khan) moved around two flanks of Sikhs, slaying all they met with.

Rebellion of Suraj Mal

This year Suraj Mal who was a very power zamindar (landlord) and whose ancestors had been receiving favours of great Moghul kings, rebelled and captured many areas. He was aware that in this running fight some ten thousands Sikhs were slain and the day is still remembered by them as that of Ghallughara or great scrimmage[55].

---

[55]   *Ten thousand Sikhs were slain and the day is still remembered by them as that of ghallughara or great scrimmage*. Abdali committed another outrage by razing to the ground the Sikh temple called Harmandir built by Guru Arjun Dev at Amritsar and desecrated the 'pool of immortality' by killing cows on its bank and throwing their bones and debris of the temple into the water."

. . .

"And now Afghan sacrilege roused the Sikh to their highest exertion and united them in the closest bond by unquenchable thirst of a vengeance that was a sacred duty. The noblest and the basest passion of human breast were united in a national resistence to the alien beyond the Indus and his local associates. Durani's rule in the Panjab became impossible in future."

. . .

"With the departure of Abdali in December 1762, Sikh aggression revived and aggravated by the misrule of his lieutenants who, like all Afghans, had no administrative capacity or honesty, and administration broke down on the rock of finance."

. . .

The city of Lahore was captured in April, 1764 by three Sikh leaders Lehna Singh, Gujjar Singh and Sobha Singh, the three chiefs dividing "the city between themselves and each ruled over and administered his portion as its master. Thus peace at last returned to Lahore but not prosperity. The city continued in desolation and misery till its revival under Ranjit Singh."

. . .

Abdali committed another outrage by razing to the ground the Sikh temple called Harmandir built by Guru Arjun Dev at Amritsar and desecrated the 'pool of immunity' by killing cows on its bank and throwing their bones and debris of the temple into the water.

My going to Agra

On that occasion I went to Akbarabad (Agra) after thirty years and paid visits to the shrines of my father and uncle. Most of the poets came to meet me considering me the high priest of the art (poetry).

Sahib turned out to be a Sunny[56]

(Narration) I heard a world of praise for him and met him but he turned out to be empty headed. In short he did not understand the substance of the talk. I had hardly taken a breath when he started his foolish talk that most the young men of these days were Rafzai[57] and they talk rubbish to slander their elders. My rosary from the land of Imam (chief priest) which clouded the meditation of puritans like him was evidence that I too was inclined toward Rifoz. If that was so I should leave him alone. I replied, "I myself was doubtful (whether you were a Rafzai or not) but thank god that Sahib (you) turned out to be Sunny." The idiot did not understand the hint and

---

"The whole country from Jhelam to Satluj, was partitioned among Sikh chiefs and their followers, as the plains of Sirhind had been in the year previous. Ahmed Shah's atrocity on their holy city was avenged in his own manner. Numerous mosques were demolished and Afghans in chains were made to wash the foundations with the blood of hogs."

. . .

The above account is based on Misc. Tracts of G Forster who adds, reservoir of Amritsar which in preceding year they had filled up . . . Though the Afghan massacre and persecution must have been deeply imprinted on their minds, the Sikhs did not, it is said, destroy any prisoner in cold blood."

—'Fall of the Moghul Empire' Vol-II, pp 348-353

[56]   Sunny and Shias are two main branches of Islam. While the former hold all the four Khalifs to be rightful descendants of the prophets, the latter only considers Ali prophet's son-in-law to be the only rightful descendant.

[57]   A group of people who deserted Ali, the prophet's son-in-law, meaning the people of little faith

was pleased. When he found it in tune with him, he started uttering more absurdities. I came away disgusted.

Oh! My Country (July to October 1762)

(Narration) I used to go for a walk and a view to the river's bank in the morning and evening. Its situation has very good surroundings. In short these were gardens on one side and fort and mansions of the rich nobility on the other as if a stream ran through heaven. I was known in the place for meaningful dialogue. Handsome innocents of black lashes as also well-groomed and well-dressed gentry, puritans and poets would not leave me alone and they held me in regard. Twice or thrice I went round the city and met scholars, fakirs and poets of the place but did not come across anyone of intelligence, meeting whom this restless heart could find some repose. I wondered whether it was the same city which had men of perception, men of perfection, writers, wise men, religious scholars, conversationalist, physicians, Sufis, scholars of Hadis (Islamic scripture), teachers, dervaishes, advocates, sheikhs, mullahs (priests), extempore reciters of Koran, high priests, caller's to prayer, and which had schools, monasteries, abodes of dervaishes, guest houses, houses and gardens. There was no place where I could sit and amuse myself. There was not even a man with whom I could exchange for sometime a little small talk. There was only a frightening ruin seeing which I felt very sad and came back. Thus I spent four months in the beloved land. I had tears in my eyes. I departed and came to Suraj Mal's forts.

Removal of Mir Qasim (August 1763)

(An Event) Coming here I heard that a war had broken out between Mir Qasim, the ruler of Bengal and Christian traders (in other words East India Company) who had settled there sometime back. There in Bengal, the people and landlords were tired of his (Mir Qasim's) untold oppression. They, therefore, did not side with him. Ultimately defeated he came to Azeemabad. (Patna) which fell within his domain, along with his vanquished army, money and jewels and limitless movable property. The English men came there in pursuit. He wanted the city to be sealed and to fight again. But his army turned their back and he was defeated again carrying along his arms and provisions he entered the border of Shujah-ul-Daula's domain along with nine thousand of his soldiers. The English gave up the war for the present and did not initiate anything further. When he reached the vicinity of Benares, after pitching his tents there, he wrote to Shujah-ul-Daula, "I have come depending on your help. If you help me and come to fight the Christians who are opposed to our religion, the expenses of your army will be borne by my officials." He (Shujah) replied, "In the first place, you come here and obtain the King's employment. In the presence of the king, whatever is decided will be accordingly acted upon." That ill-fated man, unaware of the conspiracy, on the basis of assurances of some greedy go-betweens crossed the river Ganga below the said city (Benares) and entered the army camp with provisions, arms and five hundred elephants and encircled it. But when the avaricious people of the other side saw his fabulous wealth, the intentions were shaken and sending some old bandicoots they treacherously imprisoned him. After two, three days at the instance of some shortsighted people, the minister snatched away all the wealth in cash, jewels, provisions, horses, elephants, bulls, camels, tents, floors and he was left with nothing. Those perfidious ones, who had acted as brokers, did not care for the treaty entered into and went back on their word. That helpless man had come in the hope that someone would help him but coming here he became even more distrustful. When seeking refuge he knocked at the Minister's door, the Begum, the mother of Shujah-ul-Daula got him awarded some amount as his daily pension from the government.

I leave this story here for now I have another tale to tell.

Skirmish of Suraj Mal (December 1763)

(An event) Suraj Mal was a brave Sardar (Chief). His elder son, Jawahar Singh had the idea of ruling the state in his mind. Therefore, he had earlier shed blood of many in a fight against his father and he had himself sustained a couple of serious wounds. In those days he went to Farrukhnagar which is a city of three days journey west of Shahjahanabad and which had a common boundary with his father's domain. He attacked the landlord (of Farrukhnagar) whose father was posted as Munssif of criminal court in areas around Delhi. The stalemate was prolonged; the landlord was not prepared to compromise and he fought with all he had. When two months had passed like this Suraj Mal proceeded in that direction with a large army and came to Raja Nagar Mal for saying goodbye. He (Nagar Mal) advised him not to go lest he became a cause for starting bigger strife for Najib-ul-Daula was nearby. If Najib-ul-Daula made a common cause of Islam, war might break out. And then there was one more thing, the other side had a fort, an army, and if he gave a pitched battle and war became prolonged his (Suraj Mal's) prestige as a great chief would suffer. In the book of statecraft it had been written that if your servant could deliver the goods, the chief should not ask his son to go and if son could deliver, he himself should not go. But irony of fate is that when death is hovering around, one does not listen to wise words. He (Suraj Mal) listened to this advice (of Raja Nagar Mal) with one ear and let it go through another. In short he went and arrested the ruler of that state (Farrukhnagar). His army started committing atrocities and looted houses of the gentry. The brothers of the ruler of Farrukhnagar who were with Najib-ul-Daula raised a hue and cry and expressed their helplessness to Najib-ul-Daula[58]. He, on their behalf requested Suraj Mal to forgive them for these people had been punished enough. But he did pay any heed and he fearlessly advanced towards Shahjahanabad (Delhi). Najib-ul-Daula showing indifference to fight; got the gates of the city closed and remained immured inside. The arrogant one (Suraj Mal) crossed the river with a flourish and conflict with him (Najib-ul-Daula) became the cause of a great chaos[59]. His (Najib-ul-Daula) humaneness was in no doubt. He sent repeated messages to the effect that he had no intention of fighting him (Suraj Mal). This was why he was not taking out his army. The poor people of the city were needlessly being subjected to hardship and his siege here was inappropriate. He (Suraj Mal) did not send even a single reply with any humanity but sent an impetuous message, "I will go back only after settling with Nawab's

---

[58] This was no doubt the cause of strife and final battle between Suraj Mal and Najib-ul-Daula but Mir has completely omitted any mention of the real reason of Suraj Mal inexorably punishing Farrukhnagar at the risk of alienating the powerful Najib-ul-Daula with whom he had hitherto friendly relations.

The real cause of the rift between Suraj Mal and Najib was the former's attempt to enforce law and order in the immemorial robber's den known as Mewat and guard the roads leading out of their kingdom, brought about an open war between Suraj Mal and Najib, the patron of the harbourers of these robbers." Suraj Mal had captured Farrukhnagar which was a Baluch fiefdom of Masavi Khan who was arrested and confined in Bharatpur fort. Najib demanded the release of the said Khan and his family. However, Najib tried to avert war with Suraj Mal but was provoked by the latter into it. During Suraj Mal's siege of Farrukhnagar, Najib marched from Najibad to Delhi which the former took as a hostile act.

—'Fall of the Moghul Empire' Vol-II, pp 321-322

[59] In his own army

army. If they could come out of city early, I will be grateful for I have other chores to attend to. Otherwise my army would go out of my control. Every morning and evening it wants to launch an attack on the city. That chief (Najib-ul-Daula) said, "Ok, we will definitely come out tomorrow morning and you and show you the mettle of our army."

(Copy) One person who was performing the duty of an emissary between the two told me that at midnight he (Najib-ul-Daula) ordered his army to cross the river and he himself laid down. After sometime he awoke and said that he saw a strange happening in his dream. The people inquired what it was. He said, "On a tree, one big crow was perched and around him many crows were gathered and were cawing. I passed that way and brought down the crow with one arrow. All the remaining crows seeing the death of that crow flew away simultaneously. In all probability I will be victorious. God willing I will ride in the morning and will dispose of that blackguard."

When the morning arrived, the heavens drew the sword of the event. The bugle of war was sounded and Najib-ul-Daula riding an elephant crossed the river and resolutely took up positions to fight. The enemy advanced with his army arrogantly and demonstratively. Musketeers got busy in firing their muskets and veterans started assessing strategies. The chief (Najib-ul-Daula) was already burning with anger and was fighting with his usual courage. The other side's chief (Suraj Mal) also pitched himself for a determined battle and did not hesitate in waging a war of attrition.

When Rohillas started dual sword attack, Suraj Mal hid himself within the folds of his army and not knowing that cruel death was in wait for him, he bypassing them (Rohillas) attacked the army which was close to the city. There was a great hue and cry. From the heart of Najib-ul-Daula's army, a few columns of standing rushed to their help and stemmed this onslaught. In that storm, he (Suraj Mal) was the one destined to die, was fatally injured, fell from the horse to his death. But no one then knew he was Suraj Mal. The people were talking among themselves that when his horse would appear, it would in its rein bring doom. They knew not that in his frontal attack he himself had become a morsel for death. Since that time and up to the evening there was no fighting. There he was dead and here Najib-ul-Daula's soldiers were fearing that the night was approaching and that it might happen that he (Suraj Mal) would ambush them at night and murder them.

After the evening the Jat army had dispersed and had gone away. On this side they remained prepared for battle on their horses and elephants till midnight. But all of them were apprehensive of the weird silence for there was no sound from the other side. The fear was lest the enemy attacked taking them by surprise and created havoc for them. The spies of the army scanned the area around two to three Kos but found not even a fledging of a sparrow. At the night's end the spies came with the news that they heard from the villagers that a group passing in disarray was saying, "Alas, the chief like Suraj Mal got killed and we, the ungrateful lot ran away thus fearing for our lives leaving his corpse in the field of battle." This showed that in the fight of the evening with the defending army's frontlines, he was killed and his army fled.

These things were being talked about when the morning dawned and one rider brought a severed hand and this was the dried hand of his (Suraj Mal) which had a nasoor (running abscess). The other people also recognized it and joyful celebrations started. When it got confirmed, the pursuit of fleeing army started and they went after them. Had these Rohillas crossed the river they would have caused a whole lot of destruction. But Raja Nagar Mal wrote to the Nawab that this bounty of such a glorious victory had been gained at no cost, it would be appropriate now to treat it as a blessing and go back and that there was a large gathering here and if Jats fought with courage, there would be a difficult situation. Najib-ul-Daula had a matured head and good heart[60]. He saw Raja's (Nagar Mal's) letter and went back. Jawahar Singh when he heard this news was shell shocked. But he was externally keeping his cool. Settling down on the throne he started thinking

---

[60] About Najib's life and character, Sarkar writes: "A poor illiterate Afghan of the Umer-Khel clan, sprung from the humblest home and without a friend or patron in India when he migrated to this country as a grown up man with a son, sought his bread by entering Ali Mohd Ruhila's service in the humble capacity of a foot soldier. Najib Khan rose by sheer ability and strength of character to the highest position in the realm and guided the fortunes of the empire of Delhi as its supreme regent for a full decade. In the combination of first rate military and administrative capacity, diplomatic skill and tact in dealing with others and above all in his instinctive perception of the realities of politics of his day and on the concentration on the essentials, he had no equal in that age except Ahmed Shah Abdali. His defence of Delhi against the Jat-Maratha-Sikh army of Jawahar Singh, his running fight in grim pursuit of Sikh invaders and his storming of the mud fort of Buana with mere dismounted cavalry and no guns illustrate his consummate generalship in three different types of warfare."

—'Fall of the Moghul Empire' Vol-II, pp 298-99

of amassing a new army. In courage, in bravery and in goodwill, he was hundredfold better than his father. God, give not wealth in the wrong hands.

The Reality of Kings Army and the Minister

(An event) It so happened that Shujah-ul-Daula misled by some inexperienced and incompetent people who were close to him, thought out of greed that if the province of Azeemabad (Patna) came into their hands with a little bit of effort, it would be as good as free. Taking Shah Alam (the King) with him, he marched with the army that wards. The Christian's leader (Regent or the Chief of the English), after reinforcing the arrangements for the defence of the city wrote to them that they had finished the one with whom they had an enmity and banished him from this land[61]. Now they had nothing to do with the Nawab (Shujah-ul-Daula) and the King (Shah Alam).

They knew not what the provocation for this move (movement of troops). If the idea was to force them into submission to their authority, there was no need to go into the futile trouble for they were already subordinate and subservient to their authority. If the intention was to uproot them at the instigation of ignorant nouveau riche, they could hardly do anything about it. The people in high places had temperament of a roaring flood whose course followed its own vagaries and that they were mere dust and grass in its way. What resources had they to withstand it? The ruling chief's temperament was comparable to a storm. They were a mere fistful of dust. What wherewithal had they to stop its course?

But the king's ignorant people who were sans wisdom and discernment interpreted this writing as a sign of cowardice and impotence of the British and insisted on their advice to advancement. When around Azeemabad the opposing forces clashed, the English took a firm stand with their guns and some ungrateful wretches started looting the treasure of their Moghul master. The English advanced with great courage. One of Nawab's protégé named Isaha Khan was killed fighting bravely. The King looked on as a mere spectator. The result was defeat. The Nawab who was fighting in the outskirts of the city saw no point in holding on and with a few remaining companions proceeded towards his own province. Performing such a long journey in a day and a half, he came to his own abode. From there he

---

[61]   Reference here is to Nawa Qasim Ali Khan

proceeded to Farrukhabad along with his womenfolk after taking necessary cash and material.

What a Befitting Tit for Tat

Even though the world is not place for instant reward or punishment, sometimes it is a coincidence that one meets with immediate nemesis. The disgraceful defeat of this large army was the retribution for the betrayal by them of Qasim Ali Khan.

Pension of Shah Alam

There the Englishmen capturing tents and armament of war took the King along with them and proceeded confidently ahead. After seven eight days they reached Avadh (Faizabad) which is Shujah-ul-Daula's place. In gratitude for victory which was beyong all their imagination, they harmed no one. After a week they sent the King to Allahabad after awarding him a monthly pension of rupees two lakh so that he should confine himself to that place. Now it was for them to decide the dispensation of the country.

(An Event) In the meantime, to avenge the killing of his father, Jawahar Singh invaded Nijib-ul-Daula with a large army with the help of Malhar Rao, the matter which has already been narrated earlier, and laid siege to Delhi. The people were tired of the expensiveness of food articles. The battle and killings continued for nearly two months. Imad-ul-Malik who was thinking of evading this war, came out of the Bharatpur fort with his near ones (women and children) and sending the unwanted people to Farrukhabad, joined hands with Jawahar Singh.

Imad-ul-Malik

Nawab Imad-ul-Malik is a man of parts of these times. He is man of great merits. Thus he writes five to six letters (in calligraphy) in his pleasing hand. He writes enjoyable verse in Urdu and Persian and is very kind to fakir (Mir) in his present condition. Whenever I presented myself to him I was always rewarded one way of the other.

Shujah-ul-Daula Seeks British Help

(An Event) The condition in which Shujah-ul-Daula was placed was that the people on whose help he depended for his stay in Farrukhabad were found to be indifferent and lacking in goodwill. He was constrained to make friends with Malhar, about whom has been written earlier, and gathering an army, took them to fight the British. When the opposing forces met, there were heavy showers of cannonballs from both the sides. The bands of Deccan army to show their bravery took on the artillery at its mouth with spears. The Christian army quietly evaded the encirclement and attacked with cannon fire so fiercely that Deccanis were uprooted and their boast was brought to naught. In panic they ran away vanishing into thin air. In two three days they reached Gwalior which is at a distance of three days' journey from Agra and where the Maratha ruler lived and this area was in their domain. In a few days they rectified their dispersed state of affairs and got ready to wage war against Jawahar Singh. On the other side Shujah-ul-Daula's claim was finished. He risking his life went alone to the British. They (the Englishmen) treated him with goodwill and they relinquished everything. Leaving his provinces to him they went away to Azeemabad (Patna). When (the king's and ministers') ignominy was removed, Shujah-ul-Daula again wore the mantle of ministership (30 August 1765) and settled down contentedly in his abode, that is in Avadh.

Battle Between Jawahar Singh and Maharattas

(An Event) There (Jat domain) ill-fated Maharattas came to Jawahar Singh's borders with a large army and looted most of the villages. Jawahar Singh who was really a very brave man came out of his fort and recruiting eight to nine thousand Sikhs who in those days had come to that district took them along and fought. When the battle started, those ill-fated ones (Maharathas) were routed and these Sikhs became busy in killing, looting and rounding up (men of the opposing side). Thus they rounded up five hundred men along with one of the Maharatta) chiefs and did to dust their prestige as soldiers. Since Malhar was a proud man, when he suffered one defeat after another, he died of the trauma of anguish and misery after a journey of three to four days.

Marathas Enter into Peace

In the meantime Raghunath Rao who was well known chief of Deccanis reached with a large army and created turmoil in that land by invading one of the landlords adjoining the borders of Jawahar Singh. The said landlord was friendly with Jawahar Singh to whom he wrote that if Marahattas overcame him, they would certainly try to annex his (Jawahar Singh's) state too. It was thus imperative that he (Jawahar Singh) came to the border which was in his (the said landlord's) interest too. This young man (Jawahar Singh) of great guts went with a huge army and crossing Chambal which is a famous river, pitched their tents on the other side (of the river). Marathas, becoming restless, started making fervent efforts. But even when both the sides were busy in placing their armies in battle positions that an uproar arose about the impending arrival of Shah Abdali. His very name was terrifying to Maratha chiefs. Thus they ran to their homes in an unholy hurry and they entered into truce in exchange for the release of the prisoners (Marathas) arrested in the war of Malhar. The dear one (Jawahar Singh) suitably punished those acting high and mighty on the strength of their collaboration with Marathas and he returned to Agra.

My Second Journey to Agra

The Raja (Nagar Mal) coming out of his forts went to Agra to meet him (Jawahar Singh). I too, on that pretext got an opportunity of pilgrimage to the tombs of my father and uncle. After about fifteen days' stay we came back.

Abdali's Invasion

This time too Shah Durrani came up to the other side of the famous river Sutluj and after suffering losses at the hands of non-descript Sikhs went back.

Skirmish between Jawahar Singh and Madhoo Singh

(**An Event**) In those days there arose bitterness between Jawahar Singh and Madhoo Singh son of Jai Singh on some matters of the State which gradually took the shape of dispute. That brave youngman (Jawahar Singh) became determined to destroy his (Madhoo Singh) domain and apparently on the pretext of meeting Raja Vijay Singh son of Bhakht Singh (about whom my miraculous pen has already written), he went to Pushkar which is big tank and bathing in which Hindus consider it as worship. Vijay Singh, though young, was mature in his views. He came and met him (Jawahar Singh) and mediated peace between them. There were mutual promises and agreements. Rai Bahadur Singh's elder son of the Raja (Nagar Mal) who was a brave and courageous youngman had accompanied Jawahar Singh in this journey for a holy dip in the tank. When he and Jawahar Singh's returned from there the chiefs of Madhoo Singh breaking the agreement started hostilities. Till the noon time the battle of guns and arrows continued. Finally the Rajputs the votaries of ignorance descending from their horses took out their swords and attacked fiercely. Many of them (on Jawahar Singh side) were routed. However, finally these brave youngmen (Jawahar Singh and Rai Bahadur Singh) fighting with great courage warded off this great danger. By the evening both the armies were exhausted. The fire of hatred is, however, still burning on both sides and their helpless subjects are getting burnt in it like grass and straw. Let us see what comes out of the screen of destiny.

Perfidy of the Sikh Army

(**An Event**) When Jawahar Singh came and settled down in his forts, the Rajputs army started brutally looting the populace and sheltering behind Deccani's (Marathas) they started destroying the habitations. In those days an army of Sikhs, was present on the other side of the river Jaun. The ruler there (Jawahar Singh) entering into understanding with them (Sikh army) fought the enemy. There was a lot of massacre and destruction. Finally Jawahar Singh evicting the enemy forces sent Sikh chiefs in their pursuit and considered going himself as inappropriate. These treacherous people (Sikh army) entered into conspiracy with them (Rajputs) and betrayed Jawahar Singh. When Jawahar Singh saw their (Sikh army) perfidy, he was very upset. But luck favoured him as Raja Madhoo Singh died of his illness and his army chiefs were constrained to return after making peace and these unreliable Sikhs too went away by another way.

Murder of Jawahar Singh

(**A Big Event**)And it so happened that in the meantime Jawahar Singh went to Akbarabad and in a single assault of the sword by some wretched one bid farewell to this world. His brother Rao Rattan Singh became the ruler of the State. This evil man was at all times in a State of drunkenness and committed extreme atrocities on the people. In short in a period of ten months he ill-treated all and sundry. Consequently he was knifed to death by an alchemist. Now his minor son Kesri Singh was made the chief. The power passed into the hands of the servants (of the court) and (because of that) the entire work (of governance) went haywire[62]. Now the coterie looking after the affairs of the state made Nawal Singh, the fourth son of Suraj Mal who was nowhere in the running as that (minor) boy's deputy. If he performs his duties in orderly manner it will be for the good otherwise to all appearances the matters (it seems) have deteriorated.

When the dissensions within this community persisted and it resulted in the State's management passing into the hands of menials, Nawal Singh and his younger brother Ranjit Singh who was connected with Kumhair fort stood up for fighting each other[63]. For about fifteen days a battles of guns and muskets raged. But because the fort was strongly secured, Nawal Singh was constrained to retreat after negotiating peace. Even though seemingly two brothers had patched up but what can one do to cure inner rancour? Jia Ram who was Ranjit Singh's army chief and his prime minister went to the army of Deccanis who were hovering around at a distance of four to

---

[62] "Rattan Singh had seen war at the head of a Jat Corps against Marathas in Bundelkhand and north Malwa early in 1768; but immediately after coming to the throne he gave himself up to pleasure and pomp. As new lord of Braja Mandal, he made pilgrimage to Vrinda Van and held the grandest and most costly entertainments on the banks of Jamuna, at which 4000 dancing girls were assembled. He had picked up Gosain Rupanand, a Brahmin monk reputed to be master of alchemy, and engaged him to procure the philosopher's stone. The sharper after draining the Raja of money for sometimes, at last found no other way of avoiding punishment for his imposture than to murder his dupe during an experiment for the transmutation of metals in the privacy of his tent. He was instantly cut down by the Raja's servants . . . The leading Jat general now surviving was Dhan Singh, brother-in-law of Nawal Singh and he was entrusted the regency on behalf of Rattan Singh's infant son Kesri Singh.
—'Fall of the Moghul Empire' Vol-III, pp 43-4

[63] "Brains and character alike were wanting among successors of Jawahar Singh and, in addition, the lack of strongman at the head of the state let loose all the selfishness and factious spirit among the members of the royal family which completed the national downfall in a few years."
—'Fall of the Moghul Empire' Vol-III, pp 43-4

five days journey and pandering to their greed he brought Maratha chiefs into his territory. These Maharathas who are these days assuming airs of importance, had then come in miserably poor condition with him (Jia Ram) and settled down around the walls of Kumhair fort and they were worried to an extent as to ask everyone, "How much army has Nawal Singh? And how well they fight? Had Nawal Singh not moved from his place, he would not have suffered so much loss and the Maharattas would have left with whatever little they could get as guests. But Nawal Singh's inexperienced army launched a decoit like attack near Govardhan which is a place of pilgrimage for Hindus. They did it like this that there were a hundred of them here, two hundred there, a thousand here and five hundred there. Thus, wherever any group was, it remained isolated. None could reach to help the other. The inevitable result was to be that the pleasant breeze of victory was to flutter the Deccani banners. This side's (Nawal Singh's) horses, elephants, camels and a large quantity of military equipment fell into the hands of chief of other side (Maharattas). Despite inflicting such a defeat, they (Maharattas) could not even do this much that they carry out sit in around Nawal Singh's forts. They contented themselves with whatever they got and crossed the Jaun river and pitched their tents in Doaba (between the two rivers). When their stay there became protracted, Najib-ul-Daula[64] who was a farsighted man thought that this calamity would not pass on its own. Lest they harmed the city (Delhi) he with an eye of the believer came, along with his son and brother and whatever army was with him, faced Maharatta chiefs and so long he was alive, he did not let Deccanies cast their eyes on the city. When he died of his old chronic disease, his chiefs fell out with his son Zabita Khan on some trifle. Finally Zabita Khan leaving everything went away to Shakkartal and they (Marathas) pitched their tents near the city (Delhi).

In Kaman

When the Jat misrule and mishandling (of administration) crossed the limits and living in the city became unsavoury, Raja Nagar Mal decided to leave along with twenty thousand families of Delhi who had settled down here because of him and were tied to his benign self. He sought permission from these chiefs to leave but those cruel people were secretly toying with the idea harassing them. They kept putting off the Raja and they wanted him to

---

[64]   About Najib see foot note under Skirmish of Suraj Mal

cancel his idea of going and then (finding the opportunity) quietly pounce on them high handedly. When he (the Raja) became certain that these people were not letting them go but were placing obstacles in their way, he, placing his faith in God, did what a chief's obligation was. In other words taking both his sons, he rode out of the fort and these became engrossed in helping the needy so that no one, man, woman and child was left behind by him in danger. With merciful intervention of God and with the blessings of his own benevolent nature, he along with this huge caravan entered in two to three days Kaman city which is situated on the border of Jaipur where Raja Prithvi Singh son of Raja Madho Singh had recently been made the ruler. We, the afflicted ones, are with this caravan by virtue of being in service (with the Raja) and let us see whether our livelihood keeps us here or takes us elsewhere.

My Arrival in Delhi

(**An Event**) In those days it came to be known that the shadows of the banners of royal good luck were hovering over Farrukhabad. The Raja sent me as emissary to Hassam-ud-Daula who had an access to the King. Going there I settled terms and conditions (of collaboration). On his side his younger son who was not happy with me for my contacts with his elder brothers, suggested (contrary to the agreement) that it would be better to join Deccanies. Thus he did not join the King's army and proceeded towards the city. I too was constrained to accompany them in ignominy along with members of my household. When I reached the city (Delhi), leaving my wife and children in Arab Serai, I distanced myself from their caravan. (After two to three days I met Rai Bahadur Singh and acquainted him of my state of affairs. That gentleman spared no effort in trying to alleviate my plight to the utmost of his capacity).

Attack on Zabita Khan

At these times, Scindia who was a mighty chief among Deccani chiefs bringing the King in lead entered the city (Delhi). Even a few days had not elapsed when Maratha chiefs decided among themselves to invade Zabita Khan son of late Najib-ul-Daula, taking the King with them. The King made an excuse of his illness (to evade) but it was of no avail.

My Journey to Shkartal

On this occasion I went along with the royal army. Those people made Nawab Zabita to flee without a fight. His possessions and property were seized and his wives and sons were taken into custody. They (Marathas) did not give the King anything beyond two hundred infirm horses and a few old and torn tents. The King was very disappointed on account of this act of Marathas[65] but what could he do? The Marathas were an arrogant lot (about their power) and here (on the Emperor's side) there was neither money, nor power. When they did not get money (salaries) the employees of the King started confiscating the estates of the gentry here and humiliated most of them. Immediately after the flight of Zabita Khan and his army, The Gujjars and Mewaties living in the environs of Shukartal plundered the masterless tract worse than Marathas ever did. When the victors arrived at that fort they found only sacked and blazing houses. Only a few pieces of artillery, too heavy to be removed, were secured by Marathas.

The defeat of Zabita Khan, his flight and appropriation of his estates by Marathas and Emperor was the beginning of a swift end to Rohilla fiefdom except for two and a half months of his son Ghulam Qadir's occupation of Delhi between July 1788 to October 1788 during which he carried out

---

[65]   Mir's scratchy narration is far from accurate. In so far as abandonment of Shukartal is concerned, there was no prize left in that fort. Immediately after the flight of Zabita Khan and his army, "The Gujjars and Mewaties living in the environs of Shukartal plundered the masterless tract worse than Marathas ever did. When the victors arrived at that fort they found only sacked and blazing houses. Only a few pieces of artillery, too heavy to be removed, were secured by Marathas."

However, there was a dispute between the Emperor and Marathas over the division of property and treasure seized by them at Pathorgarh. Sarkar has described it thus:

"The Marathas were vexed with the breach of agreement made at the beginning of the campaign. On the imperial side it was alleged that the faithless Marathas had seized all the artillery and treasure of Zabita Khan, as well as his elephants, horses and other property, and offered only a worthless fraction to the Emperor."

—'Fall of the Moghul Empire' Vol-III, pp 38-40

blood curdling mayhem to which we will revert towards the end of this book. In so far as Zabita Khan is concerned this is what happened to him:

"When in the last fight before Ghausgarh Zabita Khan was cut off from his fort by the advance of Afrasiab Khan's column and driven into the Sikh camp, he found himself possessed of nothing except the clothes he stood in. All his property and treasure, all his wives and sons had been left behind in Ghausgarh and all these passed into the hands of imperialists in the course of a week. The destitute Ruhila chief and his vanquished Sikh allies fled fast from Doab and retired to Sikh settlement in Karnal district west of Jamuna. Here Zabita Khan lived for many months, on the bounty of his former allies. He had no money or followers and no landed possession now; but Sikhs had enjoyed subsidies from his father year after year as his munshi Mansukh Rai reminded them and they generously took up the cause of penniless friendless exile. To cement their alliance Zabita made a public profession of Sikh religion being baptized as Dharam Singh[66]. To such a depth had fallen the heir of the champion who had held aloft the banner of Islam in Northern India for thirteen years."

—'Fall of the Moghul Empire' Vol-III, p 294

At last the patience of the Emperor was worn out and on 3rd May harsh altercations broke out between him and the envoy of Marathas and the latter went away in anger. However, on the 11th a compromise was patched up through Sindhia, and out of property officially attached at Pathargarh, one half was given to the Emperor, one fourth to Peshwa and the remaining quarter divided among the Maratha Sardars, but the elephants, cash and jewels remained unshared. The Emperor's demand was for money and Sindhia promised him two lakhs. But this was only a fraction of what was seized. As a Maratha agent reported from Nagina on 9th May, lakhs and lakhs worth of booty was appropriated by Maratha officers without crediting it either to the Peshwa or to the Emperor.

The defeat of Zabita Khan, his flight and appropriation of his estates by Marathas and Emperor was the beginning of a swift end to Rohilla fiefdom except for two and a half months of his son Ghulam Qadir's occupation of Delhi between July 1788 to October 1788 during which he carried out

---

[66]   Hence the saying:

Ek guru da do chela
Aadha Sikh aadha Ruhila

blood curdling mayhem to which we will revert towards the end of this book.

Pension from Wajih-ul-Daula

I came out in search of charity and went to the door of every chief of the royal army. Since I was well known for my poetry, the people would pay attention to me to give some kind of help. With their help I continued to live hand to mouth. I met Wajih-ul-Din Khan younger brother of Hassan-ul-Daula who awarded me some pension keeping in view my fame and his own capacity. However, he gave me a lot of encouragement.

Shah Alam and War with Marahattas

In short as the King was unhappy at the defiance of Marathas, he left for the city (Delhi) without their consent and came into the fort. Coming here Najaf Khan who considered himself to be a great soldier, without carefully examining the matter persuaded the king to annex the adjoining constituted district areas of the Jats. He, without consulting Hassan-ul-Daula who had close relations with Deccani chiefs, got the permission using persistence, to carry out a major campaign and collected ten thousand strong crowd of riff raff from the city and suburbs and in the very first assault they captured ten to twelve estates adjoining the city. At this he started bloating himself/ assuming airs. Being callow and inexperienced, at the instance of a few foolish people, he went astray and became bent on fighting Deccanies.

Plans of Marathas

They (Marathas) held parleys among themselves that the king these days is like fakirs (without arms and other accoutrements of war) but he was going to fight us even without power and strength. If he really acquired strength, he would harass us to no end. It would be better for them to march towards the city (leaving Doaba) and without giving him (the King) any respite, they should finish him off. If he got killed in the war, well and good. Otherwise they should capture him after dispersing his army and keep him in a beggarly state so that he ate his nan (bread of leavened flour) and salt and remained beholden to them. When this was decided Zabita Khan (son of Najib-ul-Daula) was won over by offering him the post of the commander of the army and restoring to him the estates of Saharanpur which were taken from him and merged with the areas of the king. Thus he was persuaded to join them. The Jat army was similarly enticed. Then with such a rumbustious marching as better be left unwritten, they reached the vicinity Faridabad in a week and crossed the river on foot. For two to three days there were minor skirmishes. Finally one day a regular war started. On this side (Kings), apart from Najaf Khan, Baluch and Monsieur Medec who had been cozened by Najaf Khan to leave the service of Jats to join this ill-fated army, fought bravely in the battle field[67]. When the 'Moghul' army, untrue to their salt, got frightened and took to their heels it brought humiliation on itself. Some people destined to die who did not have even proper uniforms on their bodies, died an ignominious death from the wounds they received. An army column of the other side (Marathas) seeing the field clear infiltrated into the city unceremoniously and took away royal elephants and in addition lots of goods were carried away on the heads of those fugitives. Some panicky people who had gathered there were cleared in the twinkling of an eye. Up to an hour into the midnight Hassan-ul-Din along with his few soldiers remained dug in on the sand of the western bank of Jamuna behind old fort. Then leaving the palace he came to the king. By midnight Najaf Khan too entered his haveli (mansions) leaving the unfortunate ones to their death. In this event the old city which had already sparse population was again looted. We, the poor ones, were protected by the ultimate protector. In the morning, the fighters on this side were not up to fighting so that they could take to battlefield. In the city that sheltered us, they spent the day in artillery battle by overcoming their laziness. The royal luck held on, otherwise the enemy would have blown up the sacred fort. In so far the people on this side were concerned, their strategy and the extent of

---

[67] Jats had in their service 'two very able European mercenary captions, Walter Rheinhard (popularly called Sombre or Sumroo) and Rene Medec. Of these Sambre cared for money and was every ready to desert the highest bidder, while Medec was lured away by his patriotic instinct at the call of M. Chevalier, the French chief of Chandernagar to transfer his services to Emperor's court at Delhi (October 1772) and there serve as a French agent for building up coalition against the British power in Hindustan.
                                    —'Fall of the Moghul Empire' Vol-III, pp 3-4

The other European with Jats, Sombre had been seduced by the Emperor to defect to his side.
                                    —'Fall of the Moghul Empire' Vol-III, p 65

their will to fight was exposed on the day when the very news of the arrival of Maratha army made them lose their wits. The men of artillery made an application to his holy highness (the King) to prepare for small and big guns, cannons, untilled area, gun powder, arrows, etc. The pay clerks gave the commander of artillery who was colder than ice, only one hundred rupees. If one looked on his face and moustache (the commander) one would be misled into believing that real men were like him. But that coward fearfully retreated to a corner and was not be seen by anyone so long as the battle went on. Finally the third day Hassan-ul-Daula rode out on his horse to the other side and returned with a peace treaty at their (Marathas') terms. The new city remained fortunately safe (from loot). Now Deccani Sardar (chief) is considering evicting Najaf Khan and the disloyal Moghul army at the instance of Hassan-ul-Daula. Let us see what emerges and how this ill-fated Moghuls leave the city and where they go.

In short Scindhia, who was the third chief of Deccanis, went away towards Jaipur. The other chiefs they are thinking of going to the other side of the river (Jamuna). Probably the idea is to go to Jhansi via Farrukhabad and from there cause damage to Shujah-ul-Daula's country.

Eviction of Najaf Khan (January 1773)

(An event) Since it was commonly talked about among the people of the city that chiefs like Najaf Khan and recalcitrant Moghul army were thinking of demanding their salaries and as and when the Marathas departed, this vast crowd would sit in at the door of the King and would harass the pay clerks. Therefore, Hassam-ul-Daula who was the regent told Deccanies that these people were treacherous and were rioters, they (Marathas) should consider evicting them. Thus at his instance Maratha chief who was looking for an opportunity to banish these people (Moghuls) from the city, issued the instructions not to let any Moghul remain in the city. When this matter was prolonged and the pay clerks of the King took refuge in the fort and the common citizens were ordered to remain confined in the city. These inconsequential groups of people taking positions up to Lahori Gate started fanning the fires of riots. Even though they did not have the stomach to fight Marathas but they got embroiled with them. When nothing came out of the turmoil created by them and they realized that if they fought the Marathas, they would be killed, they were constrained to leave the city and pledged obedience to Marathas. After two to three days Najaf Khan and other Moghul chiefs went to join Maratha army along with their companies.

Deccanies who never overlook giving seemingly courteous and good treatment, they did not hesitate in treating these worthless lots hospitably. But the respect they commanded in King's service, none of them knew whether it would continue here. In a few days these inconsequential people would disperse and every one of them would go in one direction or another. It was talked about that Marathas might take them along themselves up to Akbarabad and reaching there might permit them to go wherever anyone of them wanted to go.

In short these mischievous Moghuls and pugnacity incarnate Marathas might possibly leave and Hazart Zil-e-Subhani[68] (the King) with his good heartedness along with two or three copywriter clerks might live in the sacrosanct fort without any worry. Even if he comes for a stroll in the balcony a hundred times who is there who will not observe Hijab (cover one head). If he comes on foot in the bazaar where is enforcer of Hajib (wear head cover) who would proclaim, beware, keep distance. To all appearances, in the situation prevailing the people with skill might head towards the desert and the people of soldier's profession would roam around with hands stretched for alms. Everyone would go his own way. The city would become one of hustle and bustle.

The Doom of Hassam-ul-Din Khan 1773

(An Event) The new development was that when Deccanis taking Najaf Khan with them decided to cross over the river, the then minister (Shujah-ul—Daula) with the backing of Christians (Englishmen) came out of his province (Avadh). After battling it out reached Farrukhabad and confronted the Marathas. The chiefs of Deccani army found themselves not up to facing him. After spending three months in parleying, they finally sought peace. Since the minister was well known for his valour, he took this offer as a boon and accepted it. Finally after making Najaf Khan as his regent in the King's court left for his province. Deccanies (Marathas) and Poorabies (British) leaving their interests to him (Najaf Khan) went away to areas under their occupation. Hassan-ul-Daula's face turned deathly pale when Najaf Khan entered the city. For the next two to three days he remained confined to his own home out of fright. Thereafter the King after calling him to the fort, demanded account books for a few years and he was

---

68   It literally means 'reflection of God'.

taken into custody on the spot. Majid-ul-Daula Abdul Ahad Khan son of Abdul Majid Khan who was a prominent official of the Royal court, wore the crown of Dewan (Minister) of Royal estates after the transfer of Raja Nagar Mal. Finally the King imprisoning Hassan-ul-Din Khan who was the regent, handed him over to Fateh Khan Durrani in consideration of eight lakh rupees in connection with the government money and salaries of the Moghuls[69]. He (Fateh Khan Durrani) took him (Hassan-ul-Din Khan) from the fort to his (the former's) home. Now Moghuls were in charge. It was up to them to kill or spare him: Thus his ill considered actions brought the doom on his head. For three yearsFakir (Mir) was in a state when no admirer was there (to help him). Times are very bad. With faith in merciful God who is the provider for all and who is all-powerful, I was confining myself to my home. The apparent state of affairs there were that a few dear ones like Abdul Qasim Khan, the younger brother of Abdul Ahad Khan, Majad-ul-Daula, the rest, Wajih-ul-Din Khan the brother of Hassam-ul-Din Khan and Behram Khan senior's son Bairam Khan who were incomparable in their humanity—and Qutab-ul-Din Khan son of Sayyad-ul-Din Khan Khansama, even though young but not lacking in intelligence and respect for elders, in addition there was Qazi Lutf Ali who lived very orderly life. I kept meeting all of them whether I got anything from them or not. My faith in God had brought me wealth in the form of these people. It so happened some times that someone sent me something as an offering considering me to be a fakir, poet or the one with faith in God. It was something to be grateful for. Often I was in debt and I was living in dire poverty. In short this world is a strange house of untoward events.

War with Jats

(An Event) Abdul Ahad Khan who had become Dewan (Minister) of Royal estates and was close to the King became the Regent, he used to act in his own capricious ways and nobody dared demur. Royal army was in bad shape and the King was penniless. Only a few villages and cities were under his control. It was hardly possible to live on them. The Jats, meaning the progeny of Suraj Mal had captured areas up to the Shrine of

---

[69]   He means the money misappropriated by Hassam-ul-Din Khan.

(Apparently Hasan-ul-Din can be taken for the dead as he has fallen into the hands of his enemies who will not leave him alive, if it is in their power. But then it is in the hadns of God who controls all things.)

Hazart Khawaja Qutab-ul-Din Kaki which is 3 to 4 Kos (8-10 kms) from the city. Najaf Khan would plead with the King thus, "Hazrat (Sir) living this in this insipid manner, is no fun, but if we get back areas annexed by the Jats, we can get along somewhat more easily." The King would reply, "You are perhaps dreaming. Is it necessary to talk big when lowly placed?" He would say, "If it happens so, what will your Majesty give me?" The King said, "From the areas so conquered one-third will be mine, the rest is yours." Since the ill fate was hovering over this (Jat) nation, one day their army came to plains of Garli which is near the Shrine of Khwaja Mastoor Alia Ulrahmata/compassionate one) and started creating disturbance there. Najaf Khan taking along his people who were ill equipped, impatiently rushed on them. Jats, in any case, were an arrogant lot. They showed contemptuous unconcern towards these people (invaders). Minor skirmishes went on but when the regular war broke out the things titled in such a way as to end in a way beyond all imagination. In short by the evening Najaf Khan had won the battle. Royal army remained there at night munching uncooked grains and celebrating their victory. Next day they advanced and laid siege to Ballamgarh, which is a strong fort (of Jats) at a distance of 12 Kos (about 20 kms) from the city (Delhi). For a few days the war of heavy and light artillery continued. The chief of that place (the fort) told them that they (the invaders) would not be able to finish the war against Jats by capturing the fort. Instead they should go forward and win the impending war against the Jat chiefs[70]. In so far as that fort was concerned he could vacate it without a fight and hand it over to them. In spite of his youth, Najaf Khan was a mature chief who was very perceptive. Leaving the chief (of the fort) there, he proceeded ahead. When he reached Hodal which was Jat occupied area, he faced another difficulty for a huge army of the other side (Jats) confronted him there. Now one more big campaign was on his hands. The Jat chief named Nawal Singh came to him with large army and artillery. The battle raged and heavens brought death and destruction to many. Gradually the situation became fluid and the consequence of the war became dependant on the availability or non-availability of provisions. The royal army fought on empty stomachs at the expense of their lives, was repulsed and killed. However, as that nation was ill-fated, the royal army won. This side (Royal army) chiefs came down from their mounts, fought infantry battle and carried the day and that huge army of Jats went back defeated.

---

[70]   There were two of them, Ajit Singh and Heera Singh who joined hands with Najaf Khan against Nawal Singh.

Najaf Khan Wins (1775-1778)

The European named Sumro[71] (Sombre) who had courageously held on with his heavy and light artillery ran away towards the end of the day. Najaf Khan, under whose command this was achieved, gave himself a lot of airs. And whosoever heard about this happening was Sumro was given by the Mughal court a large tract in the South Rohilkhand called Sardhana between Meerut and Panipat which was governed in his absence by his wife Begum Sumro (Zeb-un-Nissa) when he was away on one battle front or another and she continued to rule the area after Sumro's death.

Begum Sumro was a living legend of her times. She was known for her charm, intelligence and intrepidity. She used to personally lead her army in the battlefield in her palanquin. She effectively frustrated through battle and wit efforts of her two neighbours, Sikhs and Rohillas to make inroad into her domain. Even though lying close to Delhi, the royal capital, her State was left undisturbed by successive rulers, Moghuls, Afghans, Marathas and surprisingly even by the British in spite of she being the widow of Sumro whom the British had every reason to hate. He had fought against the British as an ally of one party or another. East India Company knew him as butcher of Patna for he had massacred a large number of British officers held prisoners, at the behest of Nawab Mir Kasim.

Begum Sumro was known for her beauty and combined with wisdom, she was a charming personality. astute stateswoman, persuasive diplomat. She was an astounding story of success and of a meteoric rise of a dancing girl on the strength of a rare combination of beauty, brain and grit. She ruled for 54 years and the British lost no time in annexing her state after her death. Her mansion in Delhi still exists and is known as Patharwali Haveli. wonderstruck. Jat chief after going into his fort fell ill. Here, around Najaf Khan a lots of people gathered and he became great chief. Although he had no resources, he went on giving oral assurances. Whoever came was employed. In a few days a vast army like a limitless river gathered. Although he was poor, he was carrying on somehow with his oily tongue. When he realized that army would not stay with him on the basis of empty assurances

---

[71]   Najaf Khan's war with Jats took place during 1775 to 1778 whereas mercenary captain Walter Rheinhard (popularly christened Sombre or Sumro) was lured away to Emperor's side in May 1774. Sambre "cared for money and was ever ready to desert to the highest bidder."
—'Fall of the Moghul Empire' Vol-III, pp 3-4, 65

he started sending his commanders towards Jat areas. To some extent this move succeeded. He himself encircled Deeg fort which was twelve Kos (about 30 kms) from there. It so happened that the Jat chief (Nawal Singh) who was already ailing, died[72]. They (the Jats) started fighting (Najaf Khan) after placing Ranjit Singh, the younger son of Suraj Mal, on the throne. The Daroga (commander) of artillery of the fort entered into a conspiracy with the chiefs (of the invading army) who were informed of the way to intrude into the fort. Invading, they entered the fort and also benefited by looting the city. Every man of little consequence got his hands on two and odd bundle of goods. Najaf Khan got a lot of provisions and countless guns. Even the menial servants of the army became rich. After seven days' looting he marched onwards after handing over the fort to a chief. Now he turned towards Kumhair which was another fort of his (Ranjit Singh). Ranjit Singh, who had become the chief of that nation, vacated that fort and throwing away his arms aside, went away to Bharatpur which is a strong fort. These people (Najaf Khan's army) captured the city (Kumhair) and a lot of goods fell into the hands of these soldiers. The Jats were constrained to sue for peace in a message sent for the purpose. Kishori, the mother of Ranjit Singh who was a sagacious person came and appealed for peace[73].

Najaf Khan giving Bharatpur (region) to them (Jats) and postponing his campaign to some other time came to Agra which is a strong capital and which was in possession of Jats. Coming here he launched an attack to capture the fort. Since his star was in ascendance, he captured it in a short time by making entry through its walls. The chief of the fort commanding it on behalf of Jats was evicted after making promises of sorts to him. He treated the people there well and annexed the entire province. He would distribute areas in lieu of salary at his own discretion.

In a few days' time he became the lord of the entire country. All Rajahas and landlords got alarmed. Now, even if the Jats resorted to desperate act,

---

[72] Najaf laid siege of Deeg in January 1776 whereas Nawal had died earlier in August 1775.

'Fall'—Vol. III, pp 83 & 159

[73] Rani Kishori "personally waited on Mirza Najaf and humbly appealed for mercy for her husband's house. The Mirza had the statesmanship to convert a vanquished foe into a friend by restoring Bharatpur region, with revenue of seven lakhs to Ranjit Singh and leaving the fort of Kumhair to Kishori as personal gift."

—'Fall of the Moghul Empire' Vol-III, p 113

they would face such a defeat that they dare not stray towards this side. When Najaf Khan became the lord of the entire land he started assuming airs before Abdul Ahad Khan. In other words, the very existence of the kingdom depended on him. And when the King demanded in accordance with the undertaking given by him (Najaf Khan), one-third part (of the conquered territory), he submitted before the King that the entire land had been distributed amongst his people (the army) in lieu of pay and the king could take from him the price of the one third of land. The King who was not satisfied with false promises said, "You should leave that much of land." However, his (Najaf Khan's) tactics could not succeed before Abdul Ahad Khan's resolute stand. He was constrained to demarcate one third of the land (to be administered on behalf of the King and he was made the army's Generalissimo and elevated to the position of a pre-eminent Amir (chief). After some days with the King's permission he went away to Akbarabad (Agra).

Abdul Ahad Khan and Sikhs (1778)

Here Abdul Ahad Khan got the Sikhs to join him and whatever money he had, he gave it to them. Then banking on that large army, he, taking Prince Farkhanda Akhtar with him, invaded the Raja of Patiala. His real intention was to set the Sikhs against Najaf Khan as soon as an opportunity arose. Even when he was proceeding towards Patiala, it was Najaf Khan who was in his mind.

Gradually it came to transpire that many people leaving Najaf Khan's army joined the employment of the Regent Abdul Ahad Khan. However, as he (Ahad) had no experience in governing a country and was also ignorant about matters of the state, he would leave every work in hand incomplete. He held on there for sometime and then, at the instance of his Sikh allies, he entered into a peace accord with the Raja of Patiala[74]. Whatever money

---

[74]   This is not correct. He was beaten back and pursued by Sikhs of Patiala Rajah up to Panipat. The facts are different.

"The campaign proved disastrous for Abdul Ahad Khan for he and the prince had to retreat from Patiala and was pursued by Sikhs of Patiala Rajah up to Panipat. So much so, that this abortive enterprise precipitated a crisis in the Government in Delhi. By undertaking it Abdul Ahad Khan dug his own grave."

he had, was exhausted. He asked for money from the King. The King was annoyed at this demand and wrote back that he should carry on whatever way he could for he (the King) had no money.

MARTYRDOM OF HAFIZ RAHMAT KHAN (27TH April 1774)

(An Event)The prime minister, the great chief Nawab Shujah-ul-Daula who was a powerful person went out to fight Hafiz Rahmat (Khan) Rohilla who claimed equal eminence with him and was hostile to him. The enemy (Hafiz Rahmat) with ill-intentions wrote to the British that the minister, who was gathering so much army, had the intention of fighting them. Thus Governor Bahadur who is called Sahib, had come out intending to fight. The Nawab minister, who held that community in utmost respect, went to them alone and told them, "I have great regard for you but I will not put up with humiliation from anyone else whatever may happen. Either you take me to Calcutta with you or leave the affairs of the State to me." The English seeing this attitude of the minister, withdrew. They went away leaving the districts Kada (Manikpur) and Allahabad also to him. Now the heaven, the magus, brought in new trouble and things went haywire.

When the minister returned from there, many Englishmen were in the advance column of his army and they had organized themselves for the battle in accordance with their own strategy. When the Rohillas saw the roaring waves of his army, they were overawed. Zabita Khan and other chiefs along with ten to twelve thousand men expressed their desire to obey (Shujah) submitting, "We people are well-wishers of the Minister's well-being and we will not disobey him." The minister, keeping God's mercifulness in mind ordered them to take position in the rear of his army, even though some of his chiefs cautioned him that these people were treacherous and should not be trusted lest they betrayed in the midst of battle. But the minister was really a brave man. Frowning it away he said, "I know their might. In no time I will crush them."

"The prince's presence undoubtedly proved the salvation of the Moghul army. The glamour of the imperial name had not yet totally disappeared and Sikhs shrank from going to the extreme in their attack on Padishah's son, contenting themselves with loot only. If Abdul Ahad Khan had been alone, he would not have returned alive from his ill-judged and ill-conceived invasion."
—'Fall of the Moghul Empire' Vol-III, p 125

Asaf-ul-Daula, the son (of Shujah-ul-Daula) who is now the prime minister, fought incessantly in the battlefield. He would raise smoke wherever he went. He would snap the chains of artillery guns with his sword. When the battle entered a decisive stage the enemy which was solid steel became softer than wax. There was so much artillery fire raining on them from this side (Asaf-ul-Daula) as to leave heaps upon heaps of the dead. When Hafiz felt the heat of the battle and found no way to escape, nor had the strength to fight, he desperately jumped into the battle and becoming indifferent to the world put his life on the hold. In one attack his group feared for its life, his very brave ones got demoralized. One of the mortars hit Hafiz Rahmat Khan on the chest and his battle lines started dispersing. The enemy's (Hafiz Rahmat Khan) head was carried away rolling it like a ball. When it was shown to the victorious army, Rohillas confirmed it (and said), every good deed is rewarded and the evil one is punished. When it became certain that Hafiz had been killed, the minister bowed in <u>Sajida</u> (bowing one's head to the ground in prayer) in gratitude. The enemy's army was looted. Their women and sons were taken as prisoners. The entire country and land came into the possession of the minister. Najaf Khan who had joined minister's forces took his leave and went back to Agra.

I Remain Confined to Home (1772)

Fakir (Mir) in these days remained confined to home. The King summoned him often but he did not go. Abu-ul-Barkat Khan, the cousin of Abdul Ahad Khan, the regent and the son of Abu-ul-Qasim Khan, the Governor of Kashmir showed his concern towards me in various ways. I would meet him on occasions. Sometimes the King would also send something through some source. On odd occasion I pen a line. That is all that remains of my world.

Death of Shuah-ul-Daula (25ᵗʰ January 1775)

After this great victory, the Prime Minister, the respected chief Nawab Shujah-ul-Daula entered his province with great fanfare and in a grand style. But Heavens eye remained set on harming the people of this world. The complaining crowd's eyes too cast an evil shadow. Thus that competent and brave Minister fell prey to such an illness that its cure became difficult. Every possible treatment was tried by Tabibs (indigenous physicians) and English doctors but to no avail. When the Minister felt that the disease was getting aggravated, as wisdom dictated, he made his son, Asaf-ul-Daula who as a person is cultured, brave, well-versed in affairs of the world, and is a spring of kindness and charity, to occupy the ministerial berth. And he himself departed from the world. The mourning over the patrarchical chief's death left the world around draped in black. This great tragedy occurred. Only in a thousand years, such a leader, who was courage incarnate and was of utmost generosity, is born.

Death of Mukhtar-ul-Daula

After a few days Mukhtar-ul-Daula in whose hands was the responsibility to administer the province and to perform the duties of ministership, was not spared by the times (fate) for he was killed at the hands of a captain of the palace guards named Basant and departed for the other world. Now Hassan Raza Khan Sarfraz-ul-Daula Bahadur got the post of Deputy Ministership. He was of serious temperament, balanced, cordial and likeable chief. The quality of kindness was pre-eminent among his likeable qualities and with excellence of conduct he keeps on winning the hearts of ordinary people as well as that of the gentry. He was kind not only to me but to many others. May God preserve him.

(**An Incident**) The King was already in state of annoyance because of the Regent's (Abdul Ahad Khan Kashmiri's) demand of money from him. He wrote to Zulfikar-ul-Daula Najaf Khan to reach here (Delhi) whatever way he could manage. Finding the King's backing he boldly departed from Agra to present himself to his Majesty. As soon as the news that chief Najaf Khan was coming reached Abdul Ahad Khan, he becoming panicky rushed to Delhi along with the prince and the Sikh army and two days before the said Najaf Khan's arrival settled down in the fort taking charge of its administration.

Najaf Khan's Period

When the news spread about Zulfikar-ul-Daula's (Najaf Khan's) arrival, the King sent the same Regent (Abdul Ahad Khan) to escort him. He went with great fanfare and met him. Both came sitting on the same elephant. Najaf Khan knowing Abdul Ahad Khan to be a hypocrite treated him well to all outward appearances and sweet talkingly he brought him to the gate of the fort. Coming there he hinted to his men that his army with small arms and artillery should rush into the fort and be in readiness taking positions at various spots. Even though there was a distance of knife's blade between these two, if Najaf Khan wanted he could have killed the Regent in one blow but he hesitated because of his obedience to the King for after all this man (Abdul Ahad Khan) was also King's employee. Firstly it was necessary to know the King's intention, then see what would happen.

Then with the turmoil in his mind he came before the King and got the permission to meet him, he saw his master (the King) was full of annoyance and wanted him (Abdul Ahad Khan) to be finished off. He came back and stopped in the middle of the Bazar and made a written submission that he did not take matters in hand earlier out of respect for His Majesty. Now he would not budge from here without taking Abdul Ahad Khan with him. Seemingly the King talked of negotiated settlement but covertly he instructed that in whatever way it was to be done, Abdul Ahad Khan should be removed from here. Since the Regent's soldiers had left out of helplessness and Sikhs remained aloof, he (Abdul Ahad Khan) in desperation wanted an assurance that Najaf did not harm him and that he was not humiliated. The King said, "I am the guarantor, you go without fear." When he saw no way out and found the time having changed for him for the worse, he came out of the fort riding an elephant. The head of chiefs[75] (Najaf Khan) who was waiting in the bazar he himself rode and took his own elephant alongside Abdul Ahad Khan's elephant, taking him to his own home and kept him confined there. Some days were spent in procrastination telling him (Abdul Ahad) that todayhe would go to the King, tomorrow he would take him to the King and finally he told him that there would be no point in his (Ahad) going there (to the King) and that it was better for him to stay with him (Najaf Khan). But he did not touch his belongings. He fixed a sum of rupees twenty per day for his expenses from his own coffers and a few servants were also left with him. He (Najaf) himself became busy with the matters of many that chiefs would not get an opportunity to pay a courtesy call on him. Only the day he presented himself before the King, could the King's court be held. Otherwise the King would while away his time in the company of selected courtiers. Since he (Najaf Khan) was young and Shahjehanabad (Delhi) a bewitching place, his friends beguiled him towards fast life and over indulgence. He got so much engrossed in the use of harmful stuff and

---

75   To be precise Najaf Khan was till then Commander-in-Chief of the Royal Army but assumed all powers after the then Regent was deposed.

sensual fun with women that that his body started losing vitality[76]. Finally he became afflicted with consumption. The physicians tried their utmost to treat him but with every medication his ailment worsened. When in despair (for his life) he would say wistfully that he wanted nothing but only to stay alive. During his illness, times underwent another change.

My Migration from Delhi (1782)

Fakir (Mir) was confined to his house and wanted to go away from the city but the want of means did not let him step out. Somehow for the protection of my honour and prestige, the Nawab, the Prime not send for him? Nawab Salar Jung son of Ashaq Khan Mutmin-ul-Daula who was the younger brother of Ashaq Khan Najam-ul-Daula and maternal uncle of the Prime Minister, in view of his long standing relations with my step-maternal uncle, said that if Nawab Sahib was kind enough to provide something for the journey, Mir would definitely come. It was ordered that it should be so done. He (Salar Jung), after obtaining some amount for travel expenses from the government (of the Nawab) wrote me in a letter thus, "The respected Nawab is summoning you. In whatever way you can, get yourself here." I was already in a state of despondence. I proceeded to Lucknow as soon as I received the letter. Since it was God's will, I was on my way to Farrukhabad without any friend, companion, or help or caravan or a guide. Muzzafar Jung who was the ruling chief there (Farrukhabad) very much wanted me to stay there for a few days but there was no echo (to it) in my heart (to the suggestion). In a day or two, starting from there I reached my destination. Immediately I went to the house of Salar Jung, may God preserve him. He treated me with a lot of respect and whatever he considered appropriate for me, he conveyed in a message to exalted personage (Asaf-ul-Daula).

---

[76] Towards the end, "excess in wine and women quickly sapped Najaf Khan's vitality."

. . .

"To anyone who had followed Najaf Khan's campaign against the Jats, Ruhellas, it would be incredible, but for the authentic contemporary evidence in our possession, that this great general could now indulge in freaks of insane frivolity worthy of imbecile voluptuaries of Abdullah Qutab Shah of Golcanda or Wajid Ali Shah of Lucknow."

—'Fall of the Moghul Empire' Vol-III, p 133

Meeting Nawab Asaf-ul-Daula

After four to five days, the great honourable Nawab came by chance, to witness a cockfight. I was also present there. With his quick cognitive capacity he recognized me and said, "Are you Mir Mohammad Taqi?" Then with great goodwill he embraced me and took me along to where he was sitting and addressing me he recited his verses. I said, God be praised, the poetry of Kings is the King of poetry." He was kind enough to give me opportunity to recite my verse. That day I recited a few verses from my ghazal. When the Nawab Sahib was about to leave, Nawab Salar Jung said, "Mir has come in response to the summons, now it is up to your exalted self to bestow a place for him and whenever you wish call him into your service." Nawab Asaf-ul-Daula said, "After fixing a salary, I will inform you." After two to three days, I was sent for. I accordingly presented myself and recited a Qasida (panegyric) written for the occasion. He listened to me and very kindly took me into his service. Up till now he shows kindness and compassion towards me.

Death of Najaf Khan (April 1782)

After my coming here (Lucknow), Najaf Khan who had been ailing, died. The administration of the kingdom went haywire. A tug of war began between his protégés, Najaf Quli Khan, Afrasiab Khan and other chiefs. This tussle continued for a few days. Finally Mirza Shafi who was one of his (Najaf Khan's) brothers and was fighting Sikhs to subdue them came at the instance of the King and got Abdul Ahad Khan released identifying him as his paternal uncle. He got for him (Abdul Ahad Khan) the ministership for the management of government land and himself occupied the post of administering the state (as a successor to Najaf Khan)

Tug of War between Successors of Najaf Khan

(An Event) Since Mohammed Shafi was cruel and of truculent temperament, everyone felt endangered by him. He felt flustered by the opposition of Najaf Khan protégés and starting the war within the city, he arrested Najaf Quli Khan. Afrasiab Khan also seemingly joined Mirza Shafi. But his (Shafi's) ascendance did not last long. Only a few days had passed that a palace Daroga (captain) named Latafat who was attached to the King on behalf of the Prime Minister Asaf-ul-Daula and had, in short, some authority, conspired with one of the relatives of Sumro, the European to finish him (Mirza Shafi) off as and when they got an opportunity. They counseled the King also to the effect that this man (Shafi) was impertinent. When he (Shafi) came to know of the conspiracy, he could not exercise patience even for a little while and made his egress from the city. While leaving he took Abdul Ahad Khan also with him. When his escape came to be known to them (conspirators), they could find no trace of him.

The King sent written missives with royal seal to the people (chiefs) of the city and surrounding areas that wherever he was seen at no cost should he be spared but brought before the King. One such missive was received by the chief of Ballamgarh and this man (Mirza Shafi) was staying there. When that chief showed the King's missive to him (Shafi), he became panicky. Abandoning Abdul Ahad Khan there he made good his escape. He rested after a day or two's journey. After reaching Akbarabad (Agra) where Mohammed Beg Hamdani was ruling, he entered into an agreement with him (Hamdani) to fight the companions of the King. He (Hamdani) accompanied him (Shafi) with twenty thousand soldiers.

On his side, the European, the captain of Palace guards and other people close to the King brought the King out of the city pitched their tents on the banks of Jamuna. These people were unaware of the death hovering over their heads. They advanced aggressively to a close position. When the King saw the other side ready to fight, he sent Lalafat Ali and the European[77] to bring him (Shafi) around. They pounced on them arresting[78] the Captain of Palace guards and killing the European. The King defended himself courageously. In any way their strength did not carry any conviction with the King. They lingered on gaining time in parleys and bringing many people to their side by making promises. When they realized that the King could not be won over without war, they using Abdul Ahad Khan as their emissary, made promises and took vows to obey and be faithful (to the King) and brought him (the King) to the fort from his tent. Najaf Quli Khan, Afrasiab Khan and Abdul Ahad Khan started unitedly interfering in the affairs of the State. Hamdani who had an understanding with Mirza Shafi was put off through prevarication. He left for Akbarabad taking few heavy guns and small arms with him.

Here after a few days Afrasiah Khan went into his palaces and the said Mirza (Shafi) starting the war in the city, arrested Najaf Quli Khan and

---

77   His name was Captain Pauli.
78   He was in fact blinded.

sent him to his (Shafi's) Begum (wife) who was Najaf's sister. Abdul Ahad came out of his residence and with his flattering tongue got his own way. The aforesaid Begum putting in her recommendation got Najaf Quli Khan released and sent him away to his own Jagir (estate). Gradually Mirza Shafi's came to be in firm control and he leaving the city attended to annexing more areas. Since no one was satisfied with him Afrasiab Khan came and sent for Hamdani and it was decided that Mirza Shafi should come to Hamdani's tent to welcome him. Thus they beguilingly brought him there and killed him. When he (Shafi) got killed, the star of Afrasiab Khan became in ascendance and the administration of the State came into his hands. Hamdani[79] went back to his area and he (Afrasiab) becoming the chief of chiefs of the King, took over the regency to run the affairs of the State

WELCOME OF WARREN HASTINGS IN LUCKNOW (1784)

(An Event) Here the Prime Minister, the great chief (Asaf-ul-Daula) departed to welcome Governor Bahadur who was, on his (The Prime Minister's) invitation, coming from Calcutta and who exercised predominance over the entire country. The Army's (movement) raised dust to the skies. This journey was up to Allahabad. All the Chiefs of that district knowing his (Warren Hastings) impending arrival were waiting to see him. A day before he met Nawab Gardoon Rikab who brought him to Lucknow where lay the Nawab (Asaf-ul-Daula's) residential palace. At every halt he was entertained in different styles, in the form of new tents, excellent cuisine, Turkish and Arabic horses, large sized elephants[80], expensive dress, a boatload of gems, delicious syrups, countless varieties of dry fruit,

---

[79] Mir has here underplayed Hamdani role in this episode. In fact as we will bring out in later pages Mir's statement about Hamdani are by and large factually incorrect except the fact that was a brave man and apart from that he was hardly a laudable character by any standards. Here it is sufficient to mention that he was instrumental in making Mirza Shafi as the regent through whom he expected to rule but was out manoeuvred by others. Mirza Shafi himself being abrasive and aggressively ambitious could hardly have become his (Hamdani's) tool. When he realized that he personally stabbed Mirza Shafi with his own dagger near Deeg fort while pretending to embrace him.
    —'Fall of the Moghul Empire' Vol-III, pp 78-79

[80] Asaf-ul-Daula had more than a thousand elephants.
    —Ranking's 'Army of Moghuls' p 13

the new and novel gifts of the area and swords manufactured in the south and the west, Tashkandi bows (being exhibited everywhere). When he came to earthly heaven Lucknow and entered the palace, myriad coloured floors were laid, all corners of these were redolent with scent. In every direction of the house, rose water had been sprayed. There were decorated bed spreads, scented dresses, incomparable velvet floors, walls with silver coatings; the palace was decorated with curtain and frills. The fragrance of spring had laid a unique carpet. That house exceeded the spring's domain. Roasted pistachios and almond and English eatables provided as an accompaniment of drinks. For the nights there were dancers looking like fairies, nay, far excelling the houries of heaven in their attractiveness. Flower vases of glass and porcelain tastefully selected were arranged. Shelfs were overflowing with fresh dry fruit. There was western dance, a carnival of rejoicing. In short this was the house of joy with an air of festivity. In the evening there are lighting followed by fireworks. The sparkling stars and missiles (types of fireworks) were reaching up to the skies. The scene of lighting was captivating the heart and shining moonlit night looked as if it was day. The tent sequined in gold was spread out with such a finesse that sun had never shone on such a one. The chiefs were busy in supervising (these arrangements). Rajas were preoccupied with entertaining the guest. The poets connected (with the occasion) and robust youth were busy in singing praises of the guest. Every house was tastefully decorated. Everywhere shades were spread out. There was flowing water; vases of narcissus were arranged in such a line as to give the impression of a garden bedecked below. The ice was looking better and more pleasing than the melted silver. The flummery of myriad coloured flowers was there whose syrup was sweetness incarnate. There were different kinds of rotis (bread) on the eating table. The almond nan (a sort of fluffy bread) had been prepared with finesse. Rich milk white sweets were putting sun to shame. The fresh nan (bread) was so hot as to instill youth in the old. If I was to praise the paper thin nan, it would fill volumes. Seeing ginger nan tingled the palate. Meats of different varieties cooked twice in onion were served. All the guests were enjoying. Different kinds of kabab-e-gul (rose kabab) were freshly and finely made and kabab-e-Hindi was so tastefully salted as to captivate the heart. Kabab-e-kandhari was pulling the connoisseur to itself. Kabak-e-sang (hard) was a solace to the tired travelers. Kabab-e-varq (silver paper) were fried in a unique manner as to pander to the palate. And maroof (famous) kababs too were delicious. Before every one ten dishes had been placed. There were different varieties of pallaos (rice cooked with meat and/or vegetables) and soups. Unique were the bounties.

This Guest and that Host

He was the guest, one of affluence and the host was such as the Nawab, the minister. The one was guest of such eminence and such an opulent host. The guest was of immaculate propriety and the host, the ruler of large state. Such a guest full of wisdom and such a hospitable host, the world had never seen, nor did the wisemen ever hear of. In that manner, mutual parleys and consultations went on day and night over a period of six months.

Tie Up With the British

When the news reached the King every one of the chiefs there (Delhi) became worried for himself. Abdul Ahad Khan sent his men there (to the English) and entered into a tie up with them. Afrasiab Khan, etc. got apprehensive of the coming of English there. Since being powerful they would use the King as their puppet and they (Afrasiab Khan and company) would be removed. Better it would be to take the King to Agra. There they should collect the people and tie up the Marathas who had captured the Gohadwalla State (Gwalior) of the Rana and then negotiate with the British. If it came to fighting (the English) so be it. Otherwise they should live there (Agra) in the same great style. Thus they proceeded taking the King from Delhi to Agra and on the way took Abdul Ahad Khan as a prisoner.

Prince Jawan Bakht

(An Event) When these people reached the said city, the prince Jawan Bakht ran away from here and came to the Nawab Minister (Asaf-ul-Daula) and the British. Those people (Afrasiab Khan and the King) in their anxiety entered into agreement with the Maratha who took their side and started negotiating for the return of the prince (Jawan Bakht). But now the English dragged on their feet for they had the administration of their own land, in other words Calcutta in their minds.

After a few days he (the English) bid farewell to the Prime Minister and left taking the prince with them. At the departure the exalted Nawab gave such countless gifts to the employees of the Sahib (Warren Hastings) as could hardly be imagined. Every person was given a horse, an elephant and a long coat and every menial was loaded with gifts.

Murder of Afrasiab Khan(2nd November 1784)

When Sahib (Warren Hastings) went away by way of the river, the Nawab Minister returned to permanent headquarters (Lucknow). The Marathas and Afrasiab Khan decided to wage war on Mohd Beg Hamdani. The latter too did not yield any ground and became ready to fight. In the meantime a man of Mirza-Zainul-Din the brother of Mirza Shafi stabbed Afrasiab Khan with a dagger from which he died within a couple of days. These days there is no chief worth the name around the King. In all probability the Marathas will come to rule. After these incidents, armies of Maratha and Hamdani clashed. When they could not overcome him, he was arrested through deception[81]. Here Sahib (Warren Hastings) who had taken Prince Jawan Bakht sent him back from there. Thus the prince came back. Now he will stay back here or present himself before the King. For the time being he is under the wing of the exalted Nawab. He is doing whatever the Nawab Minister tells him to do.

Narration of Hunt (November 1784)

Here fakir (Mir) is with the Nawab of the exalted status (Asaf-ul-Daula) and is spending his days praying for him. The great men went for hunting up to Bahraich. I was also riding along. I wrote a poem Shikar Nama (Narration of Hunt). He once again rode to go for hunting and went up to the foot hills of northern mountains (Himalayas). Although people during this long journey suffered great ups and downs but they had never seen such atmosphere, such breeze and such hunting. After three months they came back to their headquarters, Lucknow. Fakir (Mir) wrote another Shikar

---

[81] Mir had migrataed to Lucknow in 1782. Thus his narration of events after that is not a firsthand account but it is based on hearsay. Therefore, his version of some of events is full of inaccuracies and incorrectness, as pointed out in footnotes.

Mir's statement that Hamdani was arrested by Maratha army through some ruse is not correct. He was crushed at Bharatpur by Sindhia and surrendered to him. Mahadji Sindhia showed clemency to him and appointed him as one of commanders of his army which he deserted four years later to join Rajputs to fight against Marathas. Hamdani as has been written earlier was a man sans any sense of loyalty.

—'Fall of the Moghul Empire' Vol-III

Nama (Narration of Hunt) and recited it before him (Nawab). Nawab Sahib selected two of the ghazals. Shikar Nama (Narration of Hunt) and with great finesse rendered them into five liners. It had a pleasant quality of fineness. He liked one of the ghazals in a particular style and asked for another one in the same mode. With God's grace that too was written. With his blessed tongue he praised it and conveyed his appreciation of my poetic efforts. In those days, he (the Nawab) due to change of climate, became unwell after ten days of Muhharam. Treatment was given but illness, by malignance of fate, got prolonged. The people were given alms and bounties for bringing luck. Everyone prayed for his good health. The ultimate physician (God) whose grace bestows cure, cured him for which we and people were grateful. World exists on God's will.

Rule of the Maratha (1785)

Since none was left amongst the men of Najaf Khan who were at the helm of affairs, the Maratha (Madhavji Scindia) who was in nearby Gwalior was overjoyed to assume power. The king made the Maratha his regent and humiliated Najaf Khan's men[82]. Now in most of the matters only Maharatta is consulted and all actions are executed according to his wishes. The Maratha army too has reached Shahjahanabad (Delhi) and it is well known that he has acquired complete control. The Sikhs who were looting the area surrounding the city (Delhi) have become cautious as they cannot fight the Marathas and in the battlefield they cannot even match the dust

---

[82]   In the original Persian text Mir talks about the Maratha being made the regent without giving his name. His Urdu translator gives the name as Madhavji Scindia but it is actually Mahadji Scindhia. He has confused the regent's name with that of Peshwa Madhavji.

Contrary to what Mir says, Mahadji Sindhia was, according to all historical evidence, a reluctant man to be at helms of affairs in a tottering Empire whose public property, wealth and revenues were misappropriated by successive regents and Army chiefs leaving royal coffins empty.

"All his acts showed that he valued his solid conquest in Malwa more than the empty dignity of the regency of an insolvent empire. Even when Emperor threw himself upon Mahadji's neck and entreated him to save the state by undertaking to be its helmsman, Maratha general hesitated for full fortnight till the hopeless disruption forced his hands . . ."

—'Fall of the Moghul Empire' Vol-III, p 205

raised by them (Marathas). The King who was camping outside the Agra city departed after a few days for Delhi and arresting Abdul Ahad Khan sent him to Aligarh which is in possession of Najaf Khan's sister and many of the men of Najaf Khan's army are assembled there. Now the Maratha is the master of the country. He does what he wants. He doles out some amount to the King[83] and takes him along wherever he (the Maratha) wishes. Thus he remained in the city for a month, then he took the King to Aligarh. There was fighting for ten fifteen days. Finally there was a truce and the Begum was banished from from the fort and she was allowed to go after taking a part of Najaf Khan's assets[84].

Invasion on Rajputs (August 1787)[85]

He took the King to invade Rajputs. They fought back. The King after making peace with Rajputs came back to the city and the Maratha remained in Agra. But the invading the Rajputs again was constantly in his mind.

Thus he invaded them again. Rajput Rajahs invited Hamdani who was a chief of Najaf Khan and made friends with him. The war broke out. Hamdani showed courage and was killed fighting. In his place his nephew Mirza Ismile Beg became the chief. He fought with fortitude and got rid ofMaratha mischief. They were squarely defeated. Marathas armaments and other means of armament were snatched[86]. Here too Mirza Ismile came

---

[83] *Mahadji Sindhia had awarded a pension of one lakh rupees a year to the King Shah Alam. The reason for laying siege of Aligarh fort was that royal treasury was empty for Najaf Khan's successors had looted it and wealth had been taken to Aligarh fort. In words of Sarkar, Mahadji had no wish to ill-treat Afrasiab's family if they acted honestly by the State and delivered without concealment or thefts the public property in late regents keeping . . . But they were determined to grasp at everything and cheat the infidel from Deccan."

—'Fall of the Moghul Empire' Vol-III, p 206

[84] Mahadji Sindhia reached Aligarh in the third week of November 1785. A part of Najaf Khan's assets taken as mentioned by Mir, consisted of 65 pieces of heavy artillery, 16 maunds of gun powder, one thousand rounds of lead and rupees forty thousand in cash

[85] This refers to battle of Tunga which is near Lalsoot.

[86] None of the statements made here in regard to Hamdani and Marathas losing all their armament are correct. Firstly Hamdani after his crushing defeat at Bharatpur at the hands of Mahadji Sindhia was shown clemency by the latter who made him a commander in his army. He never had any sense of loyalty, as

in pursuit and evicted them from the city and laid siege to the fort. The battle for the fort became prolonged. The Marathas saw his advantage lying elsewhere[87]. The King came out of the city (Agra) and went towards Najaf Quli Khan whose fort was in Rewari. There was fierce fighting there. Finally getting some cash and goods from Najaf Quli Khan he came back to the city (Delhi).

Ghulam Qadir Rohilla (July-October 1788)

In the meantime Zabita Khan's son whose name was Ghulam Qadir and who after his father's death was in occupation of Saharanpur, came to acquire strength and got the Sikh army to join him and he annexed most of the areasof Doaba (between the two rivers). Closing on the King he demanded money from him. The King refused point blank. Now he (Ghulam Qadir) took position on the other side of the river (Jamuna) to wage war. Thus fighting went on for a month. Although the King had neither the army nor strength but he gave a determined fight and got rid of this calamity. Ghulam Qadir went away and captured areas around Agra. Here Mirza Ismile who had been laying siege to Agra fort came to join hands with him (Ghulam Qadir) realizing the latter's strength. They entered into an agreement to fight the Marathas in tandem. After a few days Mahadji Scindia came invading intending to go beyond Chambal. In those days Prince Sahib-e-Alam

---

pointed out in earlier footnotes. Secondly he was not, contrary to Mir's claim, killed bravely fighting. In fact he was silent spectator on his elephant under shade of a tree when a cannon ball hit the tree and on rebound knocked him down tearing one side of his body open and then the branch broken by the shot fell on him crushing him underneath.

The statement that arms and other means of warfare were snatched from them (Marathas) is also incorrect. The battle itself was described by French mercenary De Boigne in 'Carriere', "Though sanguinary, but not decisive." Though Maratha army remained under siege in Agra fort for a few months, the tide turned in Mahadji's favour when he destroyed Mirza Ismile Beg's army, under the walls of Agra fort, as a fighting force on 17th June 1788. When Ismile Beg escaped into Agra city only fifteen troops were left with him. He escaped crossing the river Jamuna on his horse.

'Fall of the Moghul Empire' Vol-III, pp 256-265

[87]   Maratha saw his advantage lying elsewhere', means that he suspended his Rajput campaign for his programme for Malwa.

was present there but he remained indifferent and war had to be faced by Mirza Ismile alone[88]. But he fought bravely and won the battle. Marathas ran away towards Gwalior area where he ruled.After a few days he came with the fresh army to fight the battle raged on all sides of Agra and finally Mirza Ismile was defeated[89]. Ghulam Qadir remained a silent spectator. The said Mirza ran away and came to Ghulam Qadir but found him absorbed making schemes of his own and paid no attention to him (Ismile). He was constrained to leave for his own native place after living with him (Ghulam Qadir) for a few days.

Atrocities of Ghulam Qadir Khan

The Nazir (Representative) of the King had adopted Ghulam Qadir as a son. He wrote (to Ghulam Qadir) to come telling him that the King did not listen to him, meaning that he (the King) was not willing to abandon the Maratha. They both went to the city. The King himself had no power. At the instance of the treacherous Nazir, he (Ghulam Qadir) making the administrative arrangements of the fort, deposed the King and meted out such a treatment as did not behove him. Princes were put to untold humiliation. A lot of wealth fell into his hands. He blinded the King and put another on the throne[90]*. When he was in full control, he put even the Nazir into prison and started harassing the residents of the city. When his oppression crossed all limits, he fell out with Mirza Ismile over a trifle. In

---

[88]   Mir's account is mixed up. Mahadji was regent to Delhi Durbar on whose behalf he was trying to subdue recalcitrant Mirza Ismile and the rebellious Rohilla. Why should Mir expect the Royal Prince to join the rank of these rebels?

[89]   The detailed account of these battles has been given in the footnote to preceding write up under under Invasion on Rajputs.

[90]   Mir, while writing about the atrocities of Ghulam Qadir has touched only a tip of the iceberg. Earlier Imad-ul-Malik had enacted a similar ghastly scene by blinding King Ahmed Shah. Mir, in one of his verses refers to these tragic events of blinding the Kings:

> Shahan ke kehle jawahar thi khak-e-pa jin ki
> Unhe ki aankhon mein phirti salain dekhein

> Kings whose dust of the feet was precious collyrium
> I saw their eyes being pierced by needles

fact in brutality Ghulam Qadir Khan Rohilla should rank among the worst tyrants of history.

To give the harrowing details of his outrages against the King, the princes, princesses and even the palace servants, we quote verbatim from Sir Jadu Nath Sarkar's, 'Fall of the Moghul Empire':

"On the fifteenth (July 1788), the weak Emperor was tricked by his Nazir into granting audience to Ghulam Qadir. Thus began the last Afghan occupation of Delhi which lasted for two and a half months from 18 July to 2nd October 1788. It inflicted unspeakable suffering and dishonour on the royal family and ruined the prestige of the empire beyond recovery. Shah Alam was deposed (30 July) and blinded (10 August), tender children and helpless women were done to death by denying them food and drinks for daystogether, princes were flogged, princesses were dishonoured, servants were beaten till they died, the entire palace area, as well as mansions of the rich outside the fort were turned upside down by digging for a concealed treasure, the palace was denuded of its property and royal family its youthful beauties to gratify Ruhila's passion. It was a dance of demons for nine weaks."

—'Fall of the Moghul Empire' Vol-III, pp 301-302

Equally ghastly was his treatment of the King Shah Alam:

"On the 10th August, in a frenzy of vindictiveness and avarice, Ghulam Qadir had needles driven through giving him anything, that dear one (Ismile) entered into agreement with the Maratha. In the meantime Maratha army had also drawn near and some of their chiefs had entered the city. The Rohilla immured himself in the fort and at night sneaked away through Khizri gate. He took along with him, his army, its accoutrements, cash and wealth along with princes and the Nazir. He took positions near Shahdra to fight. When the the eyes of Shah Alam. Next day, in an unimaginable brutality he called for the court painter and made him draw a picture of himself as he knelt on his half dead master's bosom and carved out one eyeball with his dagger, while other eye ball was extracted by Qundhari Khan. The wounded old man was left for days together without a drop of water; three valets were killed and two water carriers wounded by Ghulam Qadir with his sword in order to deter others from relieving the royal distress in secret."

—'Fall of the Moghul Empire' Vol-III, p 310

The Maratha chief saw his obduracy they crossed the river and forced him to fight. Some time they had the upper hand and another time that wretched man. When a month passed in these skirmishes, a chief from Deccan named Ali Bahadur[91] came engaged Rohillas in war. In two, three skirmishes he captured him (Ghulam Qadir). He snatched from him the wealth and princes and put him in prison and made the same blind Shah Alam the King. He handed over the fort to Jats. Now they give a hundred rupees a day to King and they rule over the entire country. They killed the wretched man (the Rohilla) inflicting great humiliation on him[92]. Now the Maratha (Scindia) is the King. He does what he wants. Let us see how long this situation lasts.

At first Mahadji with equal humanity and policy, pampered Ghulam Qadir for sometime with rich food and clothing in order to induce him to reveal the hiding places of his Delhi plunder. But this plan had to be given up when his hands were forced by his master. On 28th February 1789 Sindhia received a sharp letter from Shah Alam telling him that if he did not extract Ruhilla's eyes and send them to him, he would abdicate the throne and retire to Mecca in the guise of a beggar, and this would expose his regent and manager to public execration. So on 3rd March he ordered the Emperor's chief secretary and the physician Hakim Akmal to go to Ghulam Qadir's prison, extract his eye balls, cut his nose and ears, and put them in a casket to be sent to the emperor. Then the rebel was taken to a place 12 miles from Mathura whereafter further mutilation of his hands and feet (Islamic legal punishment for robbery), he was at length put to death and his body hung from a tree. When the casket reached Delhi, Shah Alam's revenge was gratified as the blind old man fumbled its grisly contents and felt that his wronger had been really paid back in his own coin. Islam is a by-product of Judaism. The Mosaic law of an eye for an eye and tooth for tooth was thus fulfilled."

---

[91] He was a Maratha general who was born of a Muslim courtesan Mastani Begum and Peshwa Baji Rao-I's grandson. The state of Banda was given to him by Marathas. Sarkar calls him Rana Khan. According to him, Maratha troops of Mahadji led by his best general Rana Khan captured Ghulam Qadir along with three thousand of his soldiers in Meerut in December 1788

[92] Ghulam Qadir and other prisoners were sent to Mahadji at Mathura where they arrived on the last day of the year 1788

Moral and the End (In short)

This world is a strange place of happenings. What kind of houses got dilapidated and what kinds of youngmen died. What vanities of garden were rendered barren? What gatherings became fictitious? What flowers withered? What youth year passed away? What meetings got disrupted? What caravans departed? What dear ones suffered humiliation? What types of people came to power? This discerning eye had seen various happenings and the ears had heard a lot.

APPENDIX III

Khwab-O-hyal

(Dream or Fantasy)
(i)In Orignal
Dream or Fantasy)
(Translation of Khwab-O-Khyal)

Happy is the one
Who is no more
Known to all is my plight
My life sorrows saturated
Anxiety torn
Yearnings hundredfold
deserted my heart
Immured was I in this world
Dispersed was my heart
So was my livelihood
Never free from worry
about/sustenance
Fated to be caught up
in coils of beloved's locks
Not a day passed off
in peace at home
I knew not what rest was
As I raised my head
sudden fell the blow
And all friends turned foes
Time turned me into a waif
Frenzy seized me
Mornings and evenings
Losing myself at times
In withdrawal
At other times I would sit with a stone in my hand
Drowned in the sea of sorrow
at times and the head
filled with anxiety at another
The state delusionary
stretched so far
that my madness
spanned the skies
On fire was I set
by the full moon
Fearing it so much
that I would faint
Delusion so possessed me
Fear left me lifeless

I saw a face in the moon
That made me lose
my appetite and sleep
Scared, though I was
of the moonlight
Could not, but, help
look towards moon
The fairy from the moon
towards me would gaze
filling me with fear
driving me into daze
I would fret and foam
at the mouth
My friends feared for my life
Removed was everything
from my room
Some would be wary
of being near me
others anxious about me
out of love
A few with tears in eyes
overwhelmed with sorrow
Others would rend their clothes
Suffering for me
If I gazed at the face
in the moon
my eyes would shed blood
And if I wont
extreme restlessness
Would seize me
What my eyes saw
they did not believe
But the face in the moon
haunted my heart
Ever remaining present
in my conscious
and unconscious states
Wherever I looked
I saw that face

The same one in a thousand place
Her rolling eyes
played havoc with me
Eyelashes would cast
long lasting spells
If my eye looked at plaited lock
it was like walking on razor's edge
My life's desire dwelt
at the corner of her lips
Her smile rendered me lifeless
Ah! ask me not
What her mouth looked like
For words are not enough
to describe it
And fresh rose
Will be ashamed to face it
Ashamed will be deer's musk
before the fragrance of her locks
Beauty incarnate
from top to toe
Lifetime would one like
to spend with her
She would look sometimes
with moon's mirror in hand
and would be drunk
with her own loveliness
Another time she would appear
as an immaculate image on the wall
Then suddenly walk away
behaving sometimes like a lover
At another time be a preening self
Every word of hers
an ambrosia
She would talk to me
with sweet warmth
Revealing at times her fascinating face
Another time she would veil it
behind luxuriant loose hair
Her moods volatile

Now critical, now kind
Now friendly, now enemy like
Now her arms enfold me
Now becomes hostile, full of spite
Now indifferent, now loving kindness
When I try to touch her
there is only an empty air
What is it if not hallucination
Night after night
I suffered this fate
The face that my fantasy created
kept me company
As the dawn set in
She would set out towards moon
Leaving me to face
the darkness of the day
I shook and shivered
like a bamboo frail
Recalling the perfect
Cypress like contours
Pale I became
Ill I looked
Incoherent in speech
Sounded like a fairy tale
Someone fetched an exorcist
to chant incantations
Another brought a charm locket
to wear
Shown was I to physicians
And made to drink
Undrinkables
Whatever prescription administered
turned inimical to my nature
Prolonged was the treatment
Efforts concerted to cure
turned out to be
a futile exercise
My heart became
increasingly crowded

with hallucinations
Remained I inwardly as before
with my senses dispersed
Restless was I wherever I went
Neither at ease at home
nor outside
My head filled
with insane uproar
My heart pulled me
towards desolation
of hills and desert
My head's craving
dwelt in the collar of my heart
And wind pulled the sleeve
of my heart
towards the desolation of the desert
Head remained lost
in the coiled locks
My steps followed
the sound of my shackles
Madness persisted so much
My friends proposed confinement
I was shut up in a cell
The fire of insanity
flared there too
I was fed with bread
once a day
The water too was given sparingly
What happened to my pursuit
of knowledge?
I did not have time
even for sighing
The lone passage for air
was a ventilator
Fear kept people away from me
Apprehending what might
befall them
My mind sans any sense
No contact

with discernment, perception
The cell I was confined in
narrower than a grave
Its doors remained
closed for hours
There sometime I would
regain my wits
Then I could come out and rest
Friends tried cure of all sorts
sans blood letting
But once they let out blood
They let out too much
Rendering me breathless
Bleeding went on for long
Unconscious was I
throughout the night
Though an uproar awoke me
I could hardly open
my eyes
And the hand that bled me
Still carried the knife
I was back to square one
The torture of bleeding me
Starting all over again
Scalpel was used on me so much
as to get blunted
The blood spread over my clothes
The wound reached almost
my jugular wein
The blood warm dripped on
Inebriated with wine of unconsciousness
became too weak to speak
Opening eyes was a torture
For days I laid
with the head on the pillow
Long lasted the state
of stupor
On uncertain feet I stood
My body wobbled

like a bamboo frail
Walking I reeled head to feet
like whistling morning breeze
Weakness brought further misery
A little relief I felt
vanished as if it never was
But mind could now centre somewhat
Eyes could focus a little
Weakness slowly started departing
and the strength returning
Who really bothered
about my life
But made was I
of a sterner stuff
Strength started returning
to my limbs
for destined I was
to live in this world for some more time I, the
weak one returning from far off
having gone near the death's vale
Illusions, delusions
Started fading into dimness
And face from the moon
became nebulous
Quietly Started receding my madness
Along with the fairy from the moon
Her regular visitations gone
That face appeared rarely
Looking towards me with love no longer
She would despair
hitting her head against the wall
At times reconciled to her fate
Restless at others
And then unbridled with longings
for me, shed tears
Then she would start brooding
with her hand under her chin
At times opening her heart to me
She would chastise me

for being unfaithful
Sometime that envy of moon
would put her hand on her heart
Looked with wistful longings
on me at other time
when she became mellifluous
from the fire of love
Weeping sometime
She would tear off
her clothes' linings
and shred hundredfold her collar
Busy at times reciting
pangs of her heart
Then she would go back
to a state of motionlessness
like an image of anxiety
engraved on a wall
She would bid me adieu
Saying, she could bear the sorrow no longer
At times she would have complaints
bitter enough on her lips to ooz misery
Sometimes her eyes bestowed
such pangs of heart
forcing on me a desire for death
At times on warpath, temper rising
Another time speech full of guile
Looking into my heart
in a way strange
Alluring manner, sometimes
Revealing a state
of a lover deprived
Her speech wounded at times
At another adopted a manner
of an afflicted lover
Sometime indifference of a stranger
followed by propinquous intimacy
of love's madness
Appearing at times
in her grandeur

followed by being depressed
and tired of life
Appearing at occasions
with modesty veiled
behind love
At times restless
in various ways
Then she would hit her head
with a stone
Contemptuously indifferent at times
Then suddenly abusive
Followed by message of love in the wind
She would say
O! Cruel in love
Soften your heart
Be ashamed of rejecting
so much of love
Sometimes walked arrogantly indifferent
Another time she would assure me
of there being no madness in me
Sometimes speech that did me good
That, O, you false one
remember my words
Mir, I can come no more openly
And the time for our friendship is gone
In short you look without hope
for the delusionary figure
gone towards the moon
Never again she appeared
in that fashion
nor seen in her earlier manifestation
Heart exposed to those meetings
and their trappings
is now in repose
I sleep day and night
But sometime the shadow
in the moon
reveals its illusionary shape in dreams
I tried forgetting it

but it would come with renewed force
In the flicker of an eye
would I see the known face
Which would, as her wont
Vanish on her own
Now I sleep with felicity
The pulse of my dream
is firmly in the hand
of my wish
sitting back I feel
the heavy contents of my dream
But I choose to ignore
this world within a world
Thought of hers now
Stuns me into numbness
And I go to sleep
with my head on a stone
Thus lost I was to myself
My youth passed off in sleep
Never again that moon face
appeared to me, awake, asleep
Nor did I see her in dreams
Enough had I been unconscious, unaware
Enough had I slept
in fate's lap
But never did Mir see anything
comparable to the beauty of all beauties
Her dalliance with me were as if a dream or a fantasy

ABOUT THE AUTHOR

S R Sharma (1932) comes from a Landed family of Punjab,India. Early education in Urdu and Persian medium started his abiding interest and love for Urdu Poetry and the times when the great masters of the Urdu Poetry lived.

Completing his Masters (Economics), he joined as an editorial staff of Economic and Political Weekly" in Mumbai.He later worked with the Government of India as Director in the Ministry of Finance and Minstry of Defence. But the routine of a government office was not cut out for this free spirit and to follow his twin love for poetry and horticulture, he took premature voluantary retirement. Now he divides his time between Shimla where he has built an apple Orchard and Delhi.

His other published works include the much acclaimed "Select Urdu Verses" By India Publishers Distributors and collection of his English Poetry "Abyss" and "Meandering Mountains."